Philosophy and Language

"An exemplary exercise in philosophical acumen and clarity . . . if you have time to read only one book this year on the vexed question of meaning, this is the one."
Journal of Theoretical and Philosophical Psychology

"Hanfling opens up new as well as often forgotten perspectives on the treatment of age-old philosophical problems; above all he challenges us to be clear about what we are doing when we do philosophy."
Philosophisches Jahrbuch

"Hanfling's book constitutes a remarkably rich achievement. It is a long time since I last read a work of philosophy from which I have learnt so much."
Antony Flew, *Philosophical Investigations*

"Hanfling demonstrates the importance of ordinary language for philosophical inquiries . . . Even though the problems tackled in the volume are rather philosophical than linguistic, the book touches upon the fundamental issues concerning the nature of language and would be thus of interest to anybody involved in language studies."
Katia Chirkova, *Language*

"Oswald Hanfling has written a lucid, painstaking, thorough and comprehensive defence of a certain method in philosophy, a method used, consciously or not, by many philosophers."
Sir Peter Strawson, Oxford University, UK

Oswald Hanfling is Visiting Research Professor of Philosophy at the Open University. He is the author of several books including *Logical Positivism, The Quest for Meaning, Wittgenstein's Later Philosophy*, and *Wittgenstein and the Human Form of Life* (Routledge 2002).

Routledge Studies in Twentieth-Century Philosophy

Philosophy and Ordinary Language

The Bent and Genius of Our Tongue

Oswald Hanfling

Routledge
Taylor & Francis Group

LONDON AND NEW YORK

First published 2000
by Routledge
11 New Fetter Lane, London EC4P 4EE

Simultaneously published in the USA and Canada
by Routledge
29 West 35th Street, New York, NY 10001

First published in paperback 2003

Routledge is an imprint of the Taylor & Francis Group

© 2000 Oswald Hanfling

Printed and bound in Great Britain by
St Edmundsbury Press, Bury St Edmunds, Suffolk

British Library Cataloguing in Publication Data
A catalogue record for this book is available
from the British Library

Library of Congress Cataloging in Publication Data
Hanfling, Oswald.
    Philosophy and ordinary language: the bent and genius of our tongue/
Oswald Hanfling.
    p. cm. – (Routledge studies in twentieth century philosophy)
    Includes bibliographical references and index.
    1. Ordinary-language philosophy. I. Title. II. Series.
B828.36.H36   2000
149'.94–dc21   99–39028
                                                         CIP

ISBN 0–415–21779–2 (hbk)
ISBN 0–415–32277–4 (pbk)

Contents

Acknowledgements

A number of people have helped me to work out my thoughts in various parts of the book. I am grateful in particular to Michael Beaney, Michael Clark, David Cockburn, Antony Flew, Laurence Goldstein, Severin Schroeder and Roger Woolhouse. To Peter Strawson I am especially grateful for comments on chapter 10. John Hyman supplied detailed and incisive comments on the penultimate draft of the book, which enabled me to make many improvements. Most of all I wish to thank Peter Hacker, who read and commented on drafts of every part of the book. His criticism and discussion over the years have greatly sharpened my understanding of the topics in question.

Abbreviations

Concepts

CKP consequential knowledge principle
OTA ostensive teaching argument
PCA paradigm case argument

Texts

BB   *Blue and Brown Books* (Wittgenstein, Blackwell 1964)
CN   *Conceptual Notation and Related Articles* (G. Frege, transl. T. W. Bynum, OUP 1972)
CTP 'The Causal Theory of Perception' (H. P. Grice in G. J. Warnock, *The Philosophy of Perception*, OUP 1967)
EN   'Epistemology Naturalized' (W. V. Quine in *Ontological Relativity and Other Essays*, Columbia 1969)
FA   *The Foundations of Arithmetic* (G. Frege, Blackwell 1980)
ILT *Introduction to Logical Theory* (P. F. Strawson, Methuen 1952)
LPV *From a Logical Point of View* (W. V. Quine, Harper 1961)
MLR *Mind, Language and Reality* (H. Putnam, CUP 1975)
MPD *My Philosophical Development* (B. Russell, Unwin 1959)
NN   *Naming and Necessity* (S. Kripke, Blackwell 1980)
OC   *On Certainty* (Wittgenstein, Blackwell 1969)
PG   *Philosophical Grammar* (Wittgenstein, Blackwell 1974)
PHK *Principles of Human Knowledge* (G. Berkeley, Dent 1993)
PI   *Philosophical Investigations* (Wittgenstein, Blackwell 1958)
PL   *Philosophy and Linguistics* (C. Lyas (ed.), Macmillan 1971)
PMC *Philosophical and Mathematical Correspondence* (G. Frege, Blackwell 1980)
PP   *Philosophical Papers* (J. L. Austin, Clarendon 1961)

PW   *Posthumous Writings* (G. Frege, Blackwell 1979)
RFM *Remarks on the Foundations of Mathematics* (Wittgenstein, Blackwell 1978)
SS   *Sense and Sensibilia* (J. L. Austin, OUP 1962)
WO   *Word and Object* (W. V. Quine, MIT Press 1960)
WW   *Studies in the Way of Words* (H. P. Grice, Harvard 1989)
Z   *Zettel* (Wittgenstein, Blackwell 1967)

Introduction

> It is impossible, even in the most rigid philosophic reasonings, so far to alter the bent and genius of the tongue we speak, as never to give a handle for cavillers to pretend difficulties and inconsistencies.
>
> (Berkeley)

> One can't abuse ordinary language without paying for it.
>
> (J.L. Austin)

I

Philosophers often support their conclusions by reference to the use of language, pointing out that in such and such a case we might use the word A but not the word B, that we would not describe someone as X unless Y, and so on. Yet they also arrive at conclusions that are contrary to this criterion, as when they claim that knowledge is impossible or free will an illusion. When this is so, can the appeal to the ordinary use of language be set aside as a mere 'cavil'? How important is the 'bent and genius of the tongue we speak' in philosophy? Are the problems of philosophy largely about language, and to be settled by reference to the ordinary uses of words?

'Ordinary language' is an expression that is often viewed with suspicion by philosophers nowadays. One reason for this was expressed by Bertrand Russell in his intellectual autobiography, where he criticized those who are 'persuaded that common speech is good enough, not only for daily life, but also for philosophy'. 'I, on contrary', he continued,

> am persuaded that common speech is full of vagueness and inaccuracy .... Everybody admits that physics and chemistry and medicine each require a language which is not that of everyday

life. I fail to see why philosophy, alone, should be forbidden to make a similar approach towards precision and accuracy.[1]

Now it is true that the language of everyday life would not be adequate for the sciences mentioned by Russell, but is that because it is vague and inaccurate? What a person *says* in ordinary language is sometimes vague or inaccurate, but then the fault does not lie in the language: it lies in his or her use of it, and here too lies the remedy. In ordinary conversation we often ask people to be more precise or accurate and this demand can usually be met perfectly well within the resources of ordinary language and without resorting to a special terminology. Similarly, if there is vagueness or inaccuracy in a philosopher's statements, then he can be asked to clarify his meaning in ordinary language; and we might become suspicious if he is unable or unwilling to do this.

It might be thought that the charge of 'vagueness and inaccuracy' can be supported by reference to the conflation of words with one another, which develops from time to time, as when 'refute' is used to mean 'reject' and 'disinterested' to mean 'uninterested'. Such uses of language are sometimes criticized for undermining important distinctions. But, regrettable though these uses may be, do they entail that ordinary language is vague or inaccurate? No; this still depends on the context in which the relevant words are used. When a politician says 'I refute this allegation', it is clear that he is using 'refute' to mean 'reject'. But even if it were not so – if his meaning were unclear – the remedy would still be available within ordinary language: one could ask the speaker what he means and he should be able to tell us.

It is true that criticisms of ordinary language may go deeper. The word 'rights' has recently become prominent in moral discourse, where it is often used freely in any situation in which there is, in the moral sense, right and wrong. Such expressions as 'animal rights', 'children's rights' and 'human rights' are sometimes used in this way. But to this usage it may be objected that the word has, or originally had, a more specific meaning, involving certain kinds of moral obligations as distinct from others. (Typical examples are those in which a right is *bestowed*, by, say, a promise or a legal enactment.) If the word is applied more loosely, then, it is argued, moral perception may be distorted and inappropriate reasons given

---

1 Bertrand Russell, *My Philosophical Development* (Unwin 1959), 178.

for what ought or ought not to be done. Now this is a contentious matter, which cannot be cleared up simply by asking people what they mean; and neither, of course, can it be settled by describing how the word is used in ordinary language, for the objector will claim that ordinary language – what has now become an ordinary use of 'rights' – is here at fault.

This example shows that the appeal to 'what we say' is not as simple or as uniform as it might at first appear. What it does not show is that our understanding of the problem would be improved, as Russell implied, by introducing a technical vocabulary akin to those required in physics and chemistry. It also does not show that the method of 'what we say' is here irrelevant. Thus, in discussing this issue, we would certainly have to consider what *one would say* if an alleged right were challenged: comparing, say, one's reply to 'You have no right to walk on this land' with what might be said in defence of an animal right or a human right. (The relevance of linguistic philosophy to ethics will be further discussed in Chapter 8.)

This is not to deny that an introduced terminology may be useful in philosophy. Thus (to stay with the example of rights) it might be useful to give names to different kinds of rights. However, the more important objection to ordinary language philosophy is not about the exclusion of non-ordinary language; it is about *evaluating philosophical ideas* by reference to ordinary language. It is sometimes thought that this must make philosophy a trivial pursuit; and this objection too is to be found in Russell's autobiography. Here he lamented the change that had come over his former friend and pupil, Ludwig Wittgenstein, after he had adopted this way of doing philosophy.

> The earlier Wittgenstein, whom I knew intimately, was a man addicted passionately to intense thinking, profoundly aware of difficult problems .... The later Wittgenstein, on the contrary, seems to have grown tired of serious thinking and to have invented a doctrine which would make such an activity unnecessary. I do not for one moment believe that the doctrine which has these lazy consequences is true. (op. cit. 161).

If it were, he complained, it would reduce philosophy to being 'at best, a slight help to lexicographers, and at worst, an idle tea-table amusement'. Yet to anyone who has studied the later Wittgenstein's writings, the charge of 'lazy consequences' and 'idle amusement' must seem ludicrous. If we read Wittgenstein's discussions of *thinking*, for example, we cannot fail to be struck by the intensity of his efforts in

trying to give an adequate account of this 'widely ramified concept'.[2]
The truth is that getting clear about the uses of such words in ordinary
discourse can be a labour of great difficulty.

The term 'ordinary language philosophy' has, however, been
associated largely with certain Oxford philosophers of the 1950s and
1960s, and part of the trouble with it lay in the style of some of its
practitioners. The method of 'examining *what we should say when*',
wrote Austin in 1956, 'scarcely requires justification at present – too
evidently, there is gold in them thar hills'.[3] His own attempts at
justification were, however, both brief and, as I shall argue,
unsatisfactory. It was also Austin who came nearest to being guilty
of Russell's charge of replacing philosophy by mere lexicography, and
to inviting Quine's dismissive reference to 'Oxford philosophers who
take as their business an examination of the subtle irregularities of
ordinary language'.[4]

Another factor which contributed to bringing this kind philosophy
into disrepute was the occurrence, in the writings of a leading
protagonist, of rather obvious *mistakes* about 'what we would say'. In a
discussion of the will in *The Concept of Mind*, Gilbert Ryle declared
that we use the words 'voluntary' and 'involuntary' as 'applying to
actions which ought not to be done'.[5] But it is simply not true that the
word 'voluntary' is confined to actions that ought not to be done. (I
return to this example in Chapter 4.) Ryle's mistake led to a
widespread questioning of the data on which ordinary language
philosophy is based. How are the claims about 'what we say' arrived
at, and how reliable are they?

It is worth noting that this challenge, again, is at odds with Russell's
talk about 'lazy consequences'. Ryle's mistake, and other, more subtle
mistakes in the literature, suggest that to describe our uses of words is
much more difficult and more tricky than might at first be supposed;
and this will be amply illustrated in the chapters that follow.

I have mentioned some of the reasons behind the decline of respect
for ordinary language philosophy. It is unlikely, however, that this way
of doing philosophy could be written off. When people – ordinary

2 L. Wittgenstein, *Zettel* §110 (Blackwell 1967). I discuss Wittgenstein's writings on
   thinking in 'Thinking – a Widely Ramified Concept', *Philosophical Investigations* 1993
   and 'Thinking', in H.J. Glock, ed., *Wittgenstein – a Critical Reader* (Blackwell 2000).
3 J.L. Austin, *Philosophical Papers* (Clarendon 1961), 129.
4 W.V. Quine, *Word and Object* (MIT Press 1960), 259.
5 Gilbert Ryle, *The Concept of Mind* (Penguin 1963), 67.

people or philosophers – ask questions about the extent of human knowledge, the reality of free will and the nature of happiness, we must assume that the meanings of these words are to be understood in accordance with their ordinary use. And even if these meanings are set aside in the course of a philosopher's discussions, they cannot be altogether disregarded. At least the philosopher should be able to tell us why the ordinary meanings were set aside, and how the answers that he proceeds to offer are related to the original questions with the original (ordinary) meanings.

II

What is the scope of ordinary language philosophy? It is not applicable everywhere.

(i) A philosopher of science or mathematics may be interested in ideas that are far removed from ordinary language. In this case 'what we say' may still be a relevant consideration, but this will have to be understood as referring to the scientists' or mathematicians' language and not that of ordinary life. On the other hand, it may be appropriate for philosophers to enquire how those uses of language are related to the language of ordinary life. This is especially so where the same words are used. Thus it may be asked how the words 'time', 'before', etc. in Relativity Theory are related to their uses in ordinary speech. Again, not all the ideas discussed in the philosophy of mathematics are non-ordinary: that of cardinal numbers is an example. (An amusing instance of ordinary language philosophy in this area is provided by Frege in his *Foundations of Arithmetic*, which begins: 'When we ask someone what the number one is, or what the symbol 1 means, we get as a rule the answer "Why, a thing".'[6] Whatever we may think of this prediction, Frege was right to regard the word 'one' as belonging to ordinary language, and to approach his enquiry from this point of view.)

(ii) Philosophy often consists of *arguments* and disputes about their validity. Are such issues to be addressed by reference to the uses of words? It may be so. Consider the argument 'I cannot prove that I am not dreaming; therefore I cannot know that I am not dreaming'. This seems to involve an assumption about the meaning of 'know': namely, that 'being able to prove' is a necessary condition of knowing. (In Chapter 6 I discuss this and related assumptions.) But there are also

---

6   G. Frege, *Foundations of Arithmetic* (Blackwell 1980); hereafter 'FA'.

arguments of a different kind, calling for another kind of examination. Consider the starting point of Locke's empiricism: his challenge to the view that there are 'innate principles in the mind'. Locke thinks he can 'convince unprejudiced readers of the falseness of this supposition' by showing 'how men, barely by the use of their natural faculties, may attain to all the knowledge they have'.[7] But if Locke succeeds in showing this, will it *follow* that there is no innate knowledge? No; for even if people *may* get their knowledge in the way favoured by Locke, it does not follow that they must. But what is needed to evaluate such arguments is a careful comparison of premise and conclusion, rather than reflection on the meanings of words.

(iii) A further limit of linguistic philosophy appears when we turn to metaphilosophy – philosophizing about philosophy itself. Consider the claim that the questions mentioned above, about knowledge, free will, etc., are essentially about language, and to be tested by reference to 'what we say': this claim cannot itself be tested by reference to what we say. This kind of situation is also found elsewhere in philosophy. Locke's claim that all knowledge comes from experience cannot itself be proved from experience; Wittgenstein's identification of meaning with use cannot itself be proved from the use of 'meaning'; and, turning to Wittgenstein's early work, the account of meaning he gave there could not be applied to the account itself.

Let us now enumerate cases on the positive side.

(i) Questions of the form 'What is ... ?', such as 'What is knowledge?', 'What is freedom?', 'What is a cause?' and 'What is happiness?' have often been addressed by reference to the ordinary meanings of these words. This approach will be illustrated and defended in the chapters that follow.

(ii) The claims of philosophers are sometimes starkly at odds with what we ordinarily say. This is especially so in the case of negative claims, as when it is said that we can never have knowledge, that freedom of choice is an illusion, that nothing is really solid, that we never perceive anything directly, and so on. The ordinary language philosopher will insist that such claims cannot be right, even if the arguments for them seem irresistible. In this case, of course, it would be futile merely to point out that the claims are contrary to ordinary language. The arguments in favour of them will have to be examined, and perhaps the ordinary language philosopher will try to show that

---

7   J. Locke, *Essay Concerning Human Understanding* (OUP 1975) 1.2.1.

they are themselves based on confusions about language. (This will be illustrated in the chapters that follow.)

(iii) Disputes in philosophy are often about whether a given claim or hypothesis makes sense. An example is the idea that thoughts and sensations are brain-processes, or that this may turn out to be so on the basis of scientific research. The linguistic philosopher may argue, from the ordinary use of such words as 'thought' and 'sensation', that these ideas do not make sense, so that no conceivable scientific research could yield a positive (or, for that matter, negative) answer.

Another example concerns the Cartesian 'method of doubt'. Descartes tells us that he was able deliberately to doubt all of his assumptions about the world external to his mind, leaving intact only the knowledge that he was thinking. But if we consider how the word 'doubt' is used – what we mean by it – we may conclude that the idea of doubting at will does not make sense.[8]

III

The chapters that follow are arranged in two parts, roughly on the lines of 'for' and 'against'. I begin the first part with one of the major starting points of Western philosophy: Socrates' quest for definitions. Here I try to show, contrary to certain commentators, that when Socrates poses such questions as 'What is knowledge?' and 'What is courage?', his enquiry is essentially about the uses of words. This does not mean, however, that it is about words as opposed to realities. I reject this dichotomy and argue that the question 'What is courage?', for example, is about the use of 'courage' but at the same time about courage itself. To ask how the word is used – what we mean by it – *is* to ask what courage is.

The next two chapters are about two philosophers of recent times in whose work the philosophy of 'what we say' is especially prominent. Chapter 2 is about J.L. Austin, often regarded as the archetypal ordinary language philosopher. In his debate with A.J. Ayer about 'sense data', Austin vividly described the pitfalls attending those whose arguments rely on abnormal uses of language. However, in spite of my admiration for Austin's insights, I find his conception of philosophy, and his defence of the method of 'what we say when' (as he put it), unsatisfactory.

---

8   See O. Hanfling, 'Can there be a Method of Doubt?', *Philosophy* 1984.

In these respects the later Wittgenstein (Chapter 3) seems to me more perceptive. The chapter begins with his stated commitment to 'bring words back ... to their everyday use', with some illustrations of his use of this approach; but I also consider reasons for questioning his commitment to it. I then discuss an important and characteristic aspect of Wittgenstein's linguistic philosophy: his ideas about the 'bewitchment of our understanding' by language itself. Finally I consider the relation of language and 'the world' in the light of his remarks about 'the arbitrariness of grammar'.

An essential, and difficult, question about the method of 'what we say' is about its data, and this is the topic of Chapter 4. How are a philosopher's claims about 'what we say' to be tested? Are they based on empirical observation? If so, should he not enlist the aid of empirical linguists, armed, perhaps, with tape recorders or questionnaires? But what would be left, in that case, of the idea of philosophy as an *a priori* discipline? Again, what if it turned out that 'what we say' varies from person to person? And what about different languages? Are the claims of, say, Oxford philosophers specific to English or, worse, the English spoken by Oxford philosophers?

The next three chapters provide illustrations of the practice of ordinary language philosophy, rather than discussions of its nature. The 'paradigm case argument', once prominent but now largely scorned, is the subject of Chapter 5. I introduce a version of it that seems to me defensible against the usual objections and try to show how it can be effective in dealing with such questions as freedom of the will. Here and elsewhere, however, I am conscious that the philosopher's task cannot be achieved merely by pointing out that a given claim, such as the denial of free will, is contrary to the ordinary use of language. Pointing this out does show, in my view, that there must be something wrong with the claim; but to complete the task, one must show what is wrong with the arguments and not merely reject their conclusions.

Chapter 6 offers an alternative to the voluminous recent attempts to define the concept of knowledge in terms of necessary and sufficient conditions. I argue that if the definition is to be true to the actual use of the word, these attempts are misguided. The logical conditions for using the word are relative to various kinds of situations, which I describe. They cannot be captured in an overall definition.

Misunderstandings of the concept of knowledge are, in my view, responsible for the paradoxical claims of sceptics, as discussed in Chapter 7. The main error is one of idealization: imposing requirements on the possession of knowledge which go beyond what we mean by this word, as displayed in the actual use of it. Here again, as I recognize, it is not enough merely to point this out: one must also show what is behind the idealization and what is wrong with the arguments of sceptics. Of particular interest here is the 'consequential knowledge principle': that if a person knows that p, *and* that p entails q, he must know that q. It can be shown that if this is accepted, sceptical conclusions follow. The ordinary language philosopher, it appears, must either reject a principle that seems self-evident or accept a conclusion that is grossly at odds with the ordinary use of 'know'. Here, as in Chapter 5, I try to bring out the 'suicidal' tendencies of certain concepts. Arguments based on an ordinary understanding of them seem to lead to the paradoxical conclusion that they are never truly applicable.

Part II ('challenge and rejection') begins, again, with a historical precedent – that of the British Empiricists. A frequent ground of hostility to linguistic philosophy has been the feeling that 'words are not enough'. According to Berkeley, the philosopher must 'draw the curtain of words' and direct his attention to what lies behind them. Locke, Berkeley and Hume all gave emphatic expression to this view, in one way or another. I argue (in Chapter 8) that their attempts to get behind the curtain are incoherent and that, in spite of their admonitions, some of their own arguments are based, explicitly or otherwise, on claims about 'what we say'.

The appeal to reality as opposed to words has been prominent in recent discussions of ethics, where the dispute about the 'objectivity' of values has been treated as a question of ontology. Do values exist as objects in the world? If not, it is argued, such words as 'knowledge', 'true' and 'fact' are misapplied or misleading when applied to moral statements. The fundamental questions, on this view, are ontological and not linguistic: language is to be justified by reference to 'what is really there'. I argue (still in Chapter 8) that the introduction of ontology into ethics is misguided and incoherent. Here, as elsewhere, the dichotomy of 'what we say' versus what is 'really there' is itself unreal.

Ideas about the inadequacy of ordinary language (such as those quoted from Russell on pages 1–2) have led to attempts to introduce better alternatives. This may be done by proposing 'more rigorous' definitions of familiar words or by the invention of artificial logical notations, such as that of Frege. In Chapter 9 I discuss Frege's disparaging remarks about ordinary language and argue that the philosophical benefits of artificial notations are largely illusory. I also show how the redefinitions of particular words are liable to lead to confusion about the questions at issue. In this context I consider

Russell's theory of descriptions, which he first offered as a *true* account of the language concerned, but later described as a 'more convenient way of defining' that language.

The widespread rejection of the method of 'what we say' can be ascribed to various influences, but prominent among them is that of H.P. Grice, the subject of Chapter 10. Grice did not advocate the reform of ordinary language; he regarded himself, indeed, as an ordinary language philosopher. Nevertheless he sought to show that a philosopher's claims might be 'literally true' even if they appeared to violate the criterion of ordinary use. Thus the claim, made by some philosophers, that seeing an object entails *seeming* to see it, might be true even though it is contrary to the actual use of the language in question. Such discrepancies could, thought Grice, be explained away by what he called 'conversational implicature': to speak of 'seeming' in such cases would be misleading and therefore improper, but it might be true all the same. This view opened the door to a widespread relegation of the criterion of ordinary language. While recognizing the distinction between statements that are false and statements that are misleading and yet true, I do not think it can protect philosophers against objections based on what we ordinarily say.

Grice also attempted, on similar lines, to explain away the discrepancies between truth-functional connectives and their counterparts in ordinary language. In this way he condoned the assumption that forms of argument that are valid within the truth-functional system are also valid in ordinary language – an assumption that I reject, together with Grice's treatment of the matter.

Another major influence in the rejection of linguistic philosophy has come from the direction of science, and this is the topic of the final three chapters. The idea that philosophy can be insulated from scientific findings and theories has been questioned by many, but the most influential thinker in this respect has probably been Quine. In Chapter 11 I examine his arguments against the separation of philosophy from science, and the parallel separation of analytic from synthetic truths.

In Chapter 12 I defend the assumption that in knowing how to use words we know what they mean, against the 'scientific realism' of Putnam and Kripke. According to this, the *real* meanings of words are to be discovered by scientific enquiry into the real nature of the things designated. In this way, it is held, the authority of 'what we say' is undermined and the way left open for a new kind of metaphysics. These ideas are advocated in terms of 'extension' versus 'intension', but in my view what is really behind them is a dogmatic and unjustified preference for scientific criteria (or scientific 'intensions') over those of ordinary language. I also reject the idea of 'rigid designators' as used in this context.

The separation of philosophy from science has been challenged especially in the philosophy of mind, where it is thought that scientific findings and theories about the brain can help to answer philosophical questions about consciousness, thought and feeling, assuming that the latter are, indeed, brain-processes. A constant difficulty of this assumption has been to make it intelligible in terms of the ordinary, existing use of the language concerned, but according to the view discussed in Chapter 13, it is the existing language that must give way to the new science-based theories, and not vice versa. The existing language of 'belief', 'desire', etc., by which we explain human behaviour, is said to belong to an ancient 'folk psychology', whose time for replacement by a more satisfactory, science-based vocabulary is now at hand. I argue that the concepts in question are not replaceable and that the expression 'folk psychology' in this context is inappropriate and misleading.

To what extent our existing concepts are replaceable or variable is a question I discuss in various places in the book. My view is that there is an invariable core of language, and this makes it possible for the claims of linguistic philosophers to be about language as such and not merely about particular languages. To a large extent, as I try to show, our concepts – especially those of interest to philosophers – are bound up with essential human situations: they are part of the human 'form of life'.

Part I

The philosophy of 'what we say'

Its practice and justification

1 Socrates and the quest for definitions

A philosopher may be committed to claims about the uses of words even when this is not obvious. An example is Plato's tripartite division of the soul into a reasoning part, a 'spirited' part and a part concerned with bodily pleasures. This looks like a psychological theory as distinct from any claims about language; yet it is based on such claims. Thus, according to Plato, 'we call the individual courageous ... when the spirited element preserves, in spite of pains and pleasures, the precepts of reason'; and 'we call him wise by reason of that other small part ... which rules and issues these precepts ...' (*Republic* 442c). These are claims about how the relevant language is used.

It might be objected that the appeal to what we say is merely a supporting argument used by Plato to confirm his theory, which is about the soul itself. But as I shall argue, the distinction between 'real' and verbal questions is, in such cases, unreal. The claim that 'we call him wise' if he satisfies the stated condition is no different from the claim that he *is* wise in that case.

Another kind of question in Plato's dialogues, which seems more obviously to be about the uses of words, is that of *definition*, as when he asks 'What is courage?', 'What is piety?', 'What is justice?', 'What is virtue?' and 'What is knowledge?' The *Meno* starts with the question 'Can virtue be taught?', but Socrates replies that he cannot deal with it before determining what virtue *is*. A quest for definition ensues.

Another such quest occurs in the *Laches*, where Socrates asks his interlocutor to 'try to put into words what courage is' (190e). Laches replies that a man is courageous if he is 'prepared to stand in the ranks, face up to the enemy and not run away'; but Socrates points out that this is only one example of courage, whereas a definition should, he thinks, cover all examples (ibid. 192b).

In yet another dialogue Socrates is seeking a definition of knowledge. His interlocutor gives a number of examples, but Socrates makes fun of him. 'My word, you are generous, Theaitetos; so open-handed that, when asked for a single thing, you produce instead a whole variety' (*Theaitetos* 146d). What Socrates is after is not a list of examples but a single overall definition:

> My question, Theaitetos, was not 'What are the objects of knowledge?' nor 'How many kinds of knowledge are there?' We were not trying to count them, but to find out what knowledge (the thing itself) really is. (ibid. 146e)

There is a continuity between Socrates' quest for definitions and Wittgenstein's interest in that topic. Hence it is not surprising that, among his few references to other philosophers, Wittgenstein mentions Socrates as holding the view he opposed. Referring to the latter's treatment of knowledge, he commented:

> The idea that in order to get clear about the meaning of a general term one had to find the common element in all its applications has shackled philosophical investigation; for it has not only led to no result, but also made the philosopher dismiss as irrelevant the concrete cases, which alone could have helped him to understand the usage of the general term.[1]

Although Wittgenstein regarded Socrates' approach as mistaken, he shared the latter's concern about what it is to 'understand the usage of a general term'.

Wittgenstein speaks explicitly of meaning and linguistic usage, but can we be sure that this is how Socrates and Plato saw their problems? In the passage from the *Theaitetos* Socrates speaks of 'knowledge (the thing itself)', which may seem to mean that the enquiry is to be about knowledge itself as opposed to the word. And in general, when Socrates asks for definitions, his question is usually couched in the 'material' and not the 'verbal' mode: what he seems to be after is a definition of X itself rather than of the word 'X'. It may look as if the twentieth century philosopher Wittgenstein imposed his linguistic bias on an ancient text which was not meant in that way.

But when, in the quoted passage, Socrates spoke of 'knowledge (the thing itself)', he did not mean that the discussion was to be about knowledge as opposed to the word 'knowledge'; he meant that it

---

1   L. Wittgenstein, *Blue and Brown Books* (Blackwell 1964), 19–20, 26–7; hereafter 'BB'.

should be about the essential conditions of knowledge – for applying this word correctly – as opposed to a mere production of examples. This is not to say that there is no difference between knowledge and the word 'knowledge', courage and the word 'courage', and so on. Courage is a moral virtue; but this cannot be said of the *word* 'courage'. The word 'courage', on the other hand, has such characteristics as appearing in sentences, being commonly or rarely used, being an English translation of a Greek word, and so on; and these qualities are not attributable to courage itself. The same is true of words and things in general. No one would be tempted to confuse the word 'chair' with a chair or the word 'petrol' with petrol. One cannot sit on the word 'chair' or run a car on the word 'petrol'. Nevertheless the *questions* 'What is X?' and 'What does "X" mean?' may be one and the same. Let us consider how an enquiry about 'the thing itself' is to be conducted. Asked to say what knowledge or courage are, how am I to proceed? How should I investigate 'the thing itself', say knowledge, as distinct from the word? It is not as if knowledge were some kind of stuff, so that we might ask what it consists of, as distinct from asking what the word means. Such a distinction is in order in the case of stuffs, such as petrol. Most people know the ordinary meaning of 'petrol' and in that sense they know what petrol is. But in another sense they do not. Someone who asks 'What is petrol?' may want to know how the stuff is made, what its chemical properties are and so on. And to answer these questions it will be necessary to investigate the stuff itself as opposed to the word. Similarly, the question 'What is solidity?' might call for a scientific answer as opposed to an account of the meaning of this word. But these distinctions do not arise in the case of knowledge and the question 'What is knowledge?' cannot be separated from the question about the meaning of the word. This does not mean that, in asking the latter question, we *set aside* a question about the thing itself; it means that the questions are one and the same: the distinction between 'What is knowledge?' and 'What do we mean by "knowledge"?' is illusory. And the only way of approaching either question is by reference to how we use that word and words related to it.[2]

---

2 A similar point was made by Wittgenstein in a discussion of mental images:

> One ought to ask, not what images are or what happens when one imagines anything, but how the word 'image' is used. But that does not mean that I want to talk only about words. For the question as to the essential nature of images is as much about the word 'image' as my question is (*Philosophical Investigations* (Blackwell 1958) I/370; hereafter 'PI').

The 'linguistic' understanding of Socrates' questions has, however, been contested, especially in the case of moral concepts. One commentator, conceding that Plato sometimes used 'an area of ordinary language ... as his starting point', states that this was not his main interest. 'Plato is primarily interested in knowing what justice, courage, temperance consist in, in the sort of way in which a doctor might be expected to know what health consisted in'.[3]

But in what sense would a doctor be expected to know this? To this question two answers may be given, one linguistic and the other scientific. In the first place, the doctor must know what is meant by 'health' – how this word is used and under what conditions we describe people as healthy or unhealthy. This knowledge is shared by other speakers of the language, though it would be difficult and perhaps impossible to arrive at an agreed definition of the word. And secondly, the doctor would be expected to have knowledge of a scientific kind, not shared by the rest of us, about what *makes* a person healthy or unhealthy.

Now it might be true that Plato's interest in justice and the rest was, in some way, analogous to a doctor's scientific interest in health, but this would not prevent the question of meaning from having a fundamental role in his argument. The difficulty and interest of such questions is, in any case, amply illustrated in Plato's dialogues.

According to another writer, Socrates' questions about courage, etc. were not about meanings but about the human soul and its effects on behaviour.

> When Socrates asked 'What is bravery?' and so forth, he did not want to know what the meaning of the word 'bravery' was .... His question was rather the *general's* question, 'What is bravery?' – that is, 'What is it that makes brave men brave?' The general asks this question not out of interest in mapping our concepts, but out of a desire to learn something substantial about the human psyche.[4]

Socrates' questions, writes Penner, are to be compared with the question 'What is hysteria?' as it might have been meant by Freud – 'to be answered not by logical analysis, but by finding a true psychological theory' (ibid., 41). In both cases what is sought is '*explanation*. They

3   J.C.B. Gosling, *Plato* (Routledge 1973), 185–6.
4   Terry Penner, 'The Unity of Virtue', *Philosophical Review* 1973, 39–40.

are asking about inner motive-forces or states of soul' (45). In the case of Socrates, the question to be pursued is whether *the same* motive-force or state of soul is responsible for all kinds of virtuous behaviour: this, according to Penner, is what 'the unity of the virtues' is about. It turns out, according to the argument as represented by him, that the 'single entity, which makes men brave, wise, temperate, just [etc.] . . . is the knowledge of good and evil'; and this is what is meant by identifying bravery, for example, with the knowledge of good and evil (60–1). When Socrates maintains that 'justice', 'temperance', 'piety', etc. 'are names of one and the same thing', he does not mean that the *words* mean the same; he means that there is a single state of the soul which explains all these kinds of behaviour (50). The thesis is an ontological-theoretical and not a linguistic one.

I shall not question whether, to some extent at least, Socrates (or Plato) saw his enquiry as one of psychological theory rather than logical analysis. What I wish to deny, however, is that questions of meaning can be *excluded* from having a vital role in his argument. Suppose that Socrates' main interest in bravery really was what Penner calls the 'general's question' – 'What is it that makes brave men brave?'. Would it follow that he was not interested in questions of meaning? No; the question that Penner ascribes to Socrates depends essentially on the meaning of 'brave'. One might, indeed, respond to it with 'It depends on what you mean by "brave"'. (Similarly, in the case of the *Meno*, a reponse to the question 'Can virtue be taught?' might be: 'It depends on what you mean by virtue'.) According to Penner, Socrates' aim is to produce an explanatory theory. But such an aim presupposes that the phenomena to be explained have been identified. The phenomena in the present example are brave actions. But which ones are they? 'Facing up to the enemy', replies Laches. Socrates points out that this definition is inadequate.

The argument for the unity of the virtues depends on a further claim about the meaning of 'brave': that to describe an action as 'brave' is incompatible with describing it as 'foolish' or 'shameful'. In the *Protagoras* Socrates puts it to his interlocutor that those who act in daring ways without suitable knowledge or training are not brave but mad. If this were bravery, he says, then 'courage would be something to be ashamed of. Such men are mad' (*Protagoras* 350b). It is from these and similar premises that he argues for the identification of bravery and other virtues with the single virtue of knowledge. But how are these premises arrived at? How does Socrates get his interlocutor to agree that shameful and foolish actions are not brave actions? Not by putting forward a theory about the soul. He simply puts it to Protagoras that one would not describe such actions as brave. Protagoras, being a competent user of the language, is expected to recognize that this is so. If Socrates had really wanted to ask the 'general's question' ('What makes brave men brave?'), why did he not ask it? To *that* question, had it been asked, Laches might suitably have replied: 'Hearing music in the Dorian mode' (cf. *Republic* 399a); and then perhaps Socrates might have objected that this produces only one kind of bravery, etc. But this is not the discussion that Plato puts before us.

Another commentator who rejects the 'linguistic' view is Terence Irwin. According to him, the quest for definitions is a quest for moral judgements as opposed to linguistic knowledge or 'conceptual analysis'. Irwin refers to the passage in which Socrates puts it to his interlocutor that there is more to courage than 'facing up to the enemy'. One can also be courageous in the face of illness, in the face of poverty and in various other situations (*Laches* 191cd). According to Irwin, Laches' admission that this is so 'does not depend on knowledge of what "courage" means', but on 'his judgement that there is no morally relevant distinction between the cases'.[5] But there is no mention of moral judgement in Socrates' argument. He simply puts it to Laches that people in those other cases would also be described as courageous, and Laches agrees.

Whether to describe someone, or some class of people, as 'brave' – whether they deserve this description – might indeed call for moral judgement. The merits of such cases might be discussed and in the end the participants might or might not agree in their verdicts. But if this had been the kind of discussion intended by Plato, then we might have expected him to have Laches *rejecting* the candidates put forward by Socrates; after which the latter might argue that they are worthy to be included for such and such reasons. But this, again, is not the discussion that Plato wrote. Laches' ready acceptance of the candidates put forward can only be understood if Socrates was reminding him of an accepted part of meaning of 'courage', which he had apparently overlooked. The question was about the range of application of a word, such as might arise with any other word or predicate. Take, for example, the word 'game'. A latter-day Laches, asked to 'try to put into words' what a game is, might reply that it is a competitive activity with rules for winning and losing. And then a latter-day Socrates could remind Laches of uses of the word that are not covered by his definition. He could show, like the original Socrates, that the definition

---

5   Terence Irwin, *Plato's Moral Theory* (OUP 1977), 64.

gives neither necessary nor sufficient conditions for the use of the word.

In another passage in the same dialogue, Socrates argues that 'courage' is not properly applicable to animals. His reason is that animals lack the *knowledge* that is essential to courage. Now according to Irwin, this is a case in which 'a moral principle' is used to override an accepted use of language. According to the latter, says Irwin, animals provide 'recognized paradigm examples' of courage; but in spite of this Socrates denies that they are really cases of courage and 'insists on a moral principle which rules them out. This kind of argument is legitimate if he means to discover the truth about courage, but not if he means to discover what "courage" means' (Irwin 64).

But Socrates' argument depends essentially on a claim about the meaning of 'courage'. According to him, knowledge (of a kind that animals lack) is analytic to 'courage'. He expects those who are competent in the use of the word to recognize this; and that, in effect, is what happens in the dialogue. Nicias assures Socrates that he does *not* apply this word to animals, preferring to describe an animal that is unafraid of danger as 'fearless' or 'foolish' (*Laches* 196d–197b). His reason for this cannot be that he defers to a 'moral principle'; it is that he, like Socrates, regards knowledge as a logically necessary condition of 'courage'.[6]

In a further argument, Irwin refers to a discussion in the *Republic* (335a–e) about whether 'harming one's enemies' should be included in the definition of justice. Polemarchus thinks it should, but Socrates objects. A person who is harmed, he argues, becomes worse; and making someone worse is contrary to justice. According to Irwin, this is a moral conclusion, and 'a purely conceptual enquiry should have no moral implications' (op. cit. 64). If the issue were merely conceptual, he says, then Polemarchus could opt for either alternative: he could stick to his original position, or agree that it is unjust to harm an enemy. But 'Socrates does not allow these options'; he 'appeals to the interlocutor's moral judgements' to compel him to accept the second.

But there is no such appeal in the dialogue. Socrates' argument is designed to show that the initial definition of 'justice' was inconsistent

---

6 Whether they are right about this is another question. It would be surprising, however, if their claim were really contrary to 'recognized paradigm examples' of courage. But is this a proper description of the case of animals? If one were asked to give paradigm examples of courage, one would hardly choose animals for the purpose. The reason for this is, indeed, that animals lack the kind of knowledge that we would expect to find in paradigm examples of courage.

with a more considered analysis. The question is one of meaning and not moral judgement. If 'just' means 'repaying like with like', then it *is* just for me to harm those who have harmed me (and harm them to a proportionate extent); but if it means 'doing good to people' (or not 'making them worse'), then it is not. Socrates wants to persuade his interlocutor that the latter expresses the true meaning of 'justice' and that his initial definition had been a mistake. But this is not a matter of moral judgement. The question to be decided is not whether one definition is 'morally better' than another, but which one correctly describes the use of the word. Nor is this a question on which Polemarchus has an option: the correct description of the use of a word is not a matter of personal choice.

On the other hand, is it right to say that 'a purely conceptual enquiry should have no moral implications'? If this means that a person's moral behaviour cannot be affected by such an enquiry, then it is not. Polemarchus may have thought that in repaying harm with harm, one would have justice on one's side; but a 'conceptual enquiry' may get him to see that this is not so, and this may well affect his behaviour.

A commentator who is more sympathetic to a 'linguistic' understanding of these discussions is Gregory Vlastos, who describes Socrates' enquiry as 'a search for the meanings' of the relevant words. He warns the reader, however, against understanding this phrase in a way that might seem to diminish the importance of the enquiry. The latter, he writes,

> is anything but a lexicographical inquiry into contemporary Greek usage. It involves an analysis of the concepts named by those words – an analysis which may lead . . . to a radical revision of the meaning which attaches to those words in unreflective current usage.

Having quoted, by way of example, Laches' definition of 'courage' and Socrates' 'parade of counter-examples', he comments:

> These examples so stretch the application of the word as to break the traditional moral dogma that had kept courage a class-bound, sex-bound virtue. All this is accomplished . . . by simply appealing to the interlocutor's linguistic intuitions, counting on his ability to recognize instantly new cases of courage as they are brought into his ken.[7]

7   G. Vlastos, *Platonic Studies* (Princeton 1981), 411, note 3.

In this passage the linguistic, conceptual aspect of the enquiry is rightly emphasized; but how are we to understand the dismissal of 'lexicography' in favour 'a radical revision of meaning'? Laches, we are told, was to 'recognize instantly' the 'new cases of courage' to which his attention was drawn. But this could only have happened if the existing concept of courage – as expressed in the 'contemporary Greek usage' which Laches shared with others – already allowed for such cases. Otherwise, why should Laches accept them? If they were contrary to current usage, then his 'instant recognition' would be unintelligible. Socrates could not accomplish 'a radical revision of meaning' merely by producing examples not conforming to the existing meaning. Suppose that 'upper-class male' had been analytic to the Greek word. Then Socrates, in bringing forward his examples as examples of courage, would simply be making a strange mistake – as if his knowledge of the language were deficient.

If it were really Socrates' aim to change the meaning of the Greek word, then he would have to set about it in a different way. One such way would be to *use* it with the new meaning, in his writings and conversation. He might perhaps explain to his readers why he thought the new, extended use justified; and he might hope that others would copy him and that in due course the new use would become the ordinary use. But this is not what is going on in *Laches*.

I have defended a linguistic reading of Socrates' enquiries against a number of alternatives. The question is not merely one of exegesis: it also concerns the general importance of linguistic enquiries. My aim has been to show that, in Plato's writings as elsewhere, questions of meaning cannot be prevented from having a fundamental place in philosophical discussion.[8] It may be felt that to read Plato in this way is to diminish the importance of what he wrote; but this, as I have also tried to show, would be a mistake.

In a famous passage Socrates compared himself with a midwife. His pupil Theaitetos's mind, he says, is 'in the throes of travail' (*Theaitetos* 148e), and his job as a midwife is to help him give birth to a truth as opposed to a miscarriage. But, he insists, the labour and the delivery

---

8 The question 'What is X?' is not, of course, always pursued as a question about the use of 'X'. An interesting example is the question 'What is justice?' in the *Republic*. When Thrasymachus replies that 'justice is nothing else than the advantage of the stronger' (338c), he can hardly mean that this is how the word is actually used. His 'nothing else than' ('nothing but') indicates that he is putting forward a 'debunking' claim: all that justice comes to, he thinks, is what is enacted by the stronger parties in their own interests (338e). See A.G.N. Flew, 'Responding to Plato's Thrasymachus', *Philosophy* 1995.

must be the work of Theaitetos himself. His pupils, he remarks, have 'never learned anything from [him]; the many grand truths they bring into the world have been discovered by themselves and from within' (150d). This is readily understandable if the truths to be discovered are truths about meaning. Such truths are 'within' us, but much labour may be needed in order to arrive at a correct understanding and presentation of them. Socrates' procedure as described in these passages may be compared with Wittgenstein's method of 'assembling reminders'.[9] 'To study philosophy', wrote Wittgenstein, 'is really to recollect. We remind ourselves that we really use words in this and this way.'[10]

Questions about the role of language have also arisen with regard to Aristotle, whose reliance on 'what we say' is evident in such writings as the *Categories* and *Metaphysics V.* In the *Categories*, for example, he explains his distinction between primary and secondary substance by linguistic observations:

> Whenever one thing is predicated of another as of a subject, all things said of what is predicated will be said of the subject also. For example, man is predicated of the individual man, and animal of man; so animal will be predicated of the individual man also. (*Categories* ch. 3)

But, it has been asked, 'is the theory of categories an exercise in ontology or in linguistics? Does Aristotle classify things or words?'[11] Sometimes it looks as if he is doing ontology and merely using linguistic arguments to *support* his views about reality. Thus in support of the (ontological) claim that 'substance . . . does not admit of a more and a less', he appeals to facts about what we say: a body that is hot 'is called more, or less, hot'; whereas 'substance . . . is not spoken of thus. For a man is not called more a man now than before' (*Categories* ch. 5).

But the distinction between ontological and linguistic questions is as unreal in the case of categories as in the case of knowledge and the word 'knowledge'. To say that substance does not admit of more or less is no different from saying that we do not use substance words (such as 'a man') in that way, whereas we do use other kinds of words (such as 'hot') in that way. It is not as if Aristotle could somehow

---

9   L. Wittgenstein, *Philosophical Investigations* op. cit. I/127.
10   'Big Typescript', 419, quoted by G.P. Baker and P.M.S. Hacker, *Analytical Commentary*, Vol. 1 (Blackwell 1983), 240.
11   J.D.G. Evans, *Aristotle* (Harvard 1987), 47.

investigate the nature of substance as *distinct* from the linguistic practices. There is nothing (no 'substance itself') which stands in that relationship to what we say; and the account of how we use substance words is *ipso facto* an account of substance.

It might be objected that 'substance' is a technical term and hence not governed by ordinary usage. But this is not how the word appears in Aristotle's discussion. Aristotle does not say that he proposes to use the word in a technical sense. His explanation of it is given in terms of ordinary words such as 'a man' and the ordinary sentences in which this phrase might appear.

2 Austin

'At least *one* philosophical method'

The idea that philosophy is essentially about language is often associated with the linguistic philosophy that flourished, especially at Oxford, in the 1950s and 1960s, and which included Ryle and Austin among its leading exponents. It is probably Austin, more than anyone, who came to be regarded as the archetypal ordinary language philosopher. Austin's work on various topics has earned him an enduring place in the history of philosophy, and to do justice to it would be beyond the scope of this book. My aim will be to examine his views about the method of 'what we say' and his use of it in certain cases.

It is clear, both from his writings and from the memoirs of those who remember his lectures, that Austin was fascinated by words and meanings in themselves, independently of their relevance to problems of philosophy. While few would deny that his insights into the uses of language enabled him to make important and highly original contributions to philosophy, his interest in words sometimes laid him open to the charge of replacing serious philosophy by 'merely verbal' enquiries. Such charges may have been encouraged by some of his own remarks. In the concluding paragraphs of *How to do Things with Words* he confessed: 'I have as usual failed to leave enough time in which to say why what I have said is interesting'.[1] In another work he suggested that a good way to start on the subject under discussion would be to read through a dictionary, 'listing all the words that seem relevant'. The dictionary, he reassures us, need not be a large one: 'quite a concise one will do, but the use [of it] must be *thorough*'.[2]

When he turned his mind to the status of the linguistic philosophy that he and others were practising, his defence of it was half-hearted and unsatisfactory. In 'Ifs and Cans' he demonstrated the importance of

1   J.L. Austin, *How to do Things with Words* (OUP 1962). p. 162.
2   J.L. Austin, *Philosophical Papers* (Clarendon 1961),134 (hereafter 'PP').

this method in practice, making a major contribution to the topic of free will. Yet in concluding the essay he predicted that linguistic philosophy might one day be absorbed by 'a true and comprehensive *science of language'*. Then, he said, 'we shall have rid ourselves of one more part of philosophy (there will still be plenty left) in the only way we can ever get rid of philosophy, by kicking it upstairs' (PP 180). He apparently regarded the philosophy of 'what we say' as a temporary phase and looked forward to the day when a more satisfactory scientific treatment of the topics in question would become available. But he never explained how a 'comprehensive science of language' could replace or improve on what, for example, he had done in his essay.[3]

In another essay he observed that his method, 'at least as *one* philosophical method, scarcely requires justification at present – too evidently, there is gold in them thar hills'; but he nevertheless undertook to 'justify it very briefly' (PP 129). Ordinary language deserves the philosopher's respect, he argued, because

> our common stock of words embodies all the distinctions men have found worth drawing, and the connexions they have found worth marking, in the lifetimes of many generations: these surely are likely to be more numerous, more sound ..., than any that you or I are likely to think up in our arm-chairs of an afternoon. (PP 130; see also SS 63)

We are not, however, to think of ordinary language as 'the last word'. Although it has proved its worth in 'the practical business of life', it is likely 'to be not the best way of arranging things if our interests are more extensive or intellectual than the ordinary'. Ordinary language, he concluded, 'is *not* the last word: in principle it can everywhere be supplemented and improved upon and superseded. Only remember, it *is* the first word' (PP 133).

How are we understand this talk of the first word and the last word? The main subject of Austin's essay was the language of excuses, including such words as 'unintentionally', 'inadvertently' and 'involuntarily'. He described how these and related words are used and tried to display the difference between, say, acting unintentionally and acting inadvertently, by describing the different situations in which these words would be appropriate. But in such an enquiry 'the last

---

3 The relation of philosophy and linguistic science will be further discussed in Chapter 4.

word' must be that of actual use. This is what a philosopher must appeal to if he wishes to show that, and how, these words differ in meaning. The fact that ordinary language can sometimes be 'supplemented', etc., does not affect this point. The enquiry is *about* those words and not about others that might be used to supplement them. If the latter were the subject of the enquiry, then it is to *their* use that the philosopher would have to refer (and defer).

What did Austin have in mind in saying that ordinary language could 'everywhere be supplemented and improved upon and superseded'? Having examined the language of excuses and of action with much insight, he concluded with a disclaimer:

> In spite of the wide and acute observation of the phenomena of action embodied in ordinary speech, modern scientists have been able, it seems to me, to reveal its inadequacy at numerous points, if only because they have had access to more comprehensive data and have studied them with more catholic and dispassionate interest than the ordinary man ... (PP 151).

He gave two examples, taken from psychological theory: 'displacement behaviour' and 'compulsive behaviour' (152).

These expressions might indeed be regarded as supplementing ordinary language (though the second might be regarded as part of ordinary language by now). It is, indeed, obvious that ordinary language is not the whole of language, and that it may be supplemented in scientific and various other ways. But that ordinary language can 'everywhere be ... improved upon and superseded' is far from obvious, and Austin's examples do nothing to support this claim. They do not show, for example, that there is anything deficient about the uses of the words discussed by Austin in his essay. Nor could they, or other scientific words, undermine the ordinary distinctions between, say, 'unintentionally' and 'inadvertently' or between 'succumbing to temptation' and 'losing control of ourselves' (146).

Another weakness of Austin's 'justification' of ordinary language philosophy is related to his false conception of the nature of language. 'Words', he wrote,

> are not (except in their own little corner) facts or things: we need therefore to prise them off the world, to hold them apart from and against it, so that we can realize their inadequacies and arbitrariness, and can re-look at the world without blinkers. (130)

But if this is how words and world are related, why, we might wonder, should we bother about words at all? Why not look at the world directly 'without blinkers', avoiding the 'inadequacies and arbitrariness' of words?[4]

Austin's metaphors are vivid but misleading and his advice is unintelligible. If one wanted to study life on the sea shore, one might be well advised to prise off the rocks lying on top, so that one might 'look at the world' concealed underneath. But how can words be prised off the world?

Take, for example, the phrases 'succumbing to temptation' and 'losing control of oneself', which Austin discussed. What could it mean to prise these phrases off in order to look at the world underneath? This, in any case, was not what Austin attempted when he wanted to bring out the distinction between them. What he did was not to 'look at the world', but to *use words,* to describe different examples of behaviour. In one of these a person helps himself to a large portion of ice cream and thereby succumbs to temptation; but this, as Austin pointed out, is not the same as losing control of oneself, which would be the case if 'I snatch the morsels from the dish and wolf them down, impervious to the consternation of my colleagues' (PP 146). In this and similar ways Austin was able to clarify these notions and exhibit the difference between them. He did not do it, and could not have done it, by 'holding words against' a non-verbal world.

In speaking in this way of our language, Austin seems to have conceived of it as akin to a map. A map may be evaluated by the extent to which its 'vocabulary' – the symbols used in it – correspond to features of the world. Thus a map with a symbol for churches may be preferred to one without; a map that distinguishes between different kinds of road, to one that shows them all in the same way; and so on. And here it is appropriate to speak of comparing the map – 'holding it against' – the world that it represents, and perhaps revising it accordingly. (In another passage Austin wrote that 'when we have discovered how a word is in fact used, that may not be the end of the matter... ; we may wish to tidy the situation up a bit, revise the map here and there ....)[5]

Language is not, however, like a map, and our 'stock of words' is not to be evaluated by comparing it with the world, as may be done

---

4   Austin's position reminds one of Berkeley's advice (discussed in Ch. 8) that 'we need only draw the curtain of words, to behold the fairest tree of knowledge' (G. Berkeley, *Principles of Human Knowledge* (Dent 1993); hereafter 'PHK'; Introduction §24).

5   J.L. Austin, *Sense and Sensibilia* (SS) (OUP 1962), 63.

with the stock of symbols employed in a map. In the early years of the twentieth century a new term, 'willow tit', was introduced into ornithology, to mark an observed distinction between two kinds of tit, formerly known under the single name 'marsh tit'. (One kind of bird has a more glossy head, its call is slightly different, etc.) Here is an addition to our stock of words which marks a distinction in the world. This improvement is not, however, like the introduction of a new symbol on a map. If the map has no distinct symbols to represent two kinds of churches, then it *cannot* show that distinction; but this is not so in the case of words and birds. The distinction between marsh tit and willow tit can be made perfectly well without using these words; indeed, it is so made in *explaining* what the words mean (i.e. that one means a bird with a more glossy head, etc.). What caused the introduction of a distinct word was not a comparison of language with the world, revealing a distinction in the world which could not be marked in the existing language; it was the preference for a more convenient way of expressing an already describable distinction.

This is not to say that new words can always be defined, or defined easily, in already existing language or that their introduction is superfluous. It is indeed obvious that a vocabulary can be enriched by the introduction of new words, which may be related to new ideas and new discoveries. But this does not undermine the point that the resources of a language do not depend, like those of a map, on a correspondence of words or symbols to things in the world.

It is sometimes said that English has a richer vocabulary than other languages. But this, if true, would not entail that more distinctions can be made in English than in other languages. Nor would it be helpful to recommend to speakers of other languages to try holding their stock of words against the world. A distinction in which Austin was interested was that between 'inadvertently' and 'automatically'. (He complained that some people had 'equated' these two words: 'as though to say I trod on your foot inadvertently means to say I trod on it automatically' (PP 146).) But what if these words were not available in another language? Could the distinction not be made in that language?

It is hardly likely that the English words discussed by Austin would have exact counterparts in other languages; they may not even be part of the vocabulary of some speakers of English. But whether the relevant distinctions are observed does not depend on the existence of a particular stock of words. This can be seen by considering how we might understand an anthropologist's report of life in a tribal society. It would not surprise us to read that in such and such case someone excused his behaviour by saying he had acted inadvertently, while in another the excuse was that one had acted automatically. Would this mean that the language of that tribe contained counterparts of the English words? This would not be necessary, and the question would probably not occur to us. The justification of the anthropologist's translation would not lie in the existence of such words, but in the nature of the relevant situations and the practical implications of whatever was said in those situations.[6] (This topic will be further discussed in Chapter 4.)

In some of his writings, including the essay on excuses, Austin's main aim was to show how a particular range of language is used. Elsewhere he was more concerned to rebut the views of philosophers on certain topics. His methodology in these writings is another cause for criticism. In the essay 'Other Minds', he discussed the claims of sceptics, proposing to test them by considering 'what sort of thing does actually happen when ordinary people are asked "How do you know?" ' (PP 45). He would oppose the sceptics' claims by drawing attention to the ordinary use of the relevant language. When a claim to knowledge is questioned, he said, the questioner 'must have in mind some more or less definite lack'; he is not expected to demand that every conceivable possibility of falsehood has been eliminated (52). Doubts are raised when there is a particular reason for doubting, and then the doubt in question is 'to be allayed by means of recognized procedures' (55). Thus there might be various reasons for doubting whether an object is real; and what kind of doubt is involved should be clear from the context or after questioning. And once this is clarified, we know what procedures would serve to allay the doubt. By contrast,

> the wile of the metaphysician [i.e. the sceptical philosopher] consists in asking 'Is it a real table?' (a kind of object which has no obvious way of being phoney) and not specifying or limiting what may be wrong with it, so that I feel at a loss 'how to prove' it *is* a real one. (55)

To the philosopher who claims that 'we are never aware of more than *symptoms* of anger in another man', he would put the question: 'But *is* this the way we do talk?' (75). We usually, he said, speak of 'symptoms' or 'signs' of anger to mean signs of *rising* or *suppressed*

---

6 Similarly, the making of promises depends on suitable situations and not on the existence or use of the word 'promise', or its equivalent in other languages. See O. Hanfling, 'Promises, Games and Institutions' in *Procs. of the Aristotelian Society* 1974–5.

anger; but, in contrast to mere signs or symptoms, we also speak of 'the actual display of anger'. And when the angry man 'has given himself away we say that we *know*' he is angry (76). Sometimes, again, a man *tells* us 'what his feelings are'; and then, 'in the usual case, we accept this statement without question, and we then say that we know . . .'. In some cases, it is true, there may be reasons for thinking that the man is pretending, etc.; but if so, there are procedures for allaying these doubts too. There is, says Austin, 'no suggestion that I *never* know what other people's emotions are' (81).

Here, as elsewhere, Austin's descriptions of language are sensitive and illuminating, but how effective are they in combatting the claims of sceptics? The sceptic was not unaware that in some cases 'we say that we know', that we sometimes 'accept [a man's] statement without question', etc. His question, however, is whether we are justified in saying these things: whether we really know.[7] Again, Austin may be right in saying that the question whether we really know is ordinarily raised only in cases in which there is a specific reason for doubting, and that there are, or usually are, procedures for allaying the doubt. But why should this impress the sceptic? To Austin's claim that there is 'no suggestion that I *never* know', etc., he might retort that this is precisely the suggestion that he is making.

Austin accuses the sceptic of 'wile' in introducing the question 'Is it a real table?' without a suitable context. But that question was not asked out of the blue, without rhyme or reason. Sceptics have put forward a variety of reasons for doubting that knowledge is possible. It is true that their doubts are not specific like ordinary ones; but that is because, according to their arguments, the impossibility of knowledge is comprehensive. And to refute their arguments something more is required than merely pointing out that their questions and doubts are out of the ordinary.

So far, the debate between Austin and his adversary seems to amount to no more than this: the latter, by means of certain arguments, produces a confrontation between what we ordinarily say and what, as he sees it, is really the case (i.e. that knowledge is impossible); and Austin, in his reply, brings out the force and nature of the confrontation, by describing in detail what we ordinarily say. It is no

---

7   A similar complaint might be made about the later Wittgenstein's treatment of his own earlier philosophy, in which he rebuts statements he had made in the *Tractatus* by pointing out that they are contrary to ordinary language. I discuss this in *Wittgenstein's Later Philosophy* (Macmillan 1989), 31ff.

wonder that, notwithstanding the insight and originality of Austin's descriptive work, the philosophers concerned have sometimes felt frustrated by this treatment of their problems. Here is one of the reasons why ordinary language philosophy fell into disrepute.

In another work, Austin opposed the view that 'we never *directly* perceive ... material objects (or material things), but only sense-data' (SS 2), with the implication that we cannot be certain that material objects really exist. In his response, he pointed out what an ordinary person might say when looking at a chair that is in front of him in broad daylight.

> The plain man would regard doubt in such a case, not as far-fetched or over-refined or somehow unpractical, but as plain *nonsense*; he would say, quite correctly, 'Well if that's not seeing a real chair, then *I don't know what is.* (10)

'The philosophers' use of "directly perceive"', he pointed out, is not the ordinary one; 'for in *that* use it is not only false but simply absurd to say that such objects as pens or cigarettes are never perceived directly' (19).

The view that what we directly perceive are 'sense-data' had been introduced by A.J. Ayer in connection with an 'argument from illusion'; and Austin quotes extensively from Ayer's book.

> A man who sees a mirage, he [Ayer] says, is 'not perceiving any material thing; for the oasis which he thinks he is perceiving *does not exist'*. But 'his *experience* is not an experience of nothing ...; he is experiencing sense-data, which are similar in character to what he would be experiencing if he were seeing a real oasis ...'.[8]
> (SS 21; the passages in quotation marks are from Ayer's book)

The term 'sense-data' was then (as reported by Austin) extended by Ayer to cover the perception of real objects as well as mirages, 'on the old familiar ground that delusive and veridical perceptions' do not differ in quality. And according to Ayer, this extension could be justified, not as representing a 'factual discovery', but as 'a new verbal usage' (SS 87).

Now Austin had no difficulty in showing how the new verbal usage differs from what we ordinarily say; and throughout his discussion he made astute observations about the latter, as opposed to the claims and

---

8   A.J. Ayer, *The Foundations of Empirical Knowledge* (Macmillan 1940).

usages of philosophers. But how relevant are these observations to Ayer's position? In the passage just referred to, the latter made it clear that he was putting forward a new usage and not trying to adhere to the existing one. Notwithstanding the intrinsic interest of Austin's remarks about the existing language, they are useless against an adversary who does not purport to adhere to this language. (Austin himself, moreover, was prepared, as we saw earlier, to concede that ordinary language 'can everywhere be ... improved upon and superseded'.)[9]

Ayer's rejoinder to Austin[10] was an impressive performance. He distinguished no fewer than seventeen arguments against the 'theory of sense-data' in Austin's text, and proceeded to rebut them one by one with his usual elegance. Most of these rebuttals rely on the fact that in presenting his theory he had not been using words in their ordinary sense. He readily admitted, for example, that 'one would not ordinarily say that the existence of the chair was uncertain unless one had some *special* reason' (285); but, he replied, the use of 'uncertain' by himself and other philosophers has a 'technical sense', which makes it immune against objections drawn from ordinary use (294). Austin, as we saw, had countered the claim that we 'never *directly* perceive material objects' (SS 2) by pointing out that this is 'not the ordinary use' of 'directly perceive', and that according to the latter 'it is not only false but simply absurd' to deny that material objects are directly perceived. But Ayer's reply to this was predictable and appropriate: 'As I have construed expressions like "directly see", it would be contradictory to speak of directly seeing material things ...' (Ayer, op. cit. 295).

Ayer conceded that the sense-datum terminology may be 'misleading', but he thought it was defensible all the same, provided that the philosopher's reasons were properly understood.

> When the sense-datum theorist says, no doubt misleadingly, that even in the most favourable conditions of perception it remains

---

9   In an early paper, ('The Meaning of a Word', 1940), Austin had been sympathetic to the introduction of new usages, by philosophers and not merely scientists.

> There may be plenty that might happen and does happen which would need new and better language to describe it. Very often philosophers are only engaged in this task, when they seem to be perversely using words in a way which makes no sense according to 'ordinary usage'. There may be extraordinary facts, even about our everyday experience, which plain men and plain language overlook. (PP 37)

10   A.J. Ayer, 'Has Austin Refuted Sense-Data?' and 'Rejoinder to Professor Forguson' in K.T. Fann, ed., *Symposium on J.L. Austin* (Routledge & Kegan Paul 1969).

uncertain whether the chair exists, what he must be understood to mean is that the statement that the chair exists does not follow logically from any statement, or indeed from any finite number of statements, which are limited to describing the content of the observer's experience. (286)

He drew attention to 'the far-reaching implications of even so unambitious a statement as that this is a table'. The object must 'endure throughout a period of time', it must be 'accessible to touch as well as to sight ... [and] accessible to different observers', and it must 'continue to exist even when no one is perceiving it' (290). Ayer thought that by pointing out what is involved in the assertion that this is a table, he would be able to 'overcome' the resistance that may be felt to the introduction of technical terms such as 'visual experience', and to the idea that the statement about the table represents an 'inference' from such an experience.

It looks as if Austin had simply misunderstood what Ayer had been doing. Ayer introduces his theory in language which admittedly does not conform to ordinary use; Austin points out that, and how, it deviates from ordinary use; Ayer repeats that it was not meant to conform to ordinary use, and explains (or repeats) his reasons for introducing it.

There is one place, however, in which Austin put his finger on a fundamental difficulty of Ayer's position. In a typical passage, Ayer had claimed that the difference between two accounts of the nature of perception was purely verbal and not a matter of true or false. 'If there is here to be any question of truth or falsehood, there must be some disagreement about the nature of the empirical facts. And in this case no such disagreement exists' (Ayer, quoted at SS 59).

But Austin was not prepared to take Ayer at his word in this matter. The latter, he claimed, 'does not regard [the issue] as really verbal at all – his real view is that *in fact* we perceive only sense-data'. If, he wrote, Ayer were right in describing the dispute as 'purely verbal',

> then absolutely every dispute would be purely verbal. For if, when one person says whatever it may be, another person may simply 'prefer to say' something else, they will *always* be arguing only about words, about what terminology is to be preferred. How could *anything* be a question of truth or falsehood, if anyone can always say whatever he likes? (SS 59–60) ... If we allow ourselves this degree of *insouciant* latitude, surely we shall be able to deal – in *a way,* of course – with absolutely anything. (SS 58)

In his rejoinder, Ayer maintained that this criticism had 'missed the point. It overlooks the fact that I was not operating within our ordinary conceptual scheme but considering a revision of it' (Ayer 300). But this is to ignore Austin's point that if the question of truth or falsehood were really to be set aside, then the dispute about sense data, like any other, would lose its substance.

What was at issue was the underlying nature and aim of the enquiry. If truth was not the aim, could there be any other reason for preferring the account of perception favoured by Ayer? According to Ayer, 'the sense-datum terminology is in some ways more perspicuous, and ... is therefore convenient for the purposes of philosophical analysis' (Ayer, 346). But he did not explain why it should be regarded as more perspicuous or more convenient for this or any other purpose. It is, after all, perfectly easy to describe the phenomena of illusion, hallucination and the like in ordinary language.

It is noteworthy that Ayer himself more than once described the philosophers' usage, which he condoned, as misleading; as when he wrote, in the passage quoted above, that 'when the sense-datum theorist says, no doubt misleadingly, that even in the most favourable conditions of perception it remains uncertain', etc. If this use of language is admittedly misleading, would it not be better to use a frankly technical terminology instead of words drawn from ordinary language? As it is, the reader is left, notwithstanding Ayer's disclaimers, with the impression that he really regards the existence of the table as uncertain. The attempt to use 'uncertain' in a special sense is no more satisfactory than was the description of Mr Pickwick as 'a humbug', where this word was to be understood 'without its usual connotations'.

But was it possible for Ayer to use a frankly technical terminology instead of ordinary words such as 'uncertain' and 'directly'? It is hard to see how these words could have been replaced without making nonsense of his claims. How, for example, could the word 'directly' be replaced in the claim that we never perceive material objects directly, or the word 'uncertain' in the claim that the existence of the table before me is uncertain?

Let us compare Ayer's predicament with the position of an imaginary philosopher who denies that what comes out of our taps is water. On being challenged, he explains that this is so according to *his* use of 'water': he uses the word to mean 'pure H_2O'. Here is a trivial misunderstanding which is easily cleared up. The imaginary philosopher might be advised, in the interest of clarity, to express his denial by *using* the term 'pure H_2O' rather than the ordinary 'water', and he might be accused of being perverse if he refused to do so. But Ayer's difficulty, as Austin saw, was not of this superficial kind.

The ambivalence of Ayer's position, of his wanting to eat the cake and have it, may be further illustrated by his treatment, in another essay, of moral discourse. Here he undertook to uphold the view that 'what are called ethical statements are not really statements at all'. Yet he conceded that this view 'is in an obvious sense incorrect. For, as the English language is currently used – and what else, it may be asked, is here in question? – it is by no means improper to refer to ethical utterances as statements'.[11]

Ayer was not one of those who simply ignore or brush aside the ordinary uses of language; but he thought that something could be gained from speaking in deviant and, as he admitted, potentially misleading ways. But he never showed what these gains, overriding the pursuit of truth, might be. The difficulty of Ayer's position, and the importance of Austin's diagnosis, are of more than local interest. As we shall see in later chapters, similar difficulties are faced by others who have tried to replace ordinary language by supposedly superior alternatives.

---

11 A.J. Ayer, *Philosophical Essays* (Macmillan 1965), 231. The vacillating attitudes of philosophers towards ordinary language are discussed again in later chapters.

3   Wittgenstein

Bringing words 'back to their everyday use'

Wittgenstein and ordinary language

Austin's remarks about the methods of philosophy, and his ideas about language versus reality, are open to criticism, as we have seen. His thoughts on these topics seem to have been rather sparse, for most of what he wrote about them is contained in the passages I quoted. Wittgenstein, by contrast, expressed interest in both topics at length and in various ways. In the *Tractatus*[1] he presented a correspondence theory of meaning, believing that language consists of propositions that can be analyzed into simple constituents which have meaning by standing for simple constituents of reality. At this level, 'a name means an object. The object is its meaning' (*Tractatus* 3.203). These 'names', he held, are combined in 'elementary propositions', in a way corresponding to the combination of 'objects' in states of affairs. (There is a similarity between this and the 'map theory' discussed in the last chapter.)

These ideas were, however, rejected in Wittgenstein's later writings. Meanings, he now held, cannot be identified with objects and propositions are not analyzable in the way he had envisaged. The meaning of a word is to be found in its use and the uses of words are multifarious. He illustrated this variety by a sketch introduced in the very first section of the *Investigations*,[2] in which someone goes shopping with a slip marked 'five red apples'. Each of these words has to be treated in a different way by the shopkeeper. He 'opens the drawer marked "apples"; then he looks up the word "red" in a table and finds a colour sample opposite it; then he says the series of cardinal

---

1   L. Wittgenstein, *Tractatus Logico-Philosophicus* (Routledge & Kegan Paul 1961).
2   *Philosophical Investigations* (Blackwell 1958). References are to sections of Part I.

numbers' and counts out the apples as he does so. To the question how he knows what to do with each of the words, Wittgenstein replies: 'Well, I assume he *acts* as I have described. Explanations come to an end somewhere.' And to the question 'what is the meaning of the word "five"?', he answers: 'No such thing was in question here, only how the word 'five' is used' (PI 1). To understand the nature of language we must consider how different words actually work in practice ('he *acts* as I have described'). We are not to assume that behind these phenomena there must be a systematic correspondence between elements of language and elements of reality, as had been done in the *Tractatus* and in the systems of other philosophers.[3]

The description of Austin as an ordinary language philosopher could hardly be contested; but is the same true of Wittgenstein? Some would hesitate to describe him so, perhaps because of a reluctance to associate him too closely with the Oxford philosophy to which the label 'ordinary language' came to be attached, sometimes with derogatory connotations. In a way, however, Wittgenstein's commitment to the method of 'what we say' is more radical than Austin's. The latter, as we saw, thought that words could be tested for adequacy by comparing them with 'the world', but there is no room for such evaluations in Wittgenstein's account of language, where the meaning of a word is identified with its use.

The appeal to what we ordinarily say is, in any case, prominent in Wittgenstein's writings. Given the claim that the soul is an incorporeal entity that can 'leave the body', he replied: 'Show me how the word "soul" is used, and I will see whether the soul is incorporeal ...'.[4] The word 'mind', likewise, must be understood by reference to its actual use. To the question 'Is there then no mind, but only a body?', he replies: 'The word "mind" has a use in our language; but saying this doesn't yet say what kind of use we make of it'.[5] If we consider how the word is used, then we may find it hard or impossible to make sense of the ideas in question. The same method appears in Wittgenstein's treatment of 'What is ... ?' questions of the kind posed by Socrates. Thus the question 'What is thinking?' is to be treated, according to

---

3 The positing of simple objects as ultimate objects of meaning goes back at least as far as Plato, and Wittgenstein quotes a passage from the *Theaetetus* to this effect, commenting that 'both Russell's "individuals" and my "objects" ... were such primary elements' (PI 46).

4 *Zettel* (Blackwell 1967) §127; hereafter 'Z'.

5 *Blue and Brown Books* (Blackwell 1964), 69–70.

him, by reference to how this word is used in everyday language (PI 327–8, Z 113). In other passages he opposed what he took to be *mis*uses of words by philosophers.

> When philosophers use a word – 'knowledge', 'being', 'object', 'I', 'proposition', 'name' – and try to grasp the *essence* of the thing, one must always ask oneself: is the word ever actually used in this way in the language which is its original home?

What he proposed was to 'bring [such] words back ... to their everyday use' (PI 116). Commenting on his own statement in the *Tractatus* that 'a name means an object', he now pointed out that the use of 'meaning' to 'signify the thing that "corresponds" to the word' is not a normal one. 'When Mr N.N. dies one says that the bearer of the name dies, not that the meaning dies' (PI 40).

In the *Tractatus* he had stated 'the essence of a proposition' as follows: 'The general form of a proposition is: This is how things stand' (4.5, 5.471). (What he meant by this need not be explored here.) But in his later work he applied the criterion of everyday language to that statement. The latter, he remarked, 'is first and foremost *itself* a proposition, an English sentence . . . . But how is this sentence applied – that is, in our everyday language? For I got it from there and nowhere else'. He proceeded to give an example of someone saying 'This is how things stand' in an ordinary conversation. (PI 134; cf. Z 448).

He used the same approach in combatting a number of plausible assumptions about the nature of language. One such assumption is that 'language always functions in *one* way' (PI 304), which he rebutted in the passage about five red apples and by drawing attention to the great variety of 'language-games' in PI 23 and elsewhere.[6] Another plausible assumption is that when we apply the same word to a range of different things, there must be something that they, and only they, have in common, in virtue of which that word is applicable. This idea, according to Wittgenstein, 'has shackled philosophical investigation', leading philosophers to 'dismiss as irrelevant the concrete cases, which alone could have helped [them] to understand the usage' of such words

---

6   His examples included: giving orders, describing an object, reporting an event, speculating about an event, play-acting, singing, solving riddles, making jokes, thanking, cursing, greeting, praying and others.

as 'knowledge' and others (BB 19–20). (He criticized Socrates for being at fault in this respect.)

In a famous passage in which he discussed that assumption, he used as an example the word 'game', which is applied to chess, football, patience, ring-a-ring-a-roses and other activities. One might suppose, he pointed out, that we describe them all as games in virtue of some property or properties that they, and only they, have in common. In combatting this assumption he appealed to the reader to reflect on how the word is in fact used. 'Don't say: "There *must* be something common, or they would not be called 'games'" – but *look and see* whether there is . . . ' (PI 66). We may find that what holds the concept together is not some common property, but an informal arrangement of 'family resemblances' between the various instances: 'a complicated network of similarities overlapping and criss-crossing' (66–7).

A further aspect of Wittgenstein's appeal to ordinary language is his use of the 'paradigm case argument' (though not under that name).[7] To the question 'But how *can* a previous experience be a ground for assuming that such-and-such will occur later?', he replies that this 'is simply what we *call* a ground for assuming that this will happen . . . if *these* are not grounds, then what are grounds?' (PI 480–1). Someone who questions whether we ever have good grounds for assuming that such-and-such will occur is to be reminded of the *meaning* of 'good grounds' – how this and related words are actually used; and this can be done by drawing attention to paradigm cases: 'a good ground is one that looks like *this*' (483). Again, to the question 'Was I justified in drawing these consequences?', his response is: 'What is *called* a justification here? – How is the word "justification" used?' (486).

Wittgenstein and unordinary language

The description of Wittgenstein as an ordinary language philosopher is, as I tried to show, supported both by his statements about the nature of philosophy and by examples of his method in dealing with particular problems. There are also, however, reasons for questioning or qualifying this description.

It would certainly be wrong to suppose that Wittgenstein's work consists entirely of reminders of how we use words in ordinary discourse. This would not cover his claims about the nature of philosophy itself, for instance. Nor would it cover his philosophy of

---

7   I discuss the paradigm case argument in Chapter 5.

mathematics, where he discusses expressions and ideas that are far from ordinary. Again, he sometimes made statements that seem *contrary* to ordinary uses of language, as when he said that 'the mathematician is an inventor, not a discoverer'.[8] A mathematician can indeed be described as an inventor if he invents a new system of numbers or devises a new method of calculating; but when he works out the right answer to a problem, we say that he has *found* or *discovered* the answer and not that he has invented it. Again, if he finds a way of shortening a long mathematical expression (cf. RFM 111–12), his success is described as one of discovery (though invention may be involved if, say, he introduces a new notation).

Another case in which Wittgenstein has been accused of disregarding ordinary language is his treatment of names. In the *Tractatus*, as we saw earlier, he had declared: 'A name means an object. The object is its meaning' (3.203); but in his later work he pointed out that this was contrary to the normal use of language: 'When Mr. N.N. dies, one says that the bearer of the name dies, not that the meaning dies'. If, he went on, it were true that the meaning had 'died' – if the name 'ceased to have meaning' – then 'it would make no sense to say "Mr. N.N. is dead" '; but obviously it does make sense (PI 40).

But is it right to speak of names as having meaning? According to a reviewer of the *Investigations*,

> Wittgenstein here gives the wrong reason for objecting to the identification of the, or a, meaning of a proper name with its bearer, or one of its bearers. If we speak at all of the meaning of proper names, it is only in quite *specialized* ways, as when we say that 'Peter' means a stone, or 'Giovanni' means 'John' .... But here, as elsewhere, Wittgenstein neglects the use of 'meaning'.[9]

Such examples, however, are hardly enough to show that Wittgenstein was, in general, prepared to neglect the ordinary use of this and other words, contrary to his announced intentions, as when he declared that 'philosophy may in no way interfere with the actual use of language; it can in the end only describe it' (PI 124). In the present example his error is understandable. The main question, after all, was

---

8   *Remarks on the Foundations of Mathematics* (Blackwell 1978), 99, 111; hereafter 'RFM'.

9   P.F. Strawson, *Freedom and Resentment and Other Essays* (Methuen 1974), 138–9.

whether the word 'meaning' is ever used to signify 'a thing that "corresponds" to [a] word'. According to the *Tractatus* use of language, this is so in the case of 'names'; but it is not so according to the ordinary uses of 'name' and 'meaning'. It was natural for Wittgenstein to oppose his earlier use of language by saying that a name did not *lose* its meaning when the named object ceased to exist. Perhaps he should have said that when this happens the name does not become *meaningless*: it does not become a nonsense word and its ability to contribute to meaningful sentences remains unimpaired. ('Meaningless' is not quite the opposite of 'having a meaning'.)

Another way in which Wittgenstein seems to contravene his intention to adhere to 'the actual use of language' is when he advises the reader to 'say what you choose'. If this is so – if anyone can say what they choose on the question at issue – then where, we may ask, does that leave the authority of actual use?

The advice to 'say what you choose' occurs in a discussion of proper names: of what properties must be ascribed by the user of such a name to the person named. Taking the biblical 'Moses' as an example, Wittgenstein mentions various descriptions that a user of this name might have in mind. We are not to assume, he says, that one must have 'a fixed and unequivocal' set of such descriptions in mind whenever one uses this name (PI 79, paras 1–2). Does this mean, he continues, 'that I am using a word whose meaning I don't know, and so am talking nonsense?' His reply is: 'Say what you choose, so long as it does not prevent you from seeing the facts. (And when you see them there is a good deal that you will not say)' (para 4). A commentator has used this passage to argue that the idea of treating ordinary use as 'sacrosanct' is 'quite foreign' to Wittgenstein.[10]

How are we to understand this invitation to say what we choose? Wittgenstein's position here may seem similar to that of which Austin complained in his criticism of Ayer (as quoted in Ch. 2), whereby 'every dispute would be purely verbal', so that 'if, when one person says whatever it may be, another person may simply "prefer to say" something else'. How, asked Austin, 'could anything be a question of truth or falsehood, if anyone can always say whatever he likes?' (SS

---

10 J. Schulte, *Wittgenstein: eine Einführung* (Reclam 1989). Schulte concludes, accordingly, that Strawson's objection against Wittgenstein was misconceived: that objection was based on the ordinary use of 'name' and 'meaning'; but if we are allowed, in doing philosophy, to 'say what we choose', then we may, if we like, ascribe meaning to names.

58). Again, how are we to understand Wittgenstein's reference to 'the facts'? Did he think we could find the answer to his question by examining facts as distinct from language? No; the facts in question must be those of the actual use of the language in question. The objector who describes this use as 'nonsense' must take account of *the fact* that proper names can perform their function without the backing of 'a fixed and unequivocal' set of descriptions.

It must be admitted, however, that Wittgenstein's 'Say what you choose' was misleading. For if proper names do indeed work in this way, then the description of the example as 'nonsense' must be false and the objector should not be allowed to 'choose' to describe it so. But here again, if Wittgenstein was wrong in this instance, it does not follow that he did not mean what he said in the numerous passages in which he (a) declared his adherence to the criterion of ordinary use and (b) argued in accordance with it.

Ordinary language and the 'bewitchment of our understanding'

Philosophers who, like Wittgenstein, argue from ordinary language, have sometimes been accused of trivializing their subject. Ordinary language, after all, is something that every normal adult has mastered; and one might think that philosophical understanding should be easily attainable if this is what it is about.

Now this impression could hardly survive a reading of the work of Austin, for one; for it is obvious that the thought he gave to it was far from easy and that his abilities were exceptional both in kind and in degree; and the same is true of Wittgenstein. But in the latter's work the idea that ordinary language simply, so to speak, delivers the answers is further challenged by the claim that language is itself to blame for 'bewitchment of our understanding' in philosophical matters (PI 109). He also, in a passage reminiscent of *The Pilgrim's Progress*, wrote that language 'sets traps' for us, that 'it is an immense network of easily accessible wrong turnings'. His task, he said, would be to 'erect signposts at all the junctions where there are wrong turnings so as to help people past the danger points'.[11] In another passage he thought that we are inclined, when doing philosophy, to misunderstand our own language, so that when we reflect on the uses of the relevant expressions,

---

11   *Culture and Value* (Blackwell 1980) 18.

we do not understand them but misinterpret them. When we do philosophy we are like savages, primitive people, who hear the expressions of civilized men, put a false interpretation on them and then draw the queerest conclusions from it. (PI 194)

Wittgenstein's ordinary language philosophy is characterized by its diagnostic content: not merely does he oppose the claims of philosophers by reference to 'what we say'; he also tries to explain what is behind these conflicts and confusions. This leads him to describe what he is doing as a kind of therapy and to speak of philosophical confusion as a kind of disease (PI 255). Such diseases, he says, must be allowed to 'run their natural course, and a *slow* cure is all important' (Z 382).

How, according to Wittgenstein, are the diseases caused? One of the main causes is the assumption, to which I have already referred, that 'language always functions in *one* way'. Suppose someone asked what the words in 'five red apples' *stand for*. In the case of 'apples', it would be natural to reply by pointing to some apples. But what should we say in the case of 'five'? We may be tempted to think that, if this word is to mean anything, there must be some object corresponding to it, in the way in which apples correspond to 'apples'; and thus we would be led into 'wrong turnings' which turn us away from a proper understanding of this word. In the case of 'red', we might point to some *red* apples – perhaps the same ones that we pointed to in connection with 'apples'! But the relation between 'red' and red apples is not like that between 'apples' and apples; and the idea that red (or redness) is a kind of object leads to notorious 'wrong turnings' in philosophy.

The word 'I', to take another example, might be thought to stand for an object, 'the self'. But what kind of object would this be? To identify it with the speaker's body seems unacceptable, for 'I' cannot usually be replaced by 'my body'. Rejecting this view, we might conclude that

> we use this word to refer to something bodiless, which, however, has its seat in our body. In fact *this* seems to be real ego, the one of which it was said, 'Cogito, ergo sum'. (BB 69)

But according to Wittgenstein, 'the idea that the real I lives in my body is connected with the peculiar grammar of the word "I", and the misunderstandings this grammar is liable to give rise to' (BB 66).

The assumption that language always functions in one way is especially damaging in the philosophy of mind. Suppose we ask what *remembering* consists in. In this case we are dealing with an active verb, and it is natural to regard such words as names of actions. 'Walk', for example, is the name of a physical action. Should we say that 'remembering' is the name of a mental action? It is true that certain mental activities are typically connected with remembering: we may try calling up a mental image, or we may think hard to recall the answer to a question. But it would be wrong to conclude that 'it is this inner process that one means by the word "remember"', or that 'the picture of the inner process gives us the correct idea of the use of the word "remember"'. This picture 'stands in the way of our seeing the use of the word as it is' (PI 305). The 'picture' seems to satisfy our need for something that stands to 'remembering' as walking stands to 'walking', but this is another wrong turning; and it is part of a general misconception of the nature of language.

Another misunderstanding, also involving mental processes, is due to the resemblance of such words as 'mean' and 'understand' to ordinary verbs of action. Here again there is a temptation to think that there must be a mental process that is related to 'meaning' as walking is related to 'walking'; and that this mental process is what meaning consists in. Parents sometimes admonish their children: 'I am not just saying it, I mean it.' Here it seems as if 'meaning it' is a separate activity which may or may not accompany the act of saying.[12]

The 'mental accompaniment' theory is especially tempting where there is a question of *what* one meant. In one of Wittgenstein's examples, someone who has made a remark that Napoleon was crowned in 1804 is asked whether he meant 'the man who won the battle of Austerlitz'. If so, must not a corresponding thought have been present in his mind when he spoke? 'The use of the past tense "meant" might make it appear as though the idea of Napoleon having won the battle of Austerlitz must have been present in the man's mind' at the time (BB 39, 142). Yet this assumption, again, would 'stand in the way of our seeing the use of the word as it is'; for the truth of 'I meant X' does not depend on the presence of an idea in my mind, either now or at the time when I made the remark. If that idea had been far from my mind when I spoke, it would not follow that I had not meant the man answering to that description. And the same would apply if I were asked whether I had meant the man who was emperor of France, who

---

12   An erroneous assumption of activity is involved, I believe, in Descartes' 'method of doubt'. According to this method, we can *choose* to doubt familiar truths. But doubting is not something we can do at will. (See O. Hanfling, 'Can there be a Method of Doubt?', *Philosophy* 1984.)

married Josephine, who said 'an army marches on its stomach', was painted by such and such an artist, and so on; even though it would be absurd to suppose that I thought of all these things at the time.

The assumption that language always functions in one way is also blamed by Wittgenstein for a widespread misunderstanding of sensation words, such as 'pain'. It is natural to suppose that 'pain' is related to some inner object or process, rather as, in the physical world, 'apples' is related to certain physical objects and 'eating' to a certain physical process. This is 'the grammar that tries to force itself on us here' when we think about the meaning of pain and similar words (PI 304). Now in the physical cases the same object or process can be inspected by different users of the word; but this does not make sense in the case of pains. Here, it seems, the only possible kind of inspection must be *intro*spection; and this leads to the paradoxical but widely held view that 'pain' has a different meaning for each of us and, more generally, that one person can never tell another what he feels. According to Wittgenstein, what is needed is to 'make a radical break' with the assumption that language always functions in one way; only then will the paradox disappear and a proper understanding of the word 'pain' – and pain itself – become possible (ibid.).

The assumptions I have mentioned, and the paradoxical views derived from them, have a tenacious hold on the thought of many people, both inside and outside philosophy; and much argument (or 'treatment') may be needed to 'show the fly the way out of the fly bottle' (PI 309). This may be illustrated by the work of a prominent commentator on Wittgenstein. Saul Kripke was apparently unable to believe that Wittgenstein's numerous rejections of 'accompaniment' theories of meaning were to be taken literally; and this led him to put a novel but unjustified interpretation on Wittgenstein's writings.

One of Wittgenstein's examples, as we have seen, was that of a speaker who meant 'the man who won the battle', etc., even though no such thought passed through his mind when he spoke. In another example he asks us to suppose that someone has been taught to apply the expression '+2' with examples up to 1000 and is then asked to apply it beyond this number; whereupon, to our surprise, he writes '1000, 1004, 1008' etc. The teacher protests that this was not what he meant; and the question then arises what (if anything) his meaning what he meant consisted in. 'You don't want to say', comments Wittgenstein, 'that [he] thought of the step from 1000 to 1002 – and even if [he] did think of this step, still [he] did not think of other ones' (PI 187).

This example was used by Kripke to support his claim that Wittgenstein was putting forward 'a new form of scepticism', whereby 'there can be no such thing as meaning anything by any word'.[13] Kripke admits that Wittgenstein nowhere describes himself as a sceptic and nowhere makes the denial that he ascribes to him. Why, then, did he think Wittgenstein was a sceptic? Wittgenstein, he writes, holds that 'there was no fact about me that constituted my having meant [one thing rather than another]', and from this it is supposed to follow that there is no such thing as meaning anything by any word. But how is this supposed to follow? It may seem to follow if, in the grip of a false assumption, one insists that there must be some 'fact about me' – other than simply the fact that I meant what I meant – which 'constituted' my having meant it. But this is just the assumption that Wittgenstein was concerned to reject. In another, and typical, passage he used the example of someone having meant a particular person by the word 'you'. What, one might ask, did his meaning that person, rather than another, consist in? The assumption behind this question is rejected by Wittgenstein: 'The mistake is to say that meaning consists in something' (Z 16).

Consider an imaginary Wittgenstein – let us call him Kripgenstein. According to Kripgenstein, (a) there can be no meaning something by a given word without some fact about the speaker which *constitutes* his meaning it; but (b) there are no such facts. From this we may safely deduce that Kripgenstein is a sceptic about meaning – or rather, that he denies its existence. But (a) is precisely the opposite of what the real Wittgenstein said and argued throughout his discussions of meaning.[14]

Wittgenstein's account is in accordance with 'what we would say', Kripgenstein's is not. The person who replied 'Yes, I meant the man who won the battle', etc. would *not* be committed, by what he said, to the claim that this thought was in his mind when he spoke or that there was some 'fact about him' which 'constituted' his having meant what he meant; and neither is the teacher in Wittgenstein's example committed to the existence of such a thought or fact when he says that *he meant* '+2' to produce '1002, 1004 ...', and not '1004, 1008 ...'. The view that Kripke foists on Wittgenstein is contrary to the actual use of language and leads to paradoxical consequences. It is another of those tempting 'wrong turnings' that Wittgenstein identified and where he sought to 'erect signposts ... to help people past the danger points'.

---

13   Saul Kripke, *Wittgenstein on Rules and Private Language* (Blackwell 1982), 60, 65.
14   The question of meaning something or someone ('speaker's meaning') should not be confused with that of 'word meaning', as when it is asked what a given word, such as 'knowledge', means. Both aspects of meaning were discussed at length by Wittgenstein.

(I return to the topic of 'traps' and 'wrong turnings', with more examples, in Chapters 5 and 7.)[15]

The 'arbitrariness of grammar'

Wittgenstein's aim, as we saw, was to 'bring words back to their everyday use' – rescuing them from the distortions that philosophers had imposed, or tried to impose, on them. He was also 'tempted', however, to describe what he called 'the rules of grammar' as 'arbitrary' (Z 320). Referring to our 'system of colours' and our 'system of numbers', he wrote:

> Do the systems reside in *our* nature or in the nature of things? How are we to put it? – *Not* in the nature of numbers or colours.
>
> Then is there something arbitrary about this system? Yes and No. It is akin both to what arbitrary and to what is non-arbitrary. (Z 357–8)

In what sense would such 'rules of grammar' be arbitrary? Wittgenstein often compared language with games; and in the case of games, rules are arbitrary in a straightforward way. We can alter such rules, invent games with new rules, and so on. Our participation in games is also an arbitrary matter: one can choose whether to take part in a particular game or whether to play games at all.[16] But to regard language as arbitrary in this sense would be mistaken, as well as being in conflict with Wittgenstein's position as described so far. Whereas the inventing and playing of games is a matter of choice, this is not so with the 'game' of ordinary language and its existing 'rules'. 'Our

---

15 Having presented what he regards as Wittgenstein's 'new form of scepticism', Kripke tells us that Wittgenstein also produced 'a "sceptical solution of these doubts", in Hume's classic sense' (108). What this means, he explains, is that 'we must give up the attempt to find any facts about me in virtue of which I mean [what I mean]'. Instead we must consider how the language is actually used. 'We must look at the circumstances under which these assertions are introduced into discourse, and their role and utility in our lives.' This appeal to 'actual use' and 'role in our lives' is indeed a central feature of Wittgenstein's thought; but there is no justification for describing it as a solution to sceptical doubts, for no such doubts had been introduced by Wittgenstein. (For a fuller discussion of Kripke's account of Wittgenstein, see O. Hanfling, 'Was Wittgenstein a Sceptic?', *Philosophical Investigations* 1985.)

16 For further discussion see O. Hanfling, 'Does Language need Rules?', *Philosophical Quarterly* 1980.

ordinary language' as Wittgenstein put it in another passage, is that which 'pervades all our life' (BB 59).

He was especially interested in the language with which people describe their feelings and the feelings of others. This language-game, he argued, is not something that could be eliminated.

> If I were to reserve the word 'pain' solely for what I had hitherto called 'my pain', and others 'L.W.'s pain', I should do other people no injustice, so long as a notation were provided in which the loss of the word 'pain' in other connexions were somehow supplied. Other people would still be pitied, treated by doctors and so on. (PI 403)

A similar point is made in *On Certainty*, in relation to imaginary sceptics who had tried to expunge the word 'certain' from their vocabulary, replacing it by the expression '*very* probably'. 'How', asks Wittgenstein, 'would the life of these people differ from ours?'.[17] The distinctions we normally make between 'certain', 'probable' and 'very probable' must be as apparent to those people as they are to us, and they must pay attention to them if they are not to get into trouble. They might try to *say* 'very probably' in place of 'certain', but this would be a merely verbal manoeuvre; the difference between (as we normally put it) 'certain' and 'probable' would still have to be provided for in their language.

Wittgenstein explained his talk of 'the arbitrariness of grammar' as follows:

> One is tempted to justify the rules of grammar by sentences like 'But there really are four primary colours'. And the saying that the rules of grammar are arbitrary is directed against the possibility of this justification, which is constructed on the model of justifying a sentence by pointing to what verifies it. (Z 331)

The word 'arbitrary' was introduced to oppose the idea that we can somehow justify the grammar of our language by reference to what is 'really there', but not to claim, as some commentators have thought, that it is open to us to opt for a different grammar.

'Grammar', wrote Wittgenstein, 'is not accountable to any reality'.[18] Some have taken this to mean that the reverse is true – that reality is

---

17   Wittgenstein, *On Certainty* (Blackwell 1969) 338; hereafter 'OC'.

18   Wittgenstein, *Philosophical Grammar* (Blackwell 1974), 184; hereafter 'PG'.

accountable to grammar. If this is combined with the view that grammar is arbitrary – a matter of choice on our part – then it may seem as if the existence and nature of things depends on our choice of grammar. Such a view has been advocated, and ascribed to Wittgenstein, by Richard Rorty. According to him, the fact that one cannot be mistaken about being in pain is due to a 'convention' with 'no more ontological significance than the fact that the Constitution is what the Supreme Court thinks it is, or that the ball is foul if the umpire thinks it is'.[19] But this comparison is both wrong in itself and wrongly ascribed to Wittgenstein. The American authorities could enact a law, to come into force from next year, which would bring it about that the Supreme Court is no longer in the position mentioned by Rorty; and similarly with the rule about the umpire. But what would be the parallel in the case of language? That from next Monday we are allowed to say 'I think I have a toothache, but I may be mistaken'? In a sense we are, of course, free to say this – to utter the words – already. But it is not open to us to say it and mean it. For this to be possible, the word 'toothache' would have to undergo a change of meaning. But even then, the existing concept would not go away; it would need to find expression in some other way.[20]

Another writer has claimed that, according to Wittgenstein, the existence of the colour red, for example, depends on whether 'the language-game with [the relevant] rule is played', but that 'we need not have this game' any more than the game of football.[21] But Wittgenstein did not think, nor did he say, that the existence of the colour 'red' depends on games we play with language. Nor is such a view compatible with what we normally say. It is not self-contradictory to say, for example, that plants existing long before language, or even sentient beings, appeared on earth, had such and such colours.

Another mistake about the relation between language and reality is the assumption that 'how we speak can tell us how things really are'.[22] Having raised the question how this is possible, Schwyzer replies that there are two alternatives: '*either* how we speak is a function of how things are, *or*, conversely, how things are is a function of how we speak (205). Wittgenstein, he claims, opted for the second view, thereby

19 Richard Rorty, *Philosophy and the Mirror of Nature* (Blackwell 1980), 32.
20 Such possibilities are discussed by Wittgenstein in a number of passages in the *Blue Book* (see BB 22–3, 57–9 and 72–3).
21 John Canfield, *Wittgenstein: Language and World* (University of Massachusetts 1981), 16.
22 H. Schwyzer, 'Thought and Reality', *Philosophical Quarterly* 1973.

performing a 'Copernican revolution' comparable to that for which Kant was famous (200). One of Schwyzer's examples of 'how we speak' is the proposition 'Sensations are private', taken as 'an encapsulation of what can count as a move in the language-game'. But Wittgenstein did not suggest that we could *infer* from this proposition that sensations really are private. Similarly, when he wrote that 'if we are using the word "know" as it is normally used ..., then other people very often know when I am in pain' (PI 246), he was not *inferring* that other people can know when I am in pain, from the fact that this is how we use the word. The description of this and other language-games was the end and not the beginning of his argument.

Views such as the above about the relation between language and reality are based on a 'map' theory of language, of the kind discussed in my criticism of Austin in Chapter 2. Between a map and the reality it represents there is a two-way relationship: the map can be assessed by how well it corresponds to the reality; and, given the map, we can infer from it what the corresponding reality is like. In both respects, however, language is unlike a map. The grammar of our language 'is not accountable to any reality'; but neither is it a basis for inferences about reality.

4 'What we say'

Who says?

What we say, what I would say, and what I would be prepared to say

A philosopher's claims about 'what we say' are based on personal reflection. He considers relevant examples and concludes that he would apply a given word to such and such cases and refuse to apply it to others. Discussion with others may lead him to change his mind: they may draw his attention to other examples, or to features of examples, that he had overlooked. But the appeal will still be to his personal reflection: he must be able to see that *he* would or would not be prepared to apply the word, in ordinary conversation, to those examples. How does he acquire this knowledge and how can he generalize from what *he* would say to claims about what *we* – the language-community – would say?[1]

It is a contingent fact that people use words as they do and one might therefore expect the relevant knowledge to be empirical, and subject to empirical testing. Suppose I learn, by consulting a dictionary, or by observing how others use the word, that 'pinnate' is used to describe leaves of a certain shape. This would be a case of empirical learning and subject to empirical refutation: I might discover that the word is

---

1 The move from 'I' to 'we' has been described as follows by Vendler: 'He, a competent speaker of the language, would not say ...; hence it follows that other speakers, equally competent, would not say so either' (Zeno Vendler, 'Philosophy of Language and Linguistic Philosophy', in M. Dascal, ed., *Sprachphilosophie* (de Gruyter 1988), 14. A similar view is put forward by Kai Nielsen, who quotes this passage in 'On there being Philosophical Knowledge', *Philosophical Investigations* 1992, 156–7). But knowledge of 'what we say' is not inferential, any more than knowledge of what I would say; nor would one *justify* a statement about what we would say by reference to what one would personally say.

not used, or no longer used, in the way I thought. But ordinary language philosophers are not interested in rarely used words whose meaning one might easily forget, if one had learned it at all. They are interested in language that is embedded in daily life, including such words as 'know', 'free', 'think' and 'cause'.

Is our knowledge of the use of such words empirical? It would be better to describe it as *participatory*. I do observe other people using the words as they do, but I also participate with them in that activity. The activity, moreover, is one in which each participant is constantly kept on the rails by sanctions coming from the others. If I use words in abnormal ways, I shall be under pressure to normalize my usage. I shall fail to get what I want from others, and they will let me know that I am going wrong by puzzled looks and requests to explain what I mean. Such pressures are applied even on trivial points of grammar and pronunciation, where there is no danger of failure to communicate. The child who says 'I swimmed' instead of 'I swam' is taught to mend his language and an adult who made this mistake would not be allowed to get away with it. Language is an instrument that is constantly being sharpened and fine-tuned in interaction with others. We may suppose that Robinson Crusoe's language, after many years of solitude, would be a blunt and rusty instrument, in need of restoration. It might strike his rescuers as quaint and perhaps even unintelligible.

Our knowledge of the uses of words may be compared with knowing how to play a game such as chess: here too one's knowledge is constantly being confirmed by interaction with others. There are also differences, however, between chess and language, and between games and 'language-games'. What we do in chess does not affect what we do in other games: in this sense games are autonomous. But this is not true of language-games, which form an interrelated system, making up *the human* language-game. Another difference concerns the *importance* of language-games as compared with games. A person may or may not know how to play chess, and if he knows how to play, he may choose not to do so. Now there are trivial language-games, of which the same may be said; but this is not so with language-games in general, nor with *the* language-game as a whole.

Another difference is that in the case of chess there is a specific aim: to defeat one's opponent; but there is no such aim in the case of language. In this respect it is better to compare language with certain other interactive practices. R.M. Hare has suggested that knowing how to use language is like knowing how to perform a dance such as the eightsome reel. He asks us to suppose that a dispute has arisen among experienced dancers 'about what happens at a particular point in the dance; and that, in order to settle it, [they] decide to dance the dance after dinner and find out'.[2] When the dance reaches the disputed point, one movement is accepted as correct while others are rejected as incorrect.

This comparison captures the participatory, interactive nature of language, without the unsuitable idea of an overall aim. It is especially suitable for such examples as saying 'please' or 'How do you do', where we may need actually to 'dance the dance' to settle a dispute about what happens. (Foreigners are sometimes taught that English people say 'How do you do' on being introduced; but it is doubtful whether this usually happens in practice.) But when we turn to other kinds of language, including those of interest to philosophers, the comparison with dancing is less suitable. Here one does not need to 'dance' the language concerned and wait to see what will happen. The question that interests the philosopher is not what is actually said in a given situation, which might depend on various factors; but in what it would be permissible to say. And this question can be addressed by thinking of hypothetical situations that need not be enacted.

Sometimes, indeed, philosophers make claims about imaginary, far-fetched situations that are unlikely ever to be enacted. Such claims go beyond existing linguistic practices and their security is diminished accordingly. Personal identity is a subject where such claims have been prominent; a classic example being that of Locke, who asks us to imagine that the mind of a prince, 'carrying with it the consciousness of the prince's past life, enter and inform the body of a cobbler' (*Essay* 2.27.15). What we would say in this case, according to Locke, is that the man in the cobbler's body is now 'the same person with the prince'.

Is this really what we would say? Faced with such examples, one may be uncertain what one would say. The relevant language ('same person', etc.) is here extended to situations in which it is not at home (and in which *we* are not at home); and people who are competent in the use of this language in ordinary situations may not be so when they are presented with extraordinary imaginary ones. Again, it might well be that those (perhaps the majority) who initially accept Locke's verdict would change their minds if their attention were drawn to aspects of the question that had not occurred to them. In such cases, then, the method of 'what we would say', though still applicable, is more precarious than in the case of words being used in ordinary everyday situations, which will be the subject of my discussion.

---

2   'Philosophical Discoveries', in Richard Rorty, ed., *The Linguistic Turn* (University of Chicago 1967), 216.

Linguistic philosophy and empirical linguistics

I have argued that knowledge of language is participatory, so that one's knowledge of the use of a word is constantly kept in place by interaction with others; this being so especially with words that are important in daily life. Armed with this knowledge, the linguistic philosopher, after reviewing cases that do or may occur, is able to make statements about 'what we say': about the logical conditions allowing or prohibiting the use of a word.

But what if he gets it wrong? Or what if two philosophers give different answers? Should there not be a role for empirical testing in such cases? These and similar questions were provoked by a difference between prominent ordinary language philosophers in the 1950s. Gilbert Ryle, in a discussion of the will in *The Concept of Mind*, stated that the words 'voluntary' and 'involuntary' are applied, 'with a few minor elasticities ... , to actions which ought not to be done'; while J.L. Austin had previously observed that 'we may join the army or make a gift voluntarily, we may hiccough or make a small gesture involuntarily ...'. [3] This discrepancy led some readers to question the basis and status of statements about the uses of words. 'If agreement about usage cannot be reached within so restricted a sample as the class of Oxford Professors of Philosophy, what are the prospects when the sample is enlarged?'.[4]

It seems clear that Ryle's statement was mistaken; but according to Stanley Cavell there was at least some truth in it. At least, said Cavell, one would not describe an action as voluntary unless there was something 'fishy' about it: we cannot say 'The gift was made voluntarily' about 'ordinary, unremarkable cases' ('Must we mean what we say?', PL 135, 140). But this too is incorrect. What is required is not that the case be unordinary, but merely – as for any other statement – that there be a suitable context for it. In a suitable context, however, it would be appropriate to say, for example, that someone joined the army voluntarily as opposed to being conscripted, even if there were nothing fishy or remarkable about the case.

Another mistake was made by Cavell when he wrote: 'We do not say "I know ..." unless we mean that we have great confidence ...' (PL

---

3   Gilbert Ryle, *The Concept of Mind* (Penguin 1963), 67; J.L. Austin, 'A Plea for Excuses', *Philosophical Papers* (Clarendon 1961), 139.

4   Benson Mates, 'On the Verification of Statements about Ordinary Language', in Colin Lyas, ed., *Philosophy and Linguistics* (Macmillan 1971), 125; hereafter 'PL'.

140). Contrary to this, a person may reply 'I know' on being told that the train will leave at 9.35, without thereby expressing great confidence. The point of saying 'I know' in such a context would be that one does not need to be told and not, as in some other contexts, to express great confidence. (The uses of 'know' will be further discussed in Chapter 6.)

Such errors and differences may lead to scepticism about the method of ordinary language philosophers. Should they not, after all, enlist the aid of scientific researchers to provide more reliable data? But how are we to conceive of this? Two kinds of methods, described as 'extensional' and 'intensional', were suggested by Mates (125). In the first, 'one observes a reasonably large class of cases in which the subject applies the word and then one "sees" or "elicits" the meaning by finding what is common to these cases'. (Presumably these observations would be done on a 'reasonably large' number of subjects.) But, as Mates observed, there would be uncertainties about 'what are the relevant features of the objects to which the word is applied [and] the situations in which it is applied', etc. (127). Following the *intensional* method, on the other hand, the investigator would not be merely a dumb observer: he 'asks the subject what he means by a given word or how he uses it; then [he] proceeds in Socratic fashion to test this first answer by confronting the subject with counter-examples [etc.], until the subject settles down more or less permanently upon a definition or account' (126). Mates thought of this as 'a sort of Socratic questionnaire' and pointed out that in the course of it the subject might 'give a different answer from the one he gave at first'. But if he did so, argued Mates, it would leave indeterminate whether he 'had changed his mind, or learned something new, or [found] a better way of expressing what he really meant' (129). There would be no way to differentiate 'between *finding out* what someone means by a word, and *influencing* his linguistic behaviour relative to that word' (130).

But if these methods are unsatisfactory, what others are available? Of the two methods described, it is the second, 'intensional' one, which was compared to that of Socrates, that seems closer to the actual practice of linguistic philosophy. But should not the difficulties mentioned by Mates about that method also affect the practice of linguistic philosophy – making it, indeed, impossible? The 'intensional' method is not really, however, so similar to that of linguistic philosophy. (Nor, of course, is the 'extensional' one.) Being himself a speaker of the language, the philosopher already knows what the word in question means; hence his position, unlike that of an empirical researcher, cannot be one of 'finding out'. The answer he seeks is one that – in a sense – he knows already. What he is trying to find out – or rather, to find – is a *formulation* of his knowledge: a statement of the conditions under which the word is used by those, including himself, who know how to use it. When Socrates asked 'What is courage?', for example, he was hoping to arrive at a definition of this word that he and the others could *recognize* as correct. The nature of this kind of enquiry was brought out in the *Meno*, where the question was 'What is virtue?'. Meno puts it to Socrates that their enquiry is impossible. Either they already know the answer or they do not. If the former, then there is no need to enquire; if the latter, then the enquiry cannot succeed, for they would not be able to recognize the right answer if they found it. In reply, Socrates argues (using a mathematical illustration) that in some kinds of enquiry one may be able to *recognize* a right answer even though one would not have been able to produce it unaided. (This view of the enquiry is akin to that of the 'midwife' passage, which I quoted near the end of Chapter 1.)

In this respect the philosopher's work and predicament resemble that of a person trying to discover the rules of grammar of his native language. In both cases it is a matter of making explicit a kind of knowledge that is constantly being enacted in practice. A native German speaker knows that it is wrong to use the article 'der' for the feminine accusative case even if he is unable to formulate the relevant rules until he has been taught them at school. (His position is the reverse of that of a learner of a second language who is taught the rule first and then speaks according to the rule.) The grammarian, reflecting on nothing more than familiar linguistic practices, is able to uncover and articulate such rules. In grammar, as in 'philosophical grammar', 'the problems are solved, not by giving new information, but by arranging what we have always known' (PI 109). In both cases the aim is to make explicit features of language that the participants can recognize.

The difference between Mates's approach and that of the linguistic philosopher is also apparent from Mates's talk of 'the subject' and of finding out 'what someone means' by a word. This subjective terminology is appropriate when one is enquiring about usages that may differ from person to person or from one locality to another. Here the enquirer is indeed in the position of 'finding out', and the way to find out is empirical. But this is not so when the question is about *the meaning* of a word and the word belongs to a language that the enquirer shares with his interlocutors. In that case the enquiry will be of the kind described – and pursued – in the *Meno*.

The distinction between empirical and philosophical enquiry may have been obscured by the way in which Ryle introduced his claim about 'voluntary' and 'involuntary'. 'It should be noticed', he wrote, 'that while ordinary folk, magistrates, parents and teachers, generally apply [these words] to actions in one way, philosophers often apply them in quite another way' (op. cit. 67). The second of these statements was indeed empirical: it was by observation that Ryle found philosophers applying the words 'in quite another way'. But is the same true of the first statement, about the use of these words by 'ordinary folk'? One might perhaps think, from the way Ryle put his point, that he had observed or interviewed sufficient numbers of magistrates, parents, etc. in order to arrive at that statement. But this was not so. Ryle's claim was not about two dialects, one spoken by ordinary folk and the other by philosophers: it was about the ordinary use of a word versus a deviant use. The latter might occur when people (including ordinary folk) are doing philosophy, but they would be expected to recognize the ordinary use and indeed return to it when they are not doing philosophy.

A failure to do justice to the objectivity of meaning also occurs in H.P. Grice's account of linguistic philosophy. Describing his work as a philosopher, he wrote that he was 'primarily concerned to provide a conceptual analysis *of my own* use of a given expression'. A philosophical problem, according to Grice, is essentially personal. 'Even if my assumption that what goes for me goes for others is mistaken, it does not matter; my philosophical puzzles have arisen in connection with my use of [a particular expression].' Another person may use the expression differently, and if this leads *him* into philosophical puzzles, then an analysis of *his* use of the expression may be appropriate.[5]

This is not, however, a correct account of linguistic philosophy (or any other). If philosophy were merely about dealing with personal problems in a personal way, it would not have the interest or importance that it has. But the problems concerned are not personal, and the concepts in question are not private property. It is true that a linguistic philosopher will probably begin by reflecting on his 'own use of a given expression', but his claims and conclusions could not be limited to this. Take, for example, the problem of free will: this problem is not one that arises *for me*, because of *my* use of the relevant language. That language is common property and the problem arises, or is liable to arise, for all those who participate in it. Again, suppose Ryle had expressed his point about 'voluntary' in personal terms, claiming that *he* applied this word only to actions that ought not to be

5 H.P. Grice, *Studies in the Way of Words* (Harvard 1989), 173–5.

done: he would still have had to recognize that it *is used* in a wider way, if this had been put to him.

The typical method of linguistic philosophy is not to analyze the use of an expression by someone or some group; it is to compare *the* use of it with claims or assumptions that have been made. A simple example is Wittgenstein's response to his imaginary opponent, who said 'Only I can know whether I am in pain'. The response was:

> If we are using the word 'know' as it is normally used (and how else are we to use it!), then other people very often know when I am in pain. (PI 246)

Wittgenstein was not analyzing his own use of a word – which might have left his opponent to do likewise with *his* use of it; he was appealing to the use of 'know' as shared by him and his opponent – and, of course, the reader.

Let us return to the difference between Ryle and Austin about the use of 'voluntary' and Mates's question, that 'if agreement ... cannot be reached [among] Oxford Professors of Philosophy, what are the prospects when the sample is enlarged?' (PL 125). The truth is that agreement *can* be reached among the professors at Oxford and elsewhere, but by methods other than those described by Mates. What if Ryle were reminded by one of his colleagues of examples that were contrary to his statement about 'voluntary'? He would have either to admit that he had been wrong or to explain how he might dispose of the examples while still adhering to his claim – or, perhaps, a qualified version of his claim. If he took the latter option, he would hope to get others to agree that what he now said about the word was correct. In this way progress would be made and agreement might be reached. There is no reason to suppose that Ryle would simply adhere to his original and erroneous statement. (It was, in any case, misleading to present the difference between the two philosophers as one of *disagreement*, as if they had discussed the matter and could not reach agreement. The topic of Austin's essay was not the same as Ryle's and it is doubtful whether they were even aware of the contradiction.)

'What we say' and the diversity of usage

I have criticized Grice for introducing an inappropriate personal note into his account of philosophy. Another writer who did so was Austin. Having noted that people use words in different ways, he regarded this one of the 'snags in "linguistic" philosophy' (*Phil. Papers* 131). How would he deal with this snag? He first suggested that the differences are not as widespread as might be feared. Though 'people's usages do vary', they do not vary 'nearly as much as one would think'. But what would he say about cases in which they do vary?

> Sometimes we do ultimately disagree: sometimes we must allow a usage to be, though appalling, yet actual . . . . If our usages disagree, then you use 'X' where I use 'Y', or more probably (and more intriguingly) your conceptual system is different from mine, though very likely it is equally consistent and serviceable: in short, we can find *why* we disagree – you choose to classify in one way, I in another. (132)

How are we to understand this statement? It is true that people classify things in different ways, but does it follow that they have different conceptual systems? If 'we can find *why* we disagree', then there must be, at a deeper level, a conceptual system that we share. If this were not so, then linguistic philosophy would be intolerably 'language-parochial', not merely with respect to English, but with respect to individual speakers of the language. However, the fact that people classify things in different ways is not an obstacle to linguistic philosophy: it is an aspect of the use of language that the linguistic philosopher would take into account.

Another source of worry about differences of linguistic usage has been the actually occurring erosion of distinctions between words. Familiar examples are the use of 'infer' in place of 'imply', 'refute' in place of 'reject' or 'deny', and 'disinterested' in place of 'uninterested'. Faced with such examples, one might think that the philosophy of 'what we say' is built on shifting sands.

To those who use words in a new way we sometimes say that this is not a good use of language. In Russian the word 'beauty' was formerly confined to objects of sight, and Tolstoy criticized the new, wider usage as 'not good Russian'. Or we may be tempted to say that the new usage is not true to what a word 'really' means, where 'really' is taken to mean 'originally'. Such objections cannot, however, be sustained if the new usage persists and the old slips into oblivion. 'We tell our pupils', wrote C.S. Lewis (in 1960), 'that *deprecate* does not mean *depreciate* or that *immorality* does not mean simply *lechery* because these words are beginning to mean just those things'.[6]

---

6   C.S. Lewis, *Studies in Words* (CUP 1967), 18.

How, it may be asked, can the ordinary language philosopher cope with such fluctuations? How can his claims about 'what we say' be evaluated when the uses of words are constantly liable to change? But the fact that this is so is really no more embarrassing to the philosopher than the fact that there are different languages. English and French use different sounds with the same meaning and (sometimes) the same sounds with different meanings. There may not be a one-to-one correspondence and translation may be awkward. Nevertheless, the same questions can be asked and discussed in French as in English. Similarly, if 'refute' is being discussed in today's 'correct' English, then the discussion need not be undermined by the fact that this word is now also used in another way. If necessary, it can be explained that the word is being discussed in the relevant sense.

But what if that sense disappeared, so that the distinction between the words 'refute' and 'reject' were no longer recognized? Then other words would be available to conduct the same discussion, just as other words are available in German or French. A discussion of what is now called 'refutation' might then be conducted in terms of 'showing (or proving)' a proposition to be false; while in a discussion of *inference*, 'deduce' might come to do the work of 'infer', if the latter lost its distinct meaning. Similarly, if a Russian philosopher had asked questions about 'beauty' when this word was still confined to visual objects, then he could have gone on asking the same questions, even after the change, in terms of 'beauty of objects of sight'.

On the other hand, if a Russian philosopher of today asks questions about beauty, then they will have to be understood and answered according to the present use of the word. And in general, the philosopher's questions and answers must be understood in the same way as those of any other discourse: according to the current use of the word, as shared by those who take part in the discussion. Perhaps someone acquainted with the history of a word would draw attention to its former use, and this might bring out interesting connections between features covered by the word at different times. Thus, if the meaning of 'morality' changed in the way described by Lewis, it might be useful to point out that it formerly included other qualities besides abstention from lechery. But the actual question 'What is morality?' would be properly addressed by reference to the language in which it was posed.

Now Austin, as we saw in the passage quoted above, sought to accommodate alternative usages; but he also regarded some of them as 'appalling', and with this we might agree. But of what philosophical significance is the superiority of one usage over another? Cavell tried to explain it by reference to what the speakers would or would not be 'noticing about the world'. He did so in reference to another passage from Austin (previously quoted in Chapter 2), where the latter had complained that some people use 'inadvertently' and 'automatically' as if they meant the same. Commenting on this passage, and referring to the proverbial 'butcher and baker', Cavell asked the reader to imagine a baker who practised that 'appalling' usage, and who spoke as follows: 'I use "automatically" and "inadvertently" in exactly the same way. I could just as well have said: "I grabbed the cigarette inadvertently and knocked over the decanter automatically"' (PL 159). How would Cavell respond to this? He would admonish the baker as follows:

> If you cooked the way you talk, you would forgo special implements for different jobs, and peel, core, scrape, slice, carve, chop and saw, all with one knife. The distinction is there, in the language (as implements are there to be had) and you just impoverish what you can say by neglecting it. And there is something you aren't noticing about the world. [Cavell seems now to be thinking of a cook rather than a baker.]

In this way Cavell would justify the philosopher's preference for the more discriminating usage over that of the baker. But would the baker really have failed to 'notice something about the world'? Would he be less able than Cavell or Austin to observe the relevant distinction? This would not follow from his conflation of the words in question. Similarly, if there were a dialect or language which did not contain direct counterparts of these words, it would not follow that the people concerned failed to notice the relevant distinction. It is, indeed, hard to conceive how they could fail to be aware of such distinctions, given the prevalence of certain situations in human life.

This may be illustrated by a development of the baker example, provided by John Cook.[7] We are asked to suppose that the baker has an assistant whose job it is to turn the ovens on when he arrives in the bakery at 5 a.m. One day, to save energy, he is told to do it at a later time. But next morning, out of long habit, he does it at the old time. His excuse is that he did it *automatically*. In another case the assistant 'arrives in the dark on a cold winter morning and discovers that the lights in the bakery will not go on'. He fumbles about with the master switch, succeeds in

---

7   John W. Cook, 'The Illusion of Aberrant Speakers', *Philosophical Investigations* 1982, 219.

turning the lights on, but at the same time causes the ovens to come on before the required time. He did it *inadvertently*. The difference between the situations, as Cook points out, does not lie merely in what happened, but also in what needs to be done in the future. In the first story, the baker advises his assistant: 'Put a sign on the oven door to remind yourself tomorrow not to turn on the ovens at five'; but this advice would be nonsensical in the second case (219–20). In Cook's examples the words 'automatically' and 'inadvertently' are actually used; but the relevant distinction would be recognized even if these words were not in the language. Anyone who understands the two stories, and their implications for future action, could not avoid noticing it. Again, someone reporting the stories could properly attribute those words to the protagonists in indirect speech, even if they did not say them; and similarly in the case of translating from an alien language. The distinction is not merely one that is noticed by speakers of 'correct' or 'professors'' English; it is embedded in a form of life that we share with others, including people of diverse cultures and languages.

For another illustration, let us take Austin's account of the distinction between 'It was a mistake' and 'It was an accident'. These sentences, he said,

> can *appear* indifferent, and even be used together. Yet, a story or two, and everybody will not merely agree that they are completely different, but even discover for himself what the difference is and what each means. (*Phil. Papers* 132–3)

He supplied a suitable 'story or two' in a footnote: 'You have a donkey, so have I, and they graze in the same field. The day comes when I conceive a dislike for mine. I go to shoot it, draw a bead on it, fire: the brute falls in its tracks. I inspect the victim, and find to my horror that it is *your* donkey.' In another kind of case, 'I go to shoot my donkey as before ..., but as I do so, the beasts move, and to my horror yours falls.' The first case is 'by mistake', the second 'by accident'.

In claiming that 'everybody will agree' and 'even discover for himself what the difference is', etc., Austin could rely on his readers' participation in a form of life in which situations falling under those descriptions would be bound to occur. And here again, the recognition of 'what each means' would be expressed, not merely by using the two phrases as appropriate, but also by suitable behaviour: the different ways in which the unfortunate marksman would be held responsible and the different measures that might be taken to avoid such mishaps in the future.

A similar point may be made about the difference between 'refute' and 'reject'. 'I reject this allegation' is a 'performative' statement (the rejection is performed in the very act of stating), but this is not so with 'refute' (in its distinct sense). Hence, when we hear someone say 'I refute' ..., we know immediately that this is the new, 'appalling' use of the word. (Here, as in other cases, the danger of confusion in actual conversation is often exaggerated.) Again, if we are told of a third person that he refuted an allegation, then (adhering to the correct use) we expect something more to follow: '... by pointing out that he had not been present', etc. If no such completion is provided, then we know that 'refute' meant nothing more than 'reject'.

Another difference between the two words is that if I say of someone that he refuted an allegation, this tells you something about me and not only about him: namely, that *I* regard the allegation as false and his disproof of it as valid. 'Refute' – or some equivalent expression – is what we need in such situations, which are bound to arise in our lives.

'Language-neutral' and 'language-specific'

Although the philosopher's remarks are about 'what we say' in the current language that he shares with his listeners or readers, their significance extends beyond that. If he says that 'refute' is used in such and a distinct way, then his meaning will not be confined to the use of an English word at a particular time; it will also include any other equivalent word or expression, in English or other languages. And his remark will be understood by anyone who understands the role and importance of refutation in the human language-game.

The philosopher's statements, though made, necessarily, in a specific language, are not *language-specific*. This can be so, and is so, because the same concepts exist in different languages. Thus,

> if we inquire about the *use* of 'table', then we are simultaneously and equally concerned with the *use* of 'tavola' and other equivalents in other languages – with, if you like, the concept of table.

Such enquiries, said Antony Flew, are 'language-neutral' ('Philosophy and Language', PL 65). By contrast, to observe that the English 'table' is extended to such contexts as 'water table' and 'multiplication table' is to make a point that is specific to English. The first, conceptual kind of enquiry is the province of philosophers; the second is a province for empirical linguists.[8]

But to speak of a concept that is shared by different languages is not to say that there is in each language an exactly equivalent word, as Ryle seems to have thought. Treating Hume as a linguistic philosopher, he wrote:

> Hume's question was not about the word 'cause'; it was about the *use* of 'cause'. It was just as much about the *use* of 'Ursache'. For the use of 'cause' is the same as the use of 'Ursache', though 'cause' is not the same word as 'Ursache'. ('Ordinary Language', PL 45)

But, protested Zeno Vendler, 'this is an incredible claim. How does Ryle know, without an exhaustive study of both languages, that the use of *Ursache* is the same as that of *cause*?' ('Linguistics and Philosophy', PL 252).

It is indeed unlikely that the use of a word in one language is just the same as that of its counterpart in another – that there are no language-specific differences between them; and Vendler was able to point to such differences in this case. The word 'cause', he observed, is both a verb and a noun, while 'Ursache' is never a verb.[9] If the philosopher's interest in the use of words included differences of this kind, then, as Vendler pointed out, it would be hard to separate it from the work of philologists and empirical linguists.

However, Ryle did not need to claim that the use of 'Ursache' is exactly the same as that of 'cause'. What matters is that the same questions can be discussed by a German philosopher with reference to

8   The relevant distinction was also expressed, by both Flew and Ryle, in terms of 'use' versus 'usage'. A usage, wrote Ryle, 'is a custom, practice, fashion or vogue. It can be local or widespread, obsolete or current, rural or urban, vulgar or academic'; and 'the methods of discovering linguistic usages are the methods of philologists'; but this is not so with 'use' (Ryle, 'Ordinary Language', *Philosophical Review* 1953; reprinted in C.E. Caton, ed., *Philosophy and Ordinary Language* (Urbana 1963), see 115–16). It is doubtful, however, whether the distinction between 'use' and 'usage', as *these* words are ordinarily used, is quite so clear.

9   He also drew attention to a difference between 'cause' in Hume's time and that of today's English. According to the old use, he said, the maker of an artifact would be described as its cause, so that 'tables and chairs would be caused by carpenters'; but this is not how the word is used today. Vendler's choice of 'Ursache' as an example was perhaps unfortunate in view of the existence of a cognate *verb*, 'verursachen'. But this does not affect the essential point.

the use of 'Ursache' as are discussed in English with reference to the use of 'cause'. Thus the question whether a 'constant conjunction' analysis of causation is true to the actual use of causal language is language-neutral: it can be discussed as well in German or French as in English. And what is needed to make this possible is that the uses of 'cause' and its counterparts are alike in the relevant respects, and not that they correspond in every respect.

There are also, however, cases in which no suitable counterparts are available, as they are in the case of 'cause' and 'Ursache' (and 'table' and 'tavola'). When Frege spoke of 'Bedeutung', should the translation be 'meaning' or 'reference'? Should 'Satz', in the writings of German philosophers, be translated as 'sentence' or as 'proposition'? How should Mill's 'pleasure' and 'pain' be translated into German? (More than one translation is offered.) And how are we to deal with the various differences among languages in the area of 'mind', 'soul', 'spirit', etc.? In these cases it cannot be claimed that when a philosopher enquires about the use of a word in one language, his enquiry is 'just as much about the use' of its counterpart in another, for there is no clear counterpart: the relevant uses of words are, indeed, language-specific.

Here is indeed a difficulty for philosophers – though not one that is confined to those who use the criterion of 'what we say'. The difficulty is not, however, intractable. It was, after all, possible for Ryle's *Concept of Mind* to be 'translated into dozens of languages successfully, in spite of the fact that the very word "mind" has no one-word equivalent in German, French, Hungarian etc.'[10] Let us assume that the use of 'mind' is peculiar to English. The discussions across languages are still possible because the verbal differences in question are not beyond explanation. Lacking a word-for-word correspondence, we can still explain the words of the other language and the reasons for translating them in one way or another; and the philosophers using the other language can do likewise, in that language, with regard to ours. Such discussion can, indeed, throw light on the topic in which the 'awkward' words have occurred.

Another difficulty in this area is to distinguish between a difference of vocabulary and a difference of opinion. If we cannot accept what

---

10   Vendler, 'Philosophy of Language and Linguistic Philosophy', op. cit., 32. Vendler used this example to argue that 'the main conclusions of the linguistic philosopher do not remain language-parochial'. But whereas he regarded the intertranslatability of languages as an empirical fact, resulting from a 'genetic unity ... of the human race' due to natural selection, I take a different view of it, as will be seen.

Frege, in an English translation, says about *meaning*, should we conclude that he was wrong or should we find a different translation ('reference') for his German word? Again, if we find ourselves disagreeing with Aristotle's remarks about happiness, is that because the English 'happiness' does not correspond sufficiently with the ancient *eudaimonia*, or because we have a different opinion about happiness? And did Aristotle intend his remarks to conform to the ordinary use of the Greek word or was he going beyond that?

Such difficulties cannot be resolved by simple appeals to 'what we say'. Nevertheless this criterion must have a central place in our discussions of happiness, meaning and other topics. The questions we ask about these are, after all, asked in *our* language and it is by reference to our use of these words that the answers must be sought. If the answers were not about what *we* mean by those words – not in accordance with our use of them – then they would not be answers to the questions we were asking. Reflecting on the use of related words in other languages may *help* to answer those questions, but it cannot undermine the criterion of ordinary use in the language in which the questions are asked.

Let us take the question whether love can be commanded, which is a difficulty for the injunction 'Love your neighbour as yourself'. It can be argued that an injunction to love does not make sense, since 'love' does not mean an action; and whereas it makes sense to command actions (including loving behaviour), this is not true of love itself.[11] Now this difficulty cannot be met by drawing attention to counterparts of the word 'love' in ancient languages for which the difficulty might not arise. Suppose it were true that the word 'H' in ancient Hebrew meant what we would describe as 'loving behaviour'. In that case the injunction – or rather, an injunction – couched in terms of 'H', might not encounter the difficulty I mentioned. But this would not remove the difficulty as it arises for the injunction at issue, which tells us to love and not merely to H. But, it may be said, if the difficulty is confined to modern English, how important is it? For a modern English person who takes it for granted that 'love' means love, the difficulty may be very important. Even if he is told that what was meant was not love but H, he may still want to consider the injunction as meaning what it appears to mean.

Questions about translation have also arisen about the use made by philosophers of language-specific features of grammar. Ryle, in one of

---

11   See O. Hanfling, 'Loving your Neighbour, Loving Yourself', *Philosophy* 1993.

his discussions, drew attention to the fact that such verbs as 'know', 'believe' and 'love' have, unlike 'run', 'study' and 'think', no continuous tenses: one can say that one is running, studying or thinking, but not that one is knowing or believing, etc. From such premises, commented Vendler, 'philosophers have concluded that while studying and the like are actions or processes, knowing and the like are states or dispositions'. But, he pointed out, this argument could not be expressed in German or French, for the use of tenses is different in these languages. But then, he asked,

> how should one know that other arguments of this kind will hold in languages other than English? What shall we say then? That, for instance, knowing is not a process in English? But what sort of philosophical thesis is this?'. (PL 251)

It would be wrong, however, to think that a grammatical distinction that is present only in English cannot be useful to philosophical enquiry. If there were no more to it than English grammar, then it might indeed be regarded as a local and superficial peculiarity. But may not such a language-specific feature help us to recognize a deeper distinction? The deeper distinction in this case is, of course, that between actions and processes, and states and dispositions; and no one would think that this is peculiar to English. The English grammatical distinction is a sign of the deeper one, and useful as a device for expounding it to those who speak English. But there are other, more substantial ways of distinguishing these categories. Thus, to distinguish actions from states and dispositions, it might be pointed out that a person can be said to choose whether to run, study or think, but not whether to know, believe or love. And this remark, unlike that about continuous tenses, is not peculiar to English.

It is sometimes thought that the need to use a particular language means that *truth* must be relative to particular languages; but this is not so. An anthropologist tells us of a tribe in which the word 'dead' is used so as to admit of degrees: a person with a bad illness is said to be dead; as his condition worsens, he becomes completely or absolutely dead and, finally, dead for ever.[12]

Can a person recover after being dead? Is it true that so-and-so is dead? One might think that the answers depend on which language we are speaking. But this is not really so. A word that is used in the way

---

12 C. Turnbull, *The Forest People* (Chatto & Windus), 42–4.

described would not mean 'dead'; and therefore applying the word to those people would not be describing them as *dead*. Barring miracles, it remains true that one cannot recover after being dead.

The truth of philosophical claims, likewise, is not relative to particular languages. According to Vendler, 'one cannot know something false, because in English the verb-phrase *to know that p* is used correctly only in case *p* is true' (PL 260). But the connection of knowledge with truth is not due to a feature of English. If the English 'to know that p' came to be used differently, this would make no difference to that connection. Similarly, if the word 'refute' came in due course to mean nothing more than 'reject', this would not mean that to refute a proposition would have become easier than it is now.

It can also be misleading to qualify claims about what is true or intelligible by the phrase 'as we use the words'. This was done by Isaiah Berlin in a conversation with Austin, where he put forward the following conundrum:

> Supposing a child were to express a wish to meet Napoleon as he was at the battle of Austerlitz, and I said 'It cannot be done', and the child said 'Why not?', and I said 'Because it happened in the past, and you cannot be alive now and also a hundred and thirty years ago and remain at the same age', or something of the kind; and the child went on pressing and said 'Why not?', and I said 'Because it does not make sense, as we use words, to say that you can be in two places at once or "go back" into the past', and so on; and this highly sophisticated child said 'If it is only a question of words, then can't we simply alter our verbal usage? Would that enable me to see Napoleon at the battle of Austerlitz ...?'[13]

This supposition was put to Austin, with the question: 'What should one say to the child? Simply that it has confused the material and formal modes, so to speak?'. Austin's reply, as reported by Berlin, seems to have been rather feeble on this occasion: 'Do not speak so. Tell the child to try and go back into the past .... Let it try, and see what happens then.' One wonders how the ingenious child would have received this advice. Perhaps it would have replied that if 'it does not make sense, as we use words', to say that one can go back into the past, then it cannot make sense to ask someone to *try* to do so either.

---

13   I. Berlin, *Personal Impressions* (Hogarth 1980), 114.

What was wrong with Berlin's reply, or pretended reply, to the child was to give a use of words as the *reason why* something could not be done. Given this reply, it was natural to infer, as the imaginary child did, that according to another way of using words, it *would* be possible to do what it wished; and that, furthermore, one could choose this other way if one wanted to do that. The answer to the child should not have been 'You can't do that *because* it doesn't make sense', etc., but simply: 'The wish you expressed doesn't make sense'.

To speak of going back into the past makes no more sense in French, Chinese, or any other real or imagined language, than in English. If we were told that the Chinese speak as if it made sense (that it 'makes sense for them'), then we would question the meaning of this report, as we would if we were told that in Chinese two plus two equals five. Such a report would indicate that the words had been wrongly translated, and not that what is false or nonsensical in one language is true in another. (Perhaps the imagined Chinese would be talking merely about 'going back into the past' in the familiar sense of indulging in reminiscences.) When we say that one cannot be in two places at once, or go back into the past, we are making conceptual, language-neutral points, the validity of which does not depend on the use of words in a particular language.

If the qualification 'as we use words' were in order in these cases, then it should be so for assertions in general; and this would mean that they are all, in spite of appearances to the contrary, hypothetical. The assertion that it is raining, for example, would be subject to the same qualification, which would make it hypothetical. ('As we use words, it is raining.') (This would not be the end of the matter, for the qualified statement would itself have to be qualified ('As we use words, as we use words ....'); and so on.) But the truth is that the assertion that it is raining is not hypothetical. In making this assertion we *presuppose* that the words in which it is made are being used with their current meanings; but this is not part of what is asserted.

In resisting the idea that linguistic philosophy is bound to be 'language-parochial', I have stressed the fact that, to a large extent, the same concepts exist in different languages – more so than might be thought on the basis of differences of vocabulary and structure. Chinese and English are radically different in these respects and it has been claimed that the logic of such fundamental categories as subject and predicate cannot be rendered in Chinese, so that the corresponding ontologies can have no place in Chinese thought. One might wonder, on this view, how communication with the Chinese is possible at all. But the fact is that we communicate extensively with the Chinese, in practical matters as well as others. We do business with them, and we can read the thoughts of Chairman Mao in English; and presumably *The Concept of Mind* is available in Chinese as well as in other languages.

It is no accident that concepts are shared, to a large extent, by different societies; they are part of the human condition, reflecting the needs and interests of human beings living in a social world. Wittgenstein spoke of a 'common behaviour of mankind' by reference to which an explorer coming into an unknown country would interpret the language that is spoken there. These remarks may be described as 'anthropological', concerning facts about human life. But there is also a logical constraint on what can count as 'language'. Having introduced his 'explorer coming into an unknown country', Wittgenstein wrote:

> Let us imagine that the people in that country carried on the usual human activities and in the course of them employed, apparently, an articulate language. If we watch their behaviour we find it intelligible, it seems 'logical'. But when we try to learn their language we find it impossible to do so. For there is no regular connexion between what they say, the sounds they make, and their actions; but still these sounds are not superfluous, for if we gag one of the people, it has the same consequences as with us; without the sounds their actions fall into confusion – as I feel like putting it.
>
> Are we to say that these people have a language: orders, reports, and the rest?
>
> The regularity for what we call 'language' is lacking.[14] (PI 206–7)

Languages can and do differ from one another in important ways, but there are limits. If we are to describe another language as being different from ours, we must be able to recognize it *as* a language, and to do that we must assume that we could make sense of it in terms of *our* language. This is not, as Davidson has put it, a matter of 'making translatability into a familiar tongue a criterion of language-hood' by way of 'fiat'.[15] What prevents us from describing an unintelligible production of sounds as a language is not an arbitrary decision:

---

14   'Zu dem, was wir "Sprache" nennen, fehlt die Regelmäßigkeit'. The published translation has: 'There is not enough regularity ...'. But Wittgenstein's point is not about more or less regularity; it is about the right kind of regularity.

15   Donald Davidson, *Truth and Interpretation* (OUP 1984), 186.

intelligibility is part of what we mean by 'language' and this meaning has not been imposed by fiat.

Perhaps it will be said that the 'language' of the people in Wittgenstein's example would be intelligible to them even if it could not be made intelligible to us. But what would it mean to describe such sounds as 'intelligible'? There must be more to it than the bare fact that without them 'their actions fall into confusion': the right kind of 'regular connections' must be there, even if we have not discovered them yet. And if we do discover them, then we should be able to explain, in terms of our language, what those sounds mean and how they function as 'orders, reports and the rest'. Given the description of the example, we might regard it as *highly probable* that the people there are using a language; but this would be no different from regarding it as highly probable that there really do exist intelligible connections between the sounds they make and their behaviour.

The main argument of this chapter has been 'outwards', as it were. First I tried to show how one person's knowledge of language can include a whole language community (what *we* say and not merely what *someone* says or means). Then I argued that the method of 'what we say' is not undermined by changes and variations of usage, nor by the existence of different languages. Although the claims about what we say – how a word is used – are made, necessarily, in the current language, their import extends beyond that language. The words of a current language, such as English, may have counterparts in other languages, but even where this is not so, the same concepts may still be shared in a relevant sense. Finally I argued that conceptual convergence, especially with important concepts such as interest philosophers, is not a matter of accident. This is so in two ways: first, the concepts in question reflect needs and interests that are common to the human form of life; and second, there is a logical limit to the variety of what we can call 'language'.

5   What is wrong with the paradigm case argument?

Among detractors of ordinary language philosophy it is widely agreed that no specimen of it is more worthy of repudiation than the 'paradigm case argument' (PCA). In their eyes it is a paradigm case of bad philosophy, and merely to identify an argument as an instance of it is enough to show that it is not worth further consideration.

Apart from the validity or otherwise of the PCA, it also appears that many philosophers do not *like* this kind of argument. It may seem altogether too easy a way of disposing of problems with which philosophers have wrestled for centuries. However, to say of a method that it provides easy solutions is not to give a proper reason for rejecting it; and if a philosopher is serious about getting at the truth of a problem as opposed to merely playing with it, then he cannot criticize the PCA on this ground. But does the PCA provide easy solutions? As we shall see, understanding and applying the argument is not an easy matter. Moreover, even if the PCA is a valid and useful instrument in the treatment of philosophical problems, it cannot be a complete treatment. The argument typically purports to show that a particular philosophical conclusion must be false, but not what is wrong with the arguments leading to it.

An early presentation of the PCA was that of J.O. Urmson in 1956. 'Suppose', he wrote, 'that someone looking at what we would normally regard as a typically red object expressed a doubt whether is was really red.' There are no abnormal conditions, such as bad light, defective eyes, etc.

> We would then be at a loss and probably ask him what on earth he meant by red if he was unwilling to call this red .... If we do not call *this* red, then what would we? There is no better way of

showing what the word 'red' means than by pointing to things of this colour.[1]

He went on to apply this approach to a controversy arising from Sir Arthur Eddington's popular science book, *The Nature of The Physical World*, in which the author, 'in an attempt to bring out in a vivid fashion the difference between the scientific and everyday description of such things as desks ..., said in effect that desks were not really solid' (ibid. 121). This claim, said Urmson, had been effectively refuted by Susan Stebbing in *Philosophy and the Physicists,* by means of 'the argument from standard examples', i.e. the PCA. The refutation consisted in 'simply pointing out that if one asked what we ordinarily mean by *solid,* we immediately realise that we mean something like "of the consistency of such things as desks" ' (ibid. 121).

Antony Flew, in the same year, applied the PCA to the problem of free will, as follows:

> If there is any word the meaning of which can be taught by reference to paradigm cases, then no argument whatever could ever prove that there are no cases of whatever it is. Thus, since the meaning of 'of his own free will' can be taught by reference to such paradigm cases as that in which a man, under no social pressure, marries the girl he wants to marry (how else *could* it be taught?), it cannot be right, on any grounds whatsoever, to say that no one ever acts of his own free will.[2]

Such paradigm cases, he continued, must occur 'if the word is ever to be thus explained'; they cannot themselves be 'specimens which have been wrongly identified'. Similarly, it was argued by others, sceptical claims to the effect that nothing is certain are to be confronted with paradigm cases that are definitive of the meaning of 'certain'; etc.

It was not long, however, before there appeared criticisms of the PCA which were thought to damage it beyond repair. In what follows I shall state the main objections and try to show that the PCA, if understood in a suitable way, has not been refuted and remains an important contribution to the treatment of the problems in question.

1   J.O. Urmson, 'Some Questions concerning Validity' in A. Flew, ed., *Essays in Conceptual Analysis* (Macmillan 1956), 121.
2   'Philosophy and Language', in Colin Lyas, ed., *Philosophy and Linguistics* (Macmillan 1971), 74.

The paradigm case argument and the ostensive teaching argument

There is, said Urmson, 'no better way of showing what the word "red" means than by pointing to things of this colour'. But could it not be done by pointing to things that only appear to be of this colour? There might be a world from which red things have disappeared, and nevertheless people are taught the meaning of this word by being shown things that appear to be red. Hence the existence of red things is not entailed by the fact that it is possible to teach the meaning of this word.

When we turn to such non-visual qualities as free will and certainty, the idea of teaching by pointing to things is anyway less plausible; but if we tried to do so (pointing to the man who 'wants to marry the girl', for example), then we might well be using cases that only appear to have the qualities in question. There is, we may say, more to these qualities than meets the eye. What prevents a case from being one of free will may, for instance, be something that was said to the agent in the past, and this would not be apparent from what is there now; while in the case of certainty other non-apparent conditions would be relevant.

This objection is effective against what I shall call the 'ostensive teaching argument' (OTA). The PCA, however, should be separated from this; it is essentially an argument about description and not ostension. Thus, when Flew gave his example of the man who acted 'of his own free will', it was neither necessary nor sufficient for the reader to actually observe such a man. It was not sufficient, because mere observation would not suffice to show that the man was really acting freely; and not necessary, because a *description* of the example, such as that offered by Flew, should suffice. The man wants to marry the girl, they have been in love for some time, he is not under any kind of duress, etc. Here is a paradigm case of acting freely, and by describing such examples the meaning of 'free will' might be explained. Someone who denies that this would be a case of free will cannot be using the expression with its normal meaning, and thus the meaning of his denial is itself thrown into doubt. He uses the words 'free will', but they cannot mean what they normally mean.

Whether Urmson and Flew were committed to the OTA as distinct from the PCA is doubtful; but the former was clearly present in Norman Malcolm's 'Moore and Ordinary Language' of 1942. One cannot, argued Malcolm, 'teach a person the meaning' of such words as 'certain', 'probable' and others, without 'showing him instances of the true application' of these words; and since most people have learned the meanings of these words, there must be 'many situations of the kind which they describe'.

But the fact that people have learned the meanings of these words does not entail that they were taught to them by a particular method; it does not even follow that they were *taught* to them. There is no need, however, for advocates of the PCA to get involved in disputes about learning. The essential question is whether describable cases, *whose existence is not in dispute*, are to be further described as cases (or paradigm cases) of certainty, free will or whatever it might be. Opponents of the PCA, who deny the existence of free will, for example, do not deny that there are many cases in which a person does what he wants, is not subject to abnormal influences or compulsion by others, etc. What they claim is that, in spite of this, these are not really cases of free will. And according to the PCA, as I understand it, this claim cannot be right, because such cases are paradigms by which the meaning of 'free will' could be explained, so that anyone who denies that they are cases of free will cannot be using this expression with its normal meaning.

The PCA, as distinct from the OTA, is proof against a kind of objection that was put forward by Ayer and others. 'In a society which believes in witchcraft', argued Ayer, it may be 'perfectly correct in certain circumstances to say that a person is bewitched; the symptoms which are commonly regarded as the sign of demonic possession may be quite clearly marked'. Yet, he observed, 'it does not follow ... that demons are really at work.'[3] Similarly, he argued, our society is one that believes in free will; but though the 'symptoms' which are commonly regarded as signs of free will may be 'quite clearly marked' it does not follow that free will is really present.

These cases are not alike, however. Ayer is right in saying that the activity of demons is not entailed by the presence of signs and symptoms. But in the described cases of free will, we are not dealing merely with signs and symptoms. The fact that the man wants to marry the woman, is not under any constraint or abnormal influence, etc. – these are not mere symptoms, they are what his freedom consists in. In describing the case of the bridegroom we have given a paradigm case of free will, but in describing someone who foams at the mouth and utters strange sounds we have not yet given a paradigm case of demonic possession. To do that we would need to add the further and

3 A.J. Ayer, *The Concept of a Person* (Macmillan 1963), 18.

essential point that these things are due to the presence of a demon; and no further point corresponding to this is required in the case of free will.

It is true that appearances may justify the ascription of a given property even though that property is not really present. One may be justified in describing a thing as 'red' even though it is not really red, and even though (owing to some catastrophe, perhaps) nothing is really red. And one may have perfectly good reasons for saying that Smith acted freely even though Smith was acting under a threat of which one was unaware. A paradigm case of *justification* is not necessarily a case of truth. But this is not an objection to the PCA. The claim of the PCA is only that certain cases, *whose existence is not in dispute*, must count as cases of free will, if this expression is to be understood in its normal sense.

Free will and the paradigm case argument

Although the PCA was applied to a number of topics, it has received most attention in connection with arguments purporting to show that free will is or may be an illusion. A typical feature of such arguments is that of adding a further requirement, not covered by the undisputed description, which must be fulfilled in genuine cases of free will. (This requirement would correspond to that of genuine 'demonic possession' in addition to the undisputed presence of signs and symptoms.) John Passmore, having agreed that 'we have all learnt the use of the expression "of his own free will" to cover such cases as that of the bridegroom', goes on to claim that there is more to its meaning than that. 'We have also learnt ... that a person acts of his own free will only when his action proceeds from an act of will and when that act of will has the metaphysical peculiarity of being uncaused.'[4] Now one might well, as Passmore says, 'deny ... that this criterion is ever satisfied', and perhaps conclude from this that 'there is no such thing as free will'.

But is it true that this criterion is something 'we have also learnt', as Passmore claims? Those who do philosophy may come to learn and endorse the criterion, but this is not true of people in general. And neither is knowledge or endorsement of the criterion a condition of understanding the meaning of 'free will'. A person would be said to understand this expression if he regularly used it in appropriate

4   John Passmore, *Philosophical Reasoning* (Duckworth 1971), 117–18.

circumstances, on the basis of suitable non-metaphysical criteria and regardless of his views, if any, about the acts of will postulated by Passmore. Such a person would also understand the connections between free will and related concepts such as that of responsibility, but this, again, would not involve views about metaphysical acts of will.

According to another view, an action is not freely chosen if it can be explained in terms of natural causes; and as long as we cannot be sure that there are actions that *cannot* be so explained, the existence of free will remains in doubt. Thus, 'if we knew all our "choices" to be the product of prior conditioning or hereditary traits ..., we might think that to call certain choices "free" would have a hollow ring'.[5] Here again it is suggested that more is involved in freedom of choice than what we are given in the undisputed description.

But what is the knowledge that is here hypothesized? We know already that our characters are the products of conditioning and hereditary traits; and that most of our actions are (by definition) in character. But this does not interfere with the description of them as 'free'. This description is not in conflict with the point about conditioning and heredity. To say that a particular action was predictable and thoroughly in accordance with the agent's character is not to cast doubt on its freedom. Similarly, if we said that the bridegroom's action of marrying was predictable from his having fallen in love, etc., this would not cast doubt on the statement that he was acting freely.

It may seem paradoxical that we describe actions as freely chosen even when they result from influences that are not themselves freely chosen. The influences, genetic and environmental, that make us what we are, are not subject to our choice; and this may seem to imply that when our choices are in accordance with them, we are not choosing freely. But this is not so. Using this expression in its normal sense, we describe an action as freely chosen without implying either that it was uncharacteristic of the agent, or that the influences of heredity and environment are themselves subject to choice.

This point applies also to 'agent's reasons' – those with which a person explains (justifies) what he is doing or is going to do. My reason for acting in a particular way is not itself a matter of choice, but it does not follow that when I act for a reason my action is not a matter of

---

5 Keith Donnellan, 'Paradigm-Case Argument' in Paul Edwards, ed., *The Encyclopedia of Philosophy*, 43.

choice. Again, when I do what I *want*, my freedom is not infringed by the fact that one does not choose one's wants. 'What I will not, that I cannot do' says Angelo in *Measure for Measure* (2.2.52). But Angelo's excuse is specious: he knows perfectly well that he could do what Isabella asks. That it is against his will does not entail that he is not free to do it.

A contrary view has been taken by Thomas Nagel, who claims that 'to be really free',

> we would have to act from a standpoint completely outside ourselves, choosing everything about ourselves, including all our principles of choice – creating ourselves from nothing, so to speak.[6]

But, as Nagel observes, this is an incoherent idea; and from this he concludes that the idea of being 'really free' is likewise incoherent.

There is no reason, however, for accepting Nagel's definition of real freedom. When we look for typical (paradigm) cases of free action, we certainly do not try to find cases that conform to Nagel's conditions. There are, indeed, cases that conform to those conditions to some extent – where a person adopts, or tries to adopt, an external standpoint, questioning his 'principles of choice', etc. – but these features are not characteristic of free actions, and to put the requirement of standing 'completely outside ourselves' forward as definitive of 'free action' is to introduce an artificial (and in Nagel's version, incoherent) meaning for this expression.[7]

---

6   *The View from Nowhere* (OUP 1986), 118.

7   A view similar to Nagel's is taken by Galen Strawson, who argues as follows:

> How one acts when one acts ... for a reason is, necessarily, a function of ... how one is, mentally speaking. If, therefore, one is to be truly responsible for how one acts, one must be truly responsible for how one is, mentally speaking .... But one cannot choose ... the way one is, mentally speaking .... (*Freedom and Belief* (Clarendon 1986), 28–9)

> The conclusion is that one can never be 'truly responsible' for one's actions. But the second step of the argument ('If, therefore ...') is a *non sequitur*. Acting for a reason and being responsible for one's action do *not* entail that one has chosen 'the way one is'. Strawson goes on to claim that the condition he has described 'is just the kind of freedom that most people ordinarily and unreflectively suppose themselves to possess' (30). But I believe that most people would be astonished to have this impossible condition read into what they mean by 'acting freely'.

It is true that we sometimes use the language of compulsion when speaking of actions that are chosen on the basis of suitable reasons and whose freedom is not, as far as ordinary discourse is concerned, in doubt. We speak of 'compelling' reasons; we ask 'What *made* you do that?'; we comment that, given his character, 'he was *bound* to do it' and so on. Luther tells us that when he nailed his Ninety-five Theses to the church door, he 'could do no other'; but this does not mean that he was not acting freely.[8] Such expressions *may* mean that an action was not, or not wholly, free; but this depends on the nature of the compulsion'. The same applies to such expressions as 'I had no choice'. To understand these expressions, we need to know what kind of constraint, compulsion or obligation was at work. In some cases, these will undermine the description of an action. as 'free'; in others not. A paradigm case of free action would, of course, be one in which no undermining constraints are present; but this is not to say that the normal influences of heredity and environment, or the possession of suitable reasons, would be excluded.

Another way in which the distinction between free and not free may seem to be hostage to the advance of science is that of psychiatry. If we say, writes J.R. Lucas, 'that the kleptomaniac is constrained, is under a psychological compulsion, to steal, then we lay ourselves open to the possibility that all our actions may be, in this sense, constrained'.[9] But this is to overlook the fact that kleptomania is essentially an *irrational* condition. It is because the actions of the kleptomaniac, unlike those of a normal thief, cannot be accounted for in a rational way, that his freedom of action is thought to be impaired. But it does not make sense to suppose that all of our actions might turn out, with the advance of knowledge, to be irrational.

On the other hand, is the 'compulsion' under which the kleptomaniac acts such as to deprive him of choice? No: given strong enough reasons against satisfying his craving, he may choose to refrain from doing so. What is distinctive about the kleptomaniac is not that he has no freedom of choice, but that his desires (or 'cravings') lack reasons where reasons would normally be expected, or lack reasons that would be regarded as adequate. (They may also be distinguished, by their anti-social character, from desires that would be described merely as 'eccentric'.) It may be admitted, however, that in extreme cases the kleptomaniac's freedom of choice is, at least, diminished; but

---

8 The example is discussed by Flew in 'Anti-Social Determinism', *Philosophy* 1994, 25.
9 J.R. Lucas, *The Freedom of the Will* (OUP 1970), 15.

such cases would not, of course, be selected as paradigms of free action.

It has also been argued that the reality of free choice may be contingent on the falsehood of far-fetched but not inconceivable suppositions. Peter van Inwagen asks us to suppose that all our decisions are, unknown to us, 'programmed' by a device placed in our brains at the time of birth by Martians, so that

> whenever [any] person must make a decision, the device *causes* him to decide one way or the other according to the requirements of a table of instructions that were incorporated into the device.[10]

This supposition, labelled '(M)', was used by Inwagen in opposition to the PCA. The latter, he says, cannot allow for the possibility of (M); it is concerned merely with 'how things *appear* to us' (111), and this would be exactly the same if (M) were true. Yet, he claims, '(M) obviously *does* entail that no one can act otherwise than he does' and that no one 'could have helped what he did [or] had any choice about the way he acted' (110).

But in what sense could a device placed in our brains cause us 'to decide one way or the other'? We can easily imagine a device that produces behavioural *tendencies* in us, so that, given a certain kind of situation, one will tend to respond in one way rather than another. This is easy to imagine, because it is very similar to what we have anyway: the effects of 'conditioning and hereditary traits'. We can refer similarly to the effects of certain substances in the brain, hormones, etc. These things certainly affect our behaviour, but they do not make it impossible for a person to 'act otherwise than he does'; nor do they put into question the existence of cases of free choice.

It appears, however, that Inwagen is after something more specific: a 'table of instructions' that determines not merely how one will tend to behave, but what one will actually do in a particular situation. The following example is given by him.

> If you're in early middle age and a superior humiliates you by reprimanding you in front of your subordinates, attempt to get revenge by spreading scurrilous rumours about his personal life, taking care to see to it that these rumours can't be traced back to you. (235)

---

10   Peter van Inwagen, *An Essay on Free Will* (OUP 1983), 109.

But if this 'instruction' were something placed in our brains, then it would not be an instruction in the normal sense; for an instruction is something that is available to be heard or read by the agent. And an instruction in this (normal) sense would not have the effect of determining what one will do, for when a person is instructed to do something, it is up to him whether to obey. This is just another area in which we exercise our freedom of choice: an instruction enjoins but does not determine. The extent of that freedom may depend on the sanction behind the instruction and in some cases we may feel (or claim, by way of excuse) that we had no choice. But in other cases this is not so, and being instructed to do something is not incompatible with being free to choose whether to do it.

Leaving aside the word 'instruction', could we conceive of a device of which the agent is unaware and which determines his actions in the way described in Inwagen's example? That example fails to correspond with what we recognize as human behaviour, for it would be absurd to suppose that if the antecedent ('If you're in early middle age', etc.) were satisfied, then a person would necessarily behave as described. A person placed in that situation might consider an indefinite variety of circumstances, obligations, possible consequences, etc., before deciding what, if anything, to do. Perhaps it is conceivable that creatures superficially resembling ourselves behave in accordance with such 'instructions'; but our life is not like that. One way or the other, supposition (M) cannot serve to refute the PCA. If we take it in the sense illustrated by the example, then we know it is false. If we take it in the sense of behavioural tendencies, then it makes no difference whether it is true or false.

Now supposition (M), as we have seen, was thought to entail that 'no one can act otherwise than he does'; and it is often thought that being able to act otherwise than one does is essential to free will. But is this correct? Leaving aside far-fetched suppositions, let us consider this with reference to an example from Locke. We are asked us to imagine a man who is 'carried whilst fast asleep, into a room, where is a person he longs to see and speak with' (*Essay*, 2.21.10). On waking, the man 'stays willingly in, i.e. prefers his stay to going away'. But, unknown to the man, he had been 'locked fast in' while still asleep. The man's staying in, says Locke, is voluntary: it is what he wants to do; but in spite of this 'he is not at liberty not to stay, he has not freedom to be gone'. The conclusion is that 'liberty is not an idea that belongs to volition, or preferring; but to the person having the power of doing . . .'. On this view, 'liberty' and 'free' belong with doing and not with willing. But, it is argued, since the freedom to act may be contingent on circumstances beyond our knowledge (which might include real possibilities as well as far-fetched conjectures), we can never be sure that we are free.

But would we not, in the case of Locke's example, say that the man *chose freely* to stay in? This is not what we would say if he had *known* the door to be locked; but it would not be wrong to say it in the case described by Locke. In such a case, to be sure, we might also say that the man was not, or 'not really', free to choose, meaning by this that his freedom of *acting* was (unknown to him) curtailed; but this would not be incompatible with the statement that he chose freely. The fact that staying in was what he preferred, and that his choice was not made under duress, is sufficient for saying correctly that he chose freely to stay in. The justification for describing his choosing as 'free' is just the fact that he was not choosing under duress.

To clarify the point, let us consider a more straightforward example, involving a choice between two actions. (This is not so with Locke's example, where the choice is between acting and doing nothing.) Suppose I am ordered, under threat of a penalty, to appear before a magistrate on Monday morning. This would not be a case of free choice. Before setting off, however, I consider whether to go by car or by train and decide on the former because it is more convenient. Given that this is my only reason, the choice is made freely. Later, however, it turns out that the trains were not running, so that I could not have gone by train anyway. Would it follow that I had not chosen freely to go by car? No; I chose freely, because that is what I wanted to do, on the basis of suitable reasons (reasons other than duress). Had I *known* that the trains were cancelled, then of course I could not have chosen, let alone chosen freely, between car and train. But, not knowing this, I chose, and chose freely, to go by car. If I told someone later that I chose freely to go by car, I would be speaking the truth and not merely making an excusable mistake. Perhaps, if I had found out about the trains in the meantime, I would add a rider to this effect, but this would not affect the truth of the original statement. It is also on this basis that we regard people as *culpable*. Let us suppose that, for environmental reasons, I ought not to have gone by car. In that case I would be *to blame* for having made that choice; and the fact that, unknown to me, the trains were cancelled, would be irrelevant: it would not excuse my choice.[11]

---

11   For a somewhat similar argument, see Harry Frankfurt, *The Importance of What We Care About* (CUP 1988), ch. 1.

In considering the condition 'He could have acted otherwise' it is important to distinguish two kinds of 'could'. If the 'could' is relative to constraints of which the agent is aware, then it is indeed a necessary condition of free (or wholly free) choice. But this is not so if the 'could' is relative to circumstances beyond the agent's knowledge. It is easy to conflate the two kinds of 'could' because in most cases of free choice the options between actually doing one thing and another are real and not merely apparent; but free choice and free will do not depend on this.

I have reviewed a number of arguments purporting to show that free will is or may be an illusion. The literature on this subject is vast and obviously I cannot do justice to it here. But I hope enough has been said to bring out a flaw that is typical of such arguments: to impose requirements on the use of 'free choice' and its cognates that are contrary to the actual use of this expression, as illustrated by paradigm cases. The requirement may be metaphysical, as in Passmore's conception of 'an act of will' and in Nagel's idea of 'creating ourselves from nothing'; it may be connected with scientific knowledge about the effects of heredity and conditioning; or it may be the one about being able to do otherwise, where what is meant are circumstances beyond the agent's knowledge. Such requirements, I have argued, are not recognized in the normal use of 'free choice'.

Inductive reasoning and the paradigm case argument

Urmson and Flew, as we saw at the start of this chapter, applied the PCA to a number of topics, including free will and solidity. Both writers denied, however, that the argument is applicable to the problem of induction. Their reasons were drawn from the widely accepted dichotomy of description versus evaluation.

Urmson considered how the PCA might be applied to scepticism about *validity*, in the case of both deduction and induction. It is – so the argument would run – 'meaningless to ask whether the standard examples [paradigm cases] of valid deduction are really valid .... The meaning of "valid" with regard to deductive argument is determined by these standard examples' (op. cit. 123). Similarly, in the case of inductive reasoning 'we must start from the standard examples of valid and invalid argument':

> Except by reference to such examples no meaning can be attached to the term 'valid' .... If the validity of such examples is denied,

by what standards is [an argument] being judged? ... These examples set the standard.[12] (124)

He went on, however, to deny that the PCA is applicable to validity, whether deductive or inductive. The trouble was that 'valid' has an evaluative meaning, so that 'to call an argument valid is not merely to classify it logically, as when we say it is a syllogism or *modus ponens*; it is at least in part to evaluate or appraise it; it is to signify approval of it' (126).

The PCA was, he thought, effective in dealing with 'descriptive' terms, but evaluative language was a different matter. In this case the argument could be applied only in a relative sense, depending on the evaluative preferences of a given group. Thus, 'if amongst a certain group of people the evaluative distinction between valid and invalid arguments is recognized ..., then we shall expect to find criteria ... which are generally accepted by the group' (128). And then it will be 'pointless to ask whether *for that group* there is any distinction between valid and invalid'. We ourselves are such a group and for us 'the fact that there are standard cases of validity which outside his study no one would deny, shows that the doubt when expressed in the study is absurd or at least incorrectly formulated' (129). At another level, however, the doubt is not absurd. 'Granted that this is the way in which *we* distinguish between valid and invalid ..., what good reasons have we for evaluating arguments in this way?' (130).

But how should we understand this demand for 'good reasons'? What good reasons could there be for (or against) evaluating, say, *modus ponens* as a valid form of argument? The latter is definitive (a paradigm case) of what is meant by 'good reason'. A good reason is what a person has if, for example, he deduces a proposition in accordance with *modus ponens*. Similarly – turning to induction – a good reason is what a person has if, apprised of suitable evidence, he concludes, say, that drinking coffee will keep him awake at night.

According to Urmson, however, we must ask whether there are good reasons for regarding these as good reasons. He compared the two levels of questioning with allegedly similar questions about the evaluation of apples. Given the existence of such and such criteria

---

12   Among those who had applied this kind of argument to the problem of induction were Paul Edwards, in 'Bertrand Russell's Doubts about Induction', *Mind* 1949, and P.F. Strawson in *Introduction to Logical Theory* (Methuen 1952), ch. 9.

(prescribed by an authority, perhaps) for the grading of apples in a particular country,

> we can no longer ask whether it is possible for that group to distinguish good and bad apples. But we can perfectly properly ask why they use these standards and whether we ourselves have any good reason for using them. (129)

This is true, but it will not help us to make sense of the question of good reasons for relying on *modus ponens*. In the case of apples it is easy to think of reasons for or against adopting a particular standard of grading. Such reasons might be given in debating whether, say, uniformity of size should be introduced as a criterion for 'Grade 1'. But such discussions and introductions do not make sense in the case of *modus ponens*. There cannot be an argument for adopting *modus ponens*, because this and similar standards of validity are presupposed in the very notion of argument.

Can there be arguments for (or against) distinguishing between valid and invalid in the case of induction? This would mean that we have a choice in the matter – as we have in the case of criteria for grading apples. According to Flew, indeed, 'it is necessary for each of us tacitly or explicitly actually to make our personal value commitments here'. 'Most of us', he continued, 'are in fact willing' to do this in the case of induction; but 'as philosophers we must insist' on bringing the question and choice into the open (op. cit. 74).

But how are we to conceive of choice and 'personal commitment' in this matter? Given suitable evidence, I come to believe that coffee keeps me awake at night. Here is an example of what we call 'a reasonable inference'. But this is not a matter of choice for me (or for us). I *find* the evidence to be good (fairly good, etc.) and do not *choose* to regard it so. The language of choice and 'personal value commitments' does not make sense here.[13] Again, my aim in looking at for evidence is not, as Urmson would have it, to find out what kind of evidence is accepted in a particular group (which happens to be mine). I am not interested in anthropology, but in the truth of the matter: whether coffee really will keep me awake.

The difficulty, or alleged difficulty, of applying the PCA to evaluative language is connected with a misunderstanding of the nature of the PCA, as in the following passage from Flew:

13 For further discussion see O. Hanfling, '"Is", "Ought" and the voluntaristic Fallacy', *Philosophy* 1997.

That too short a way with the problem of induction, which tries to *deduce* that induction is reasonable from the premise that people regard it so, or even that they make inductive behaviour part of their paradigm of reasonableness, will not do. (74)

Such a deduction, he pointed out, would offend against the principle that one cannot deduce a value proposition ('induction is reasonable') from a factual one ('people regard it so').

But what is wrong with this 'short way with the problem of induction' is not the step from fact to value; it is the step from what people think to what is really the case (that, as Flew puts it, 'induction is reasonable'). Of course a proposition or procedure may not be reasonable in spite of the fact that 'people regard it so'. But the PCA does not depend on deductions of this fallacious kind. (If it did, then the same objection would apply to the case of free will: we cannot *deduce* that there is free will from a premise about what people think.) The PCA is about the actual use of such terms as 'free', 'reasonable', 'valid', etc.; and this does not include the deduction posited by Flew.

In one respect the problem of induction is more tricky than others to which the PCA has been applied. Such words as 'free will', 'solid' and 'certain' are part of the ordinary vocabulary, and it is on their use in ordinary language that the PCA relies. But 'induction' is not part of the ordinary vocabulary, and the PCA cannot rely on an ordinary use of this word in dealing with the problem of induction. The relevant ordinary expressions in this case are 'good evidence', 'reasonable', etc. The introduction of the term 'induction' to cover this kind of reasoning may give the impression that it is supposed to be justified by a 'principle of induction'; and then the sceptic can direct his doubt against that principle. Flew, for one, appears to have seen the matter in this way when he denied the ability of the PCA to show that 'induction is reasonable'.

But when people justify their inductive beliefs and certainties, they do so by reference to 'good evidence' ('conclusive evidence', etc.); they do not, in addition, invoke a principle of induction or claim that 'induction is reasonable'. If the sceptic directs his doubt against this claim, he is disputing with an artificial opponent – a creature of philosophical terminology as distinct from ordinary language and ordinary beliefs. To engage with the latter, he must address such expressions as 'good evidence', 'reasonable' and the rest, arguing, for example, that no past experience can amount to good evidence and that beliefs based on such experience cannot really be reasonable. And it is to paradigm cases of 'good evidence', etc. that the advocate of the PCA will appeal in opposition to the sceptic.

The term 'induction' may also mislead in another way. It may give the impression that what is at stake is a particular method: 'the method of induction'. Given this phrase, it may seem as if induction is one method among other possible ones; and then it may reasonably be asked why this method, in particular, should be placed beyond any need for justification. Wesley Salmon, having pointed out that a moral practice that is accepted in a given society may nevertheless be questioned by a critic, thinks that the same is true of the method of induction: 'I cannot accept that induction needs no justification, just because it happens to conform to the common methodology.'[14] But 'induction' is not the name of a methodology that just happens to be common among us. Reasoning from what has been observed to what may be expected is part of what we mean by 'reasoning' and someone who did not reason in this way could not be said to have a methodology at all. Hence, as Strawson observed, 'if one asked a meteorologist what method or methods he used to forecast the weather, one would be surprised if he answered: "Oh, just the inductive method".'[15]

'The method of induction' should not be confused with 'inductive methods'. Such a confusion seems to be involved in Salmon's question, 'Are the inductive methods we regard as correct really correct?' (op. cit.). It is true that particular inductive methods may be open to question and improvement. This is so in the case of opinion polls, for example. But a challenge to particular inductive methods is not a challenge to inductive reasoning as such.

What we say and what philosophers say

The PCA is an argument from ordinary language. The idea is to describe cases which would clearly be regarded as having property P in accordance with the ordinary meaning of 'P', thus refuting the claims of philosophers that nothing has (or that, for all we know, nothing has) property P. Some philosophers, as we have seen, continue to maintain such positions in spite of the PCA.

How is such disagreement possible? And what account do these philosophers take of the facts of ordinary language? A number of different attitudes are to be found in their writings. One is expressed by Passmore when he says that the language in which philosophers' claims are made needs to be understood 'in a very special,

---

14   In R. Swinburne, ed., *The Justification of Induction* (OUP 1974), 67.
15   P.F. Strawson, *Introduction to Logical Theory* (Methuen 1952), 258.

philosophical sense'. Such assertions, he says, *'cannot* mean what, as ordinary men and women, we should naturally suppose them to mean' (op. cit. 111–12). If this is correct, then arguments based on the ordinary meanings of words are irrelevant.

But can the matter really be so simple – a case of mistaking a special meaning for an ordinary one? If so, then a simple explanation should suffice to remove the misunderstanding. That the matter is not so simple is evident from the fact that the philosophers making those claims have, after all, chosen to express them in ordinary language. Why should they do this when the danger of misunderstanding must be obvious? When a philosopher or scientist denies that tables are solid or that anything is certain, it surely looks as if they mean to deny that tables are solid or that anything is certain. If this were not so, why would they express their claims in that way, rather than choose a frankly technical terminology? (A similar point was made in Chapter 2, with reference to Ayer's defence against Austin.)

According to Passmore, the philosophers' language can be understood as emphatic. The statement 'no bodies are solid', he writes,

> is, considering the history of the idea of solidity, a quite natural way of making the point that there are no bodies which are wholly impenetrable. 'No empirical propositions are certain', similarly, is an emphatic way of asserting that it is always logically possible for an empirical statement to be false. (112)

But if a philosopher wants to emphasize the point that it is always logically possible for an empirical proposition to be false, he can do it in various, less misleading ways. He can underline his statement, go over the point more than once and so on. Why should he resort to a statement that seems to be saying something different from what, according to Passmore, he wants to say?

Another attitude to the discrepancy has been to blame ordinary language for being at fault. This attitude was expressed by Ayer when rejecting the PCA as applied to the problem of other minds.[16] Ayer conceded that to speak of 'knowing' in such situations would 'accord with ordinary practice'; but, he went on, 'the contention we have to meet is that ordinary practice is here at fault'. In support of this he supposed that the ascriptions we make may all turn out 'to be incapable of being justified'.

16   Ayer, *The Concept of a Person* (op. cit.), 32.

But what is meant here by 'justified'? Is *this* word being used in its normal sense, or in an artificial, philosophers' sense? If the former, then it can be defined by reference to paradigm cases of justification; if the latter, then the PCA has not been answered but merely set aside. It is, of course, not difficult to describe paradigm cases of the justified ascription of thoughts and feelings to others. If I tell you, perhaps with suitable behaviour, that I have a toothache, and there is no reason to think that I may be speaking falsely, then you are justified in ascribing toothache to me. This is how 'justified' is normally used. (It would not follow, of course, that I really have a toothache: a paradigm case of justification is not a paradigm case of knowledge. To describe the latter, we would need to add the assumption that I really do have a toothache.)

Sometimes, however, critics of the PCA seem to *base* their objections on ordinary language, as when it is claimed by Lucas that 'we use the word "free" ... to characterize [actions of which] no complete causal account can be given' (op. cit. 12). Passmore seems similarly to be making a claim about ordinary language when he writes that 'it is wrong to say that anything is certain if there is the slightest possibility that it will not happen', and that we 'misuse' the word, and stand to be corrected, if we do not conform to this criterion (op. cit. 115).

But is this criterion true to the normal use of the word? A person can be asked to ascertain whether a meeting will take place tomorrow, and he would be expected to answer 'yes' if, having made suitable enquiries, he were asked whether he was certain. In this case he would stand to be corrected if he did *not* answer 'yes'. And yet, of course, there is always 'the slightest possibility' – perhaps more than the slightest – that the event will not happen.

It would, however, be wrong to deny that the philosophers' claims have any basis in ordinary language. That they have such a basis is suggested by the readiness with which, in spite of their radical and apparently devastating implications, many ordinary people are inclined to assent to them. Any teacher of philosophy will know how easy, or even unnecessary, it is to make such claims plausible to students without any need for sophisticated arguments or instruction in metaphysics. The fact that the claims are so close to the philosophy of everyman gives them a special interest and importance. It appears that, despite the tensions, the 'ordinary man and woman', and perhaps the philosopher too, want to have it both ways: to preserve the ordinary distinctions, and yet to claim that they are unreal – so that nothing (or everything, as the case may be) really has property P. In this way we are led, by arguments based on ordinary language, to conclusions that are subversive of ordinary language, and to deny the validity of distinctions that we make, and need to make, in everyday life.

The arguments for denying application to 'free choice', for example, are drawn largely from the ordinary use of causal language. (Here are more of those 'traps' which, to quote Wittgenstein again, 'language sets for us'.) 'Cause' is often used in the sense of 'sufficient condition', so that if we say 'A caused B', we mean that, given A, B was bound to happen. And if this is applied to human actions it may seem as if, in assigning a cause to someone's action, we are committed to the view that he was bound to do it and not free to choose otherwise. Again, the condition about being able to *act* otherwise than one did may seem to be supported by the actual use of language, for we often express our freedom of choice by saying that we could have acted otherwise. Yet this, as I have argued, is not a necessary condition of free choice, as this expression is normally used.

In the case of 'solid', the argument for denying application to this word was drawn from criteria by which this word is normally applied. The table at which he sat, wrote Eddington,

> is mostly emptiness. Sparsely scattered in that emptiness are numerous electric charges rushing about with great speed; but their combined bulk amounts to less than a billionth of the bulk of the table ...

There was, he concluded, 'nothing substantial' about his table; 'it is nearly all empty space'.[17]

Now it is true that we would not ordinarily describe something as solid (or 'substantial') if it were no more than a collection of fleeting entities, thinly dispersed in an area of empty space. This might indeed be regarded as a paradigm of *non*-solidity. And yet the latter turns out to be identical with that paradigm of solidity, the table. How is this possible?

The answer is that the description given by Eddington was incomplete. According to him, there is 'nothing substantial' about those 'numerous electric charges'. But there is something substantial about them: the fact that they are disposed in such a way as to constitute a solid table. In this respect the composition of the table differs from that of objects such as clouds, which are only apparently solid. A cloud too consists of 'electric charges rushing about', etc.; but

---

17   A. Eddington, *The Nature of the Physical World* (Everyman 1935), 6–8.

not in such a way as to constitute a solid object. What science has taught us is not that tables are not really solid, but that they, as well as other thoroughly solid objects, are composed of electric charges rushing about, etc. But what is true of the elements of which a thing is composed is not necessarily true of the thing itself. (A page of text is composed of little black marks dispersed in what is 'mostly empty space', and the marks by themselves are meaningless; but it does not follow that the text is so.)

Eddington's argument does not prove that tables are not really solid, but it does demonstrate something important: the manner in which – and the ease with which – the accepted criteria for applying a concept may be thought to make that concept inapplicable. These points will be further illustrated in Chapter 7.[18]

---

[18] The present chapter is a much revised version of my paper of the same title in *Procs. of the Aristotelian Society*, 1990–1.

6 Knowledge and the uses of 'knowledge'

> To search for 'unity' and 'system', at the expense of truth, is not, I take it, the proper business of philosophy, however universally it may have been the practice of philosophers
>
> (G.E. Moore, *Principia Ethica*, 222).

There is a tendency, when doing philosophy, to impose idealized definitions on familiar words. These may take the form of requirements that are more stringent than those under which a word is normally used, and in such cases the idealization may be presented as the 'real' or 'strict' meaning. Thus it may be claimed that although we often speak of actions being done freely, this is not really so according to a strict meaning of 'free'; that although we speak of some actions as being done for unselfish motives, this is not so according to a strict meaning of 'unselfish'; that although we speak of two people having the same feeling or perceiving the same colour, this is not really so, strictly speaking; that although we describe tables as solid, they are not, strictly speaking, really solid; and that although we often ascribe knowledge to people, this is not correct according to the strict meaning of 'knowledge'. This kind of idealization was discussed in the last chapter and will be considered again in Chapter 7, in connection with philosophical scepticism. The present chapter is devoted to another kind of idealization, that of regimentation: replacing the situation-dependent uses of a word by a definition in terms of necessary and sufficient conditions.

In Chapter 1 I argued that the Socratic quest for definitions, in the writings to which I referred, were essentially verbal, and to be treated by reference to what we say. This is not to say, however, that he was able, by this method, to produce answers to the questions he had raised. What prevented him from doing so? He found that while it was easy to give examples of such qualities as (say) courage, it did not seem possible to find an overall definition of the concept. But, as we saw in Chapter 3, the assumption that there must be such a definition, or that our understanding must be deficient unless we can produce one, was challenged by Wittgenstein. We are not to say 'There must be . . .', but to 'look and see'. Although Socrates' approach was based on 'what we say', his assumption that there must be an overall definition was not.

Of the questions posed by Socrates, it is that about knowledge, especially, that has stimulated the efforts of philosophers of our time; and the Socratic assumption has nowhere been more powerful. In spite of setbacks suffered by the 'traditional' analysis ('knowledge' equals 'justified true belief'), the conviction remains that there must be a set of necessary and sufficient conditions for the truth of 'A knows that p'. Yet there is no good reason why this should be so.[1]

The traditional analysis seems immediately implausible if we consider negative uses of the word. If such an account were correct, then these uses should produce an indeterminacy. If 'A knows that p' were equal to a conjunction of assertions, then the negative, 'A doesn't know', must be equal to a disjunction of denials. We might expect, then, that the negative statement will leave us wondering which of the conjuncts is being denied. (Is p false?, Does A not believe that p?, Is A's belief unjustified?, etc.) But usually there is no such indeterminacy when we are told that someone does not know. 'He doesn't know that today is my birthday' I remark, commenting on the postman's surprise. Would this mean that perhaps today is *not* my birthday? On the contrary, the remark may be taken to imply, inter alia, that today *is* my birthday. Nor would the remark be taken to mean that though he believes it is my birthday, he lacks justification.

In this respect 'He knows' and its negative are to be contrasted with straightforward molecular statements. Consider, for example, a diploma that is granted to people of a minimum age, who have done such and such work, passed certain exams, etc. Then the statement that so-and-so qualifies for the diploma can be analyzed into statements about the separate requirements. And conversely, the statement that he *fails* to qualify will mean a disjunction of denials; leaving

---

1 Even the word 'bachelor', often regarded as an easy candidate for such definition, turns out to be more recalcitrant in this respect than one might assume. Not only must 'unmarried' be replaced by 'has never been married' so as to exclude widowers from being bachelors, but something further may need to be added to exclude celibate priests. There must also be provision to exclude men in societies where there is no concept of marriage and, finally, men in *our* society who, though not married, are living in a stable relationship with a woman.

undetermined the question whether not-p, or not-q, etc. By contrast, the statement 'He doesn't know' is hardly ever indeterminate in this way.

There must be some basis in the actual use of 'know' for the traditional analysis and its modifications; for without this they would hardly command any interest. It is true that many philosophers, in this area as in others, make a point of rejecting the appeal to 'what we say', but this rejection is often undermined by their way of discussing the matter. In such discussions we are commonly invited to agree that in such and such a case a person would or would not know that p (that 'it is clear' he would not know, etc.); but the only way to assess such claims is by considering whether a person would or would not *be said* to know that p in those circumstances.

Some knowledge-situations

To understand the concept of knowledge we need to consider, not merely how the word is used, but why it is used as it is – why such a concept exists in our language. A concept is shaped and developed by human needs. If knowledge is, say, justified true belief, then there must be features of the human condition which create a need for a concept with these components.

If our language did not contain the word 'know', where would the need for it arise? It would not arise in the expression or imparting of knowledge. In a language without this word people would still be able to inform one another that p or that not-q; and even in our own language knowledge that p is usually expressed and imparted by stating that p and not by using the word 'know'. Thus if someone tells me, in suitable circumstances, that it is five o'clock, then he has expressed knowledge of this fact. Sometimes the word 'know' is used to express a high degree of certainty. But this need too can be met without the word 'know'. There are plenty of words in our language for expressing degrees of certainty, from the lowest to the highest. Again, sometimes we express certainty by referring to suitable evidence ('I can see it plainly', etc.).

Where, then, does the need for 'know' arise? Where would this word be missed if we did not have it? I shall discuss the matter mainly in terms of two situations: the *enquiring situation* and the *commenting situation*. In the first, we are interested in knowledge as an ability; in the second, in knowledge as awareness.

The first kind of need arises with the existence of *questions* in the language. Sometimes, wishing to find out the truth about p, we can do so by asking someone who is able to tell us. In the most straightforward case, this does not yet require the use of 'know'. We simply ask 'p?', and are given the answer, yes or no. There is, however, a third answer which will sometimes be needed, namely 'I don't know'. It is true that in most cases 'I can't tell you' would serve equally well. But the answer 'I don't know' is more specific. It means a particular kind of inability (not, say, one that is due to a promise to keep p secret).

Another use of 'know' occurs in an enquiring situation in which we want to find out *who* can give a desired answer. This leads to such questions as 'Does he know whether p?', 'Does anyone here know?', etc., and the corresponding statements (so-and-so knows, etc.). Here again, however, one might just as well ask 'Can anyone tell me?', etc., without needing the word 'know'.

The commenting situation is very different. This time our interest is not in a person's ability to tell us the truth about p, for we know this already. It is in *explaining*, or *predicting*, a person's behaviour by reference to his awareness, or lack of awareness, of the truth. 'He knows that p.' 'I didn't know that q.' 'She doesn't know whether r.' Such statements are needed to make sense of a person's behaviour, and in predicting what they are likely to do.

There is also another situation in which, as in the commenting situation, we know (or take ourselves to know) that p, namely, the *no-need-to-tell situation*. This time we are not explaining a person's behaviour, but wondering whether to treat him as being (actually or potentially) in the enquiring situation. 'There's no need to tell him – he knows.' Here the word 'know' is needed to give a certain kind of reason for *not telling*. (This use is also common in a two-person situation, sometimes with irritation: 'You needn't tell me – I know.') Another, related need is that in which one is *unsure* about the other's state of knowledge. 'Did you know (are you aware) that p?' is what I need if I want the other to know that p, but am unsure whether he needs to be told.

This, in outline, is the schema of situations that I propose to use in evaluating the traditional analysis.[2] It is not intended to be definitive. There may be other ways of describing and arranging the essential knowledge-situations, and further kinds of situations in which the word 'know' may come to be used once it is in the language. One such use, however, deserves special comment, since it has sometimes been regarded as central to the concept. This is the use of the first-person 'I

---

2 For a somewhat similar approach, see Edward Craig, *Knowledge and the State of Nature* (Clarendon 1990).

know that p' to express a special degree of certainty. (The view that this use is central may be connected with the egocentric perspective of the Cartesian tradition.) But if my account is correct, the concept of knowledge has its roots in situations in which knowledge is ascribed, to oneself or others, for purposes other than to express certainty.

The mistake of treating 'I know that p' as central has a parallel in another concept much discussed by philosophers – that of promising. In spite of the fascination of the performative 'I promise', this expression does not take us to the heart of the concept – the situations in which the need for such a word as 'promise' arises. We can make our promises perfectly well without this word, simply by saying what we intend to do: such a statement will, in suitable circumstances, count as a promise. What matters here is not whether the word 'promise' is used, but whether the person addressed would have grounds for complaint if one did not do what one said. You would have such grounds if I had made my statement (with or without the word 'promise'), in the knowledge that you are counting on me to do what I said. It is when I *fail* to do what I said that the word 'promise' comes into its own. 'But you promised': thus you can say, in one phrase, that you understood the situation to be of that kind and that you blame me for my failure to do what I said.[3]

Similarly, one makes oneself responsible for the truth of an assertion by making the assertion, with or without the use of 'know'. And this responsibility will be stronger or weaker according to the situation in which the assertion is made. If I am aware that it is very important to you to know the truth about p, then I have a special duty to be careful in what I say. And this can be further strengthened, to any degree, by such exchanges as 'Are you sure that this is true?'; 'Yes, I have just checked'; 'This is very important to me'; etc. There is no need for the word 'know' in this situation (and similarly for the word 'promise').

Let us now consider the traditional analysis in the light of the situations I described above, starting with the most widely accepted component.

Knowledge and truth

Consider a situation in which A wants to explain S's behaviour by reference to the latter's epistemic state in relation to p. In this situation

3   For further discussion see my 'Promises, Games and Institutions', *Procs. Arist. Soc.* 1974/75.

there is, necessarily, another epistemic factor, namely A's own relation to p. Either he regards p as true, or he regards p as false, or he is uncertain whether p is true or false. The relevant case is that in which he regards p as true. His desire in that case is to comment on S's behaviour by reference to the latter's awareness or unawareness of *the fact* (as A sees it) that p. The word 'know' is adapted to this situation. It is used by someone who, when commenting on another's behaviour by reference to p, regards p as true. 'He knew there was a short cut': this explanation of S's behaviour is given by someone who regards it as true that there was a short cut.

This relation between knowledge and truth is one of presupposition. In saying 'S knows that p', A would not be stating a molecular proposition, with 'p is true' as one component. He would be telling B of S's condition, rather than informing him of the truth of p. The presupposition is similar to that of the existence of the King of France in Russell's example. To suppose that, in the present case, one might be *affirming* that p is true, would be similar to Russell's error in claiming that when one states that the King of France is bald, one is *affirming* (inter alia) that there is a King of France. (This will be discussed further in Chapter 9.)

As the existence of the King of France is presupposed both by '... is bald' and by '... is not bald', so, in the situation I have described, the truth of p is presupposed both by 'S knows that p' and by 'S doesn't know that p'. Both statements would be made by people who know, or think they know, that there is a short cut. There is a difference, however, between this case and that of the King of France, which appears when we turn to contradiction. 'S knows there is a short cut.' – 'No, he doesn't.' So far, the presupposition (that there is a short cut) is sustained. But here is another way of contradicting: 'No, he doesn't; there *is* no short cut.' This time the presupposition is cancelled. In denying that there is a short cut, the speaker has brought about a change in the situation: it is no longer a commenting situation, but one in which the *truth* of p is in dispute. And this way of contradicting has no counterpart in the other case. 'The King of France is bald.' – 'No, he isn't: there is no such person.' This reply would be incoherent: in saying 'He isn't', the speaker condones the assumption that there *is* such a person, which he then denies.

How are knowledge and truth related in an enquiring situation? This time we are concerned with knowledge as an ability. In this context 'He knows' means he is able to answer our question, and answer it truly. The relevant concept is that of knowing *whether*, rather than knowing *that*. In this situation the ascription of knowledge is made on the basis of a speaker's preparedness to state whether p and the condition of truth can be applied only in retrospect. We assume that what the speaker says is true, but withdraw the ascription of knowledge if this turns out not to have been so. Conversely, the denial of knowledge, in this situation, would be based on a speaker's inability to say whether p. (When we ask him, he says 'I don't know'.) There is also a less common situation, in which he is prepared to answer, but we have reason to think that his answer will be unreliable. In this case too we would deny that he knows. ('He doesn't know, he's merely guessing.')

What happens when we withdraw the ascription of knowledge in retrospect? The condition of being prepared to answer remains dominant over that of truth, so that the simple 'He didn't know' would be incorrect. (It would imply that he was not prepared to answer.) Suppose I ask an official at the station whether a certain train has come in, and he answers that it has. I go to the platform and find he was wrong. Later I tell someone what happened. Should I say that when I asked the official, he didn't know? I cannot say this, because the word 'know' would still carry the meaning that is appropriate to the enquiring situation. In these circumstances 'He didn't know' would mean that he was not able to give an answer. On the other hand, given the connection of knowledge and truth – derived from the commenting situation – it would also (obviously) be wrong to say that he did know. In this situation the word 'know' is more trouble than it is worth. There are other and better ways than the simple 'He didn't know', of describing the official's failure. Thus we might say that he thought he knew but didn't; or more clearly, and avoiding the word 'know' altogether, that he told me but turned out to be wrong.

So far I have tried to explain the entailment from knowledge to truth and not to question it. But does this entailment always hold? Is the claim that it does confirmed by the actual use of the word? Suppose that in a novel we find the following account of a stormy relationship: 'In spite of all that had happened between them, there was one thing he knew: she would never be unfaithful to him.' Then, so many pages later, it turns out that she had been unfaithful to him. Such 'knowledge' may also be expressed in direct speech, as in the following:

> 'I couldn't see you until I saw your arm stretched out from under the door. I thought you were dead.'
> 'You might have come and tried.'

'I did. I couldn't lift the door.'

'There was room to move me; the door wasn't holding me. I'd have woken up.'

'You don't understand. I knew for certain you were dead.'[4]

Another kind of example occurs when the entailment from knowledge to truth is put to students. Some will give as a 'counter-example' the statement that whereas we know the earth to be round, people in former times knew it to be flat. (This might also be used to illustrate 'the fallibility of human knowledge'.)

It would be futile to reply that these are not proper uses of the word 'know'. Such uses are recognized and make perfectly good sense in a variety of contexts. Do they show that the claim about knowledge and truth is false? They show that the matter is not as clear-cut as it is often taken to be. But it would be rash to give up the claim. Faced with such examples, it is appropriate to comment 'You mean they *thought* they knew'. The point of this would be that the speaker had deprived 'know' of its *distinctive* meaning: when he said 'they knew' he meant nothing other than 'they firmly believed'. The word 'know' lends itself to this shift because 'I know' is sometimes used as an expression of firm belief. In this non-distinctive sense, then, knowledge is ascribable in spite of the absence of truth, though it would not be so in the more usual, distinctive sense.

Knowledge and belief

According to the 'traditional' definition, knowledge is a species of belief ('justified true belief'), and therefore knowing entails believing. But is this really so? There is a 'subtraction argument' in favour of the entailment view. Consider a person who, at a certain time, knows that p. Subsequently a change takes place, unknown to him, whereby p becomes false.[5] We would now say he believes that p, and not that he knows that p. Yet throughout the change something remains the same: he still feels the same about p and would give the same answer if asked whether p. But if his condition now is one of belief, must not belief have been present also at the earlier time? Paraphrasing Wittgenstein's

4 Graham Greene, *The End of the Affair*.
5 See Merrill Ring, 'Knowledge: The Cessation of Belief', *American Phil. Quarterly* 1977, especially p. 53. See also John O. Nelson, 'Propositional Knowledge and Belief: Entailment or Mutual Exclusion?', *Phil. Investigations* 1982.

famous question about raising one's arm (PI 621), we might ask: 'What is left over if we subtract the fact that p is true from the fact that S knows that p?', to which the answer seems to be: 'S believes that p'.

But is it right to conclude that S believed that p when p was still true? Was belief a *component* of S's knowledge, and is it generally such a component? Wittgenstein's question was directed at the view that *trying* is a component of *doing*. The question was: 'What is left over if I subtract the fact that my arm goes up from the fact that I raise my arm?' And the answer that may suggest itself is: 'I tried to raise it'. A person who has been asked to raise his arm but was prevented by some handicap, might well say 'At least I tried to raise it'. But, as Wittgenstein went on to observe, 'when I raise my arm, I do not usually *try* to raise it'. The subtraction argument is not a reliable guide to the description of *positive* cases – where an action is *not* prevented or where p does *not* become false. One would not say one had *tried* to perform an action if one had straightforwardly performed it and neither would one say, for example, 'I believe there is a short cut' if one knew perfectly well that there is a short cut.

It might be thought that the entailment thesis can be saved by invoking H.P. Grice's principle of 'conversational implicature'.[6] Thus it might be said although 'I believe' would be inappropriate in such a case, it would nevertheless be true. It would be inappropriate, because, given that knowledge does entail belief, 'I believe' would be less informative ('weaker') than what the speaker could say (viz. 'I know'). Hence, in saying 'I believe', he would be transgressing the 'conversational' principle of providing as much information as he can and would thereby mislead the hearer, who would infer that he was *unable* to claim that he knows. Yet this, it is argued, would not affect the *truth* of 'I believe'.

But the person who says 'I believe' when he knows perfectly well would not be giving *less* information than he might: he would be giving *false* information. For in saying 'I believe it's raining' he would convey to the hearer that he is less than fully confident on the matter, when in fact he is fully confident. (The principle of providing as much information as possible is in any case open to question, as will be shown in Chapter 10.)

How would the entailment thesis work in a commenting situation? A: 'S knows there is a short cut.' B: 'So according to you, S believes there is a short cut.' Would A have to assent? It is not clear what A's response would or should be. Let us consider the role of 'believe' in our language and how a need for this word arises. One such need arises in commenting situations. The word 'know' (as in 'S knows that p') is suitable where p is taken by the commenter to be true. But we also need a word to be used when this is not so, and 'believe' (as in the comment 'S believes that p') is available for this purpose. This contrast between the two commenting situations is the reason why A, in the above example, might be puzzled and uncertain how to respond. The situation was one in which he took p to be true; but the introduction of 'believe' by B implied that *he* regarded p as doubtful or even false. Hence, when B invited A's assent to 'S believes there is a short cut', A might have responded: 'Oh – you mean there isn't?'

It is sometimes thought that the entailment from knowing to believing can be proved by a simple application of *modus tollens*. Not believing, it is claimed, entails not knowing; hence, by *modus tollens*, knowing entails believing.[7] But is it true that not believing entails not knowing? Suppose I have told S that there is a short cut and he tells me he doesn't believe it. In that case, should I answer 'No' when asked whether S knows? To say that S doesn't know would imply that the fact had not been drawn to his attention – as if he lacked *awareness* of it, rather than disbelieving what I said. In such cases I had better help myself to a longer form of words: 'I told him, but he didn't believe it.' This would be a suitable reply, in this situation, to the question whether S knows. But the reply 'He doesn't know' would not be acceptable here.

But, it might be replied, the fact remains that 'He knows' would also be unacceptable: it would *not be the case* that he knows. And it might be thought that this is enough to sustain the argument from *modus tollens*. Thus we would proceed from the premise

(1) 'It is not the case that S believes' entails (2) 'It is not the case that S knows', to the conclusion:
(3) 'It is the case that S knows' entails (4) 'It is the case that S believes'.

---

7 According to Keith Lehrer, 'If I do not believe that p, then I do not know that p'; from which he concludes: 'If S knows that p, then S believes that p' (*Knowledge* (Oxford University Press 1979), 12). Lehrer is another philosopher who dismisses the criterion of 'what we say'. His theory of knowledge is not to be 'about the meaning of epistemic words', but about 'what conditions must be satisfied in order for a person to know something' (5). But what is the source of his claim that 'If I do not believe that p, then I do not know that p'? Did he reflect on believing and knowing 'themselves', as distinct from the meaning and use of these words?

In this argument, however, there is an equivocation between the premise and the conclusion. For while 'It is the case that S believes' is equivalent to 'S believes' (both being expressions of the desired consequent), this is not so with the premise, where (1) is *not* equivalent to (1*) 'S does not believe'. For in the case described, (1) would be true, while (1*) would not be true.

The argument would also fail in situations in which the difference between knowing and believing is that between being and not being fully confident. Here the premise of the argument would be *untrue*, for it would mean that

(1**) 'It is not the case that S is not fully confident' entails (2**) 'It is not the case that S is fully confident',

which is no better than the absurd entailment from 'S is fully confident' to 'S is not fully confident'.

Let us now consider an *enquiring* situation in which 'I believe' is used. We ask someone at the station 'Do you know whether the train has left?' and he replies: 'I believe so.' A proper comment would be: 'He doesn't know; we'd better ask somebody else'. If the entailment thesis were correct, then it should be an open question whether the person who replied 'I believe so' *knows* that p. 'He believes the train has left, so perhaps he knows it has left.' But this would be absurd. Here again the difference between knowing and believing is a difference between being fully confident and not being fully confident; and the entailment view would mean, absurdly, that not being fully confident is compatible with being fully confident (that if a person is not fully confident he may be fully confident).

A similar clash between 'believe' and 'know' can occur in an *exchanging-opinions* situation. In this case, 'believe' is the common currency, because the topics in question are assumed to be matters of opinion rather than certainty. Suppose A is interested in B's opinions about economic prospects. A: 'Do you believe the Government means to raise interest rates?' B, as it happens, has inside knowledge. His reply is: 'I don't believe it, I know it.' Here it was appropriate for B, knowing that p, to *deny* that his position is one of belief.

The case of knowledge versus belief should be contrasted with that in which an emphatic expression is compatible with a less emphatic one. Consider the statement: 'I am not (merely) sad; I am *very* sad.' It would be absurd to take this speaker to be *denying* that he is sad. Being very sad does indeed entail being sad. This is not, however, a good analogy for the claim about knowledge and belief. The person who is very sad must agree that he is sad, but someone who knows that p need not, and probably would not, agree that he believes that p. In the latter case, as we saw, there is a contradiction between being and not being fully confident (having conclusive evidence and not having it, etc.); but there is no such contradiction between 'very sad' and 'sad'.

Knowledge and justification (i)

Does knowledge entail justification? Justification of what? According to the traditional analysis, it is the relevant belief that must be justified ('justified true belief'). But this cannot stand if the entailment from knowledge to belief is rejected. We can, however, speak of a *claim to know* as being justified or unjustified, so let us consider the justification requirement in this sense.

Of the situations I have described, it is the enquiring situation that produces an interest in justification. Here one is concerned to find out the truth about p; and so one has an interest in the qualifications of one's informant. Our concept of knowledge is adapted to this concern, so that, in many cases, we would not ascribe knowledge to a person unless he could satisfy us that his claim to know is justified.

This concern and this condition are there prior to the introduction of the word 'know'. Our interest in truth, and the consequent demand for reasons, exist whether the speaker says 'I know', or 'I believe', or simply 'p'. It is part of the concept of *assertion*, which is itself connected with our interest in truth. Thus, if I say there has been an accident in the next street, I must be prepared to say why I take this assertion to be true. Failing this, it would be doubtful whether I had understood what I was saying.

The justification requirement is sometimes explained in terms of the ability to *give reasons* for stating, or claiming to know, that p – being able to answer the question 'How do you know?'. But in this sense the requirement, though correct for some cases, is not so for others. I know that today is Tuesday, but would not be able to say why I take this to be so. Yet this does not put into doubt my ability to know that today is Tuesday. I know that London is the capital of England, that the Battle of Hastings took place in 1066, etc. but could not say how I know these things. I know that 'epistemology' is spelt with two e's, that eight sevens are fifty-six, that my name and address are such and such, that the earth existed 100 years ago.[8]

---

8 Wittgenstein's treatment of such propositions (in *On Certainty*) is discussed in my paper 'On the Meaning and Use of "I know" ', *Phil. Investigations* 1982. See also Norman Malcolm's examples, in *Thought and Knowledge*, pp. 181–2.

Here, and in various other cases, the language-game of 'How do you know?' is not appropriate. Again, I know what I had for lunch today, that I travelled from A to B five years ago, and so on. I also remember 'private' occurrences, such as sensations, thoughts and dreams. Asked how I know that these occurred, I might reply that I remember them. But to say 'I remember that p' is not to produce evidence for p. (Memory is not evidence for knowledge; it is a *form* of knowledge.)

In such cases we might still speak of justification, but this would have to be understood in a different way. It would mean not that one is able to produce reasons, but that for certain kinds of facts one would be justified in claiming to know without being able to do so.[9] In these cases the assumption is that a normal person can be relied upon to be in possession of the truth, even though the question 'How do you know?' would not be appropriate. And since our interest in truth is satisfied without this, we are not deterred from describing them as cases of knowledge.

In yet another kind of case, however, the justification requirement would not be applicable in this sense either. What matters in such cases is *getting it right*. We say that the squirrel knew where to find its nuts because it *succeeded* in finding them. Another case occurs typically in commenting situations, where the commenter is, or thinks he is, already in possession of the truth. For him the question *how* the other person knows may be of little interest, even where the case is one in which reasons would normally be available. Consider the case of John, who expresses, in words or behaviour, a conviction that his wife is unfaithful, but cannot give reasons. Would we say he knows? In an enquiring situation, we would not do so: our interest in learning the truth would prevent it. But what if – in a commenting situation – we already know that John is right? In that case the question *how* he knows will be of secondary interest, and hence the ascription of knowledge may stand even if no satisfactory explanation can be produced by John. 'I can't tell you how I know, I just do.'[10]

Let us also consider a case in which an enquiring situation is *superseded* by a commenting situation. In the former, we are not prepared to ascribe knowledge to Jane, because she cannot justify her assertion. But then it turns out that she was right. 'So she knew after

---

9   Compare Wittgenstein, PI 289: 'To use a word without justification does not mean being unjustified in using it.'

10   Here I go further than Bernard Williams (*Problems of the Self* (CUP 1973), 147), who describes a case in which a person may be said to know even if he only got the information from loose gossip. I claim that even this much is not necessary.

all.' 'She knew all along.' Now our interest has shifted. *Knowing* that p is true, we are no longer in the position of wondering whether to trust Jane's assertion. The fact that she 'got it right' may suffice to cause us to say that she knew.

A similar development may take place with predictions. Someone tells us there will be an economic improvement before the year is out, but is unable to give reasons. (Perhaps, in spite of this, he backs his assertion with money.) Or perhaps, having given reasons and heard objections to them, he replies lamely: 'Well, I still say . . . '. We would obviously be ill-advised to treat his assertion as a guide to truth, and would not describe him as having knowledge. But what if his prediction turned out to be true? 'So he knew after all.' 'He couldn't say how he knew, but he knew.' Of course we are not obliged to use the word 'know' in these cases, but to do so would not be improper.[11]

Cases similar to those discussed above were considered by Ayer in *The Problem of Knowledge*[12] Ayer concluded that the difference between describing and refusing to describe them as cases of knowledge is not a difference of fact; it is, rather, 'that to say that he knows is to concede him the right to be sure, while to say that he is only guessing is to withhold it' (ibid. 33). The definition of knowledge is, at which Ayer arrived was formulated accordingly. According to it, one knows that p if and only if (1) 'p' is true, (2) one is sure that p, and (3) one has the right to be sure. But this fails to accommodate yet another knowledge-situation in which 'getting it right' is what matters. Asked whether one knows the dates of the Kings of England, or the second stanza of *The Ancient Mariner*, or whether this is the way to Cambridge, one may be hesitant about giving, or claiming to know, the answer; and yet one might be said to know it if one got it right. 'I'm not sure', or 'I'm not sure I know', such a person might say; and yet his answer, if correct, might count as an expression of knowledge. ('So you did know'.)

Knowledge and justification (ii)

The argument of the last section has been that justification is not always treated as a necessary condition of knowledge. But since the appearance of an article by Edmund Gettier, the trend has been to strengthen rather than weaken the condition about justification. In his

---

11 For further examples and discussion see N. Malcolm, *Knowledge and Certainty*, (Cornell 1963), 225–7.
12 A.J. Ayer, *The Problem of Knowledge* (Penguin 1955).

much-cited article Gettier claimed: 'It is clear that Smith does not *know* that (e) is true', in spite of (e)'s being a proposition that Smith was 'justified in believing'.[13] This was so because one of the propositions on which Smith based his putative knowledge happened, as luck would have it, to be false. It followed, according to Gettier, that justified true belief is not a sufficient condition of knowledge. Many writers have responded by trying to refine the condition about justification, accepting that something more rigorous than mere justification is required. Now these attempts are obviously not appropriate for cases where (as I have argued) *no* justification is required. But even where this is required, the need for something more rigorous than mere justification varies with different situations; and here again the importance of 'getting it right' may be decisive.

In the above example, taken from Gettier, Smith was justified in believing that (e) the man who will get a certain job has ten coins in his pocket; and this proposition was true. But one of Smith's supporting beliefs – that Jones, who has ten coins in his pocket, will get the job – happens to be false. (It is somebody else, who also happens to have ten coins in his pocket, who will get the job.) And in this case, according to Gettier, 'it is clear that Smith does not *know* that (e)'. But it this really clear?

Suppose we are in an enquiring situation, and Smith tells us that (e) is true. Asked how he knows, Smith gives his reasons, among them being the belief that (d) Jones will get the job. Would we now say that Smith knows that (e)? This will depend on our situation with regard to (d). If we already know this belief to be false, then we shall not ascribe knowledge of (e) to Smith. Here again, the use of 'know' is adapted to our need. Aware that (d) is false, we can see that Smith's assertion that (e) is not a trustworthy guide to the truth.

This, however, is not how the matter would appear in a *commenting* situation. To illustrate the point, I shall use an example that is similar to Gettier's, but with practical consequences. Let the supporting proposition be:

(d*) Jones will be made director, and Jones wants Smith transferred to Birmingham,

and Smith's conclusion:

(e*) The man who will get the job wants Smith transferred to Birmingham.

13 'Is Justified True Belief Knowledge?', *Analysis* 1963.

As in Gettier's example, I shall assume Smith's belief that (e*) to be both justified and true, while his belief that (d*) is also justified, but, as it happens, false: it is Robinson, not Jones, who will get the job. And then, as luck would have it, Robinson also wants Smith transferred to Birmingham, and that is what actually happens, so that (e*) remains true.

Suppose now that, prior to Robinson's appointment, Smith is showing interest in houses in the Birmingham area and has even paid a deposit on one. Should we not say, in explaining this behaviour, that Smith *knows* he will be transferred? Here is a conversation between A and B, confidential secretaries of the firm.

A: Why is Smith so interested in houses in the Birmingham area?
B: Because he's going to be transferred.
A: How does he know that?
B: He heard from a usually reliable source that Jones is being made director, and he knows that Jones wants him in Birmingham.
A: But Jones isn't getting the job; Robinson is.
B: True. But as you know, Jones and Robinson are agreed about the transfer.

What now? Must A and B conclude that Smith *doesn't* know? Suppose this is what they say to C. Could not the latter accuse them, when the details are revealed, of having spoken falsely? The correct verdict in this case would not be that Smith doesn't know: it would be that he knows, though his knowledge is due to luck. Again, suppose Smith is commenting on his own behaviour in retrospect: 'I paid a deposit because I knew ...'. Should we say 'No, you didn't?' This would not be a correct response.

Similar conclusions would be drawn in a no-need-to-tell situation:

A: I've heard of a house in Birmingham that would suit Smith perfectly. I wonder if we ought to drop him a hint that he will be transferred.
B: No need; he knows already.
A: How does he know?
B: [as before].
A: But Jones isn't getting the job; Robinson is.
B: Well, never mind how he knows; he knows anyway. So there's no need to drop any hints.

In these and similar situations, the truth of p is already known to the speakers. Hence they are not concerned, as they would be in an enquiring situation, about Smith's qualifications to tell the truth. This question moves into the background and is not allowed to prevent the ascription of knowledge to Smith.[14]

It is also useful to consider the use of 'know' in retrospective situations. Suppose it were accepted as a historical fact that, at the battle of X, Napoleon took certain measures because he knew that the enemy would advance on his left flank; and in this way gained the victory. And now suppose that according to new research, the messenger who brought the report of the enemy's intentions was in fact subject to Gettier complications. (A suitable story could easily be imagined.) What then? Must we say that Napoleon did *not* know that the enemy would advance on the left? Is that how the history would have to be written thereafter? No: the original story would stand – though the Gettier complication might be added, space permitting, as an interesting twist.

The treatment of justification, whether in the original or the more rigorous sense, as a necessary condition of knowledge, depends on a false assumption about the nature of this and other concepts: that they can be defined in general terms without attending to the variety of situations in which they are used. It is, to quote Moore again, a case of 'searching for "unity" and "system", at the expense of truth'.[15]

---

14 Similar counter-examples can be given in response to Robert Nozick's proposal to treat the following as a necessary condition of knowledge: 'If p were not true, S wouldn't believe that p' (*Philosophical Explanations* (Clarendon 1981) 172–85). Suppose I am walking up the road in quest of the library. It starts to rain and I ask a local person which is the quickest way. He tells me to take the first passage on the right. I do so and arrive at my goal by what was indeed the quickest way. But did my informant really *know* this? What if the passage had been blocked by a road accident half an hour earlier: would he not have given the same reply? very probably he would. Applying the proposed condition, I would have to conclude from this that he didn't know it. But this is quite implausible.

15 This chapter is a much-revised version of 'A Situational Account of Knowledge', which appeared in *The Monist*, 1985.

7 The paradox of scepticism

In the last two chapters I referred to the tendency, on the part of philosophers, to impose abnormal requirements on familiar concepts, the requirements being such as to make the concept inapplicable. Nowhere has this been more evident than in the case of knowledge. But how can the existence of knowledge be doubted? The word 'know' is used every day with regard to the future, the past, unobserved objects, the feelings of other people, and so on. How can it be denied that we have knowledge in these and other areas? If knowledge were a kind of substance or process, then its existence would not be thought to follow from the mere use of the word. The fact that there is a use for the words 'fairy' and 'black bile' would not prevent us from doubting whether these things exist. But 'knowledge' does not stand for a thing or substance. And when sceptics deny the existence of knowledge, it is not this kind of existence that is at issue.

How can the existence of knowledge be doubted? Take an example of knowledge about the future. Someone asks 'Do you know whether there will be a concert tomorrow?' Having read the newspaper, and having no reason to disbelieve what it says, I reply 'Yes'. Which aspect of knowledge would a sceptic have in mind in denying that I really have this knowledge? Let us use as a starting point the 'traditional' analysis, in terms of justified true belief, as discussed in the last chapter. Would the sceptic be denying that p ('There will be a concert tomorrow') is true? He is in no position to deny this. Would he be denying that I believe, or am certain, that p? No; the fact that I am certain is not in question. What about justification? Again, I have a suitable justification for saying I know, in accordance with the normal use of 'justification'.

Returning to the first point, it might be said that the sceptic does not need to *deny* that p, but only to claim that p is doubtful. But what reason can he give for describing p as doubtful? Perhaps he will point out that p may turn out to be false in spite of the justification. But this is not enough to show that p is doubtful. We do not describe a proposition as doubtful unless there is reason for doubting it; and the bare possibility of falsehood does not count as such a reason. Confusion about this matter sometimes leads to misunderstanding of a passage in Hume: '*That the sun will not rise tomorrow* is no less intelligible a proposition, and implies no more contradiction, than the affirmation, *that it will rise*'.[1] This is sometimes taken as an expression of scepticism, but it is nothing of the sort: Hume is making a remark about the logical status of these propositions, and not about their certainty or otherwise. There is no valid argument from the premise 'not-p implies no contradiction' to the conclusion that p is doubtful. Knowing that p, and being able to suppose that p is false, are, in such cases, perfectly compatible: this is part of the logical background against which such knowledge is normally expressed and ascribed.

Could the sceptic's conclusion be based on requirements about the *sources* of knowledge? In the literature since Gettier it has been claimed that even if a person's belief is both true and justified, it may not qualify for knowledge if (unknown to him) it has come from a tainted source. This claim was questioned in the last chapter, but let us suppose it were true. Then the same comment could be made as on the condition about truth. It is not enough for the sceptic to point out that Gettier-conditions *may* be present in a given case. To prove that knowledge is impossible, he must show that they are present in all cases; but he is in no position to do this.

How then is the sceptic to argue for his claim that knowledge is impossible? His argument must be of this form: there can be no knowledge unless requirement R is satisfied; R can never be satisfied; hence there can be no knowledge. But why should we accept the first premise? We know, without specifying it, that requirement R will not be in accordance with the normal conditions for ascribing knowledge; for if it were, it would not lead to a *sceptical* conclusion, one that presents a challenge to the normal use of the word.

How, then, is scepticism possible? According to Wittgenstein, the concept of knowledge, 'as understood by philosophers, [is] created by a kind of sublimation' from the ordinary one.[2] Here, it seems, is another example of the way in which language 'sets traps for us'.[3]

1   David Hume *Enquiries* (Clarendon 1975), 25–6.
2   L. Wittgenstein, *Remarks on the Philosophy of Psychology* II, 289.
3   See Chapter 3, page 44.

Requirements that cannot be fulfilled seem to grow out of the ordinary concept, and thus to render it inapplicable. Knowledge, we might say, is a concept with suicidal tendencies. Let us consider some of those requirements in turn.

The absolute certainty requirement

It is often thought that in saying 'I know that p' one assumes a special responsibility, one that would not arise with plain 'p'. This is wrong because in many situations plain 'p' is, and is understood to be, an expression of knowledge, with the same commitment as 'I know that p' (just as in many situations 'I'll do it' counts as a promise, even though the word 'promise' is not used).

It is true that in some situations the use of 'I know' commits one to a high degree of certainty. In such cases one may be admonished 'You shouldn't say "I know" unless you are absolutely certain', and it may be tempting to regard this as a general condition for the use of 'know'. But this (as we saw in the last chapter) would be a mistake. The admonition is appropriate in some situations but not in others. It would clearly be appropriate in an 'enquiring' situation if a piece of information on which one had been counting turned out be, or were suspected of being, unreliable. But in other situations it would be out of place. In a 'no-need-to-tell' situation, the reply 'Yes, I know' would not be criticized as improper if the speaker were less than absolutely certain. The same is true of 'commenting' situations, as when 'She knew that p' serves to explain her behaviour and not to describe a special degree of certainty, on her part, of the truth of 'p'.

But what if absolute certainty *were* a necessary condition of knowledge? Here we must distinguish between subjective and objective certainty: between *someone's* being certain and *it* being certain that p – that, say, a concert will be held tomorrow. It is the second kind of certainty that is in question in sceptical arguments. (The existence of certainty in the first sense is not in doubt.) Suppose then that certainty in the second sense were a necessary condition of knowledge. Could this condition not be satisfied? According to Peter Unger,[4] it could not. In his argument, 'sublimation' of a concept occurs twice over, affecting both 'certain' and 'absolutely certain'. In the first place, he maintains that the distinction between these is untenable – that 'certain' means nothing less than 'absolutely certain'; and then it

---

4 Peter Unger, *Ignorance* (Clarendon 1975).

appears that absolute certainty is unattainable. Unger's argument is applied quite generally to words that can be qualified by 'absolutely', including such examples as 'dry', 'straight', 'crucial', 'useless' and 'flat', which he contrasts, in this respect, with such words as 'wet', 'crooked',' important' and 'useful'. According to Unger, the meaning of words of the first kind is 'absolute', even when this qualification is not inserted. Thus 'to say that something is flat is ... no different from saying that it is absolutely, or perfectly flat' (op. cit. 54); the qualification 'absolutely' is understood and hence there is no need to make it explicit. It is, he says, 'redundant as far as content goes' and 'its function appears to be mainly that of emphasis' (61).

It then appears that the condition of being, say, flat – which can mean nothing less than absolutely flat – cannot be realized. For when we look through a powerful microscope at a surface described as 'flat' (or 'absolutely flat'), we find that it is 'rife with irregularities'. In a formula reminiscent of the 'ontological argument', Unger expresses his view about what is required for a surface to be really flat: 'If it is logically possible that there be a surface which is flatter than a given one, then that given surface is not really a flat one.' Similarly, turning to the concept of certainty, he claims that 'if someone is certain of something, then there is never anything of which he or anyone else is more certain', and if greater certainty is 'logically possible . . ., then he is not actually certain of that given thing' (66–7). Following Unger's view, these concepts might be described as *asymptotic*. An asymptote is a line that is approached more and more closely by a curve whose tangent is such that the line and curve meet only 'at infinity'. Similarly, on Unger's view, the words in question can approach more and more closely to being truly applicable, but without ever being so.

But how is this to be reconciled with the fact that these words are regularly applied in actual discourse? According to Unger, the use of 'flat' in describing an ordinary surface is 'to indicate that the object is close enough to being flat' for practical purposes in a given context (69).[5] But the fact is that when we describe a surface as 'flat', this is not understood to mean 'close to being flat'. We speak of pancakes as paradigms of flatness ('as flat as a pancake'), but it needs no powerful microscope to detect irregularities on the surface of a pancake. There

---

5   This kind of argument should not be confused with that discussed in Chapter 5, about 'solid' – a word that can also be qualified by 'absolutely'. The argument there was not that tables are 'close' to being solid without really being so, but that they are far from being so. It was about the *composition* of tables and other paradigms of solidity.

are conditions, which are frequently met, for describing things as 'flat', and *different* conditions for describing them as 'nearly flat'; and in the first case it would be wrong *not* to say 'flat'. Asked whether the local bowling green is flat I must, if I am to speak correctly, reply that this is so, and *not* that it is nearly flat. (The latter might be correct for my lawn, but it would not be so for the bowling green.) Similarly, it is correct to say, in a suitable situation, that a forthcoming event is certain, or absolutely certain, even though there is always a remote possibility, at least, that it will not occur. This possibility is not being denied when we say that an event is certain, or absolutely certain, to occur. Hence, even if absolute certainty were a condition of knowledge, this would not make the possession of knowledge impossible.

On the other hand, it would be wrong to regard the 'asymptotic' view as entirely devoid of support from actual usage. (Here is another place where language 'sets traps for us'.) The person who describes a bowling green, or a table top, as 'flat' may be aware that from another point of view they are not really flat; that there is a context in which the question 'Is it really flat?' would elicit a negative answer. This answer would not contradict the original description in the original context, but the possibility of it is part of an ordinary understanding of the concept. The asymptotic perspective is also part of our understanding of 'certain': the proverbial 'Nothing is certain' is an expression of this. But this does not mean that when one speaks of being certain, or even absolutely certain, of some fact, one is using words incorrectly or even that one's use of them is not *strictly* correct. (Here it is important not confuse the property of being *more exclusive* with that of being strictly correct.)[6]

A minister tells reporters: 'The product is now completely safe.' Does he mean there is absolutely no risk? If the question were put, he might reply 'Of course there is always *some* risk.' But this would not show that he had spoken incorrectly or carelessly in the first place. Sometimes it is safe to cross the road and sometimes not. In the former case we might say, and say correctly, that it is perfectly safe and there is no risk. But, again, we might also concede that 'nothing is perfect' and that 'no risk' does not exclude every conceivable degree of risk.

---

6 Wittgenstein makes a similar point about the use of 'exact': if I tell someone that dinner 'begins at one o'clock exactly', I am not using this word in an incorrect or degenerate sense, even though the criteria of exactness here would fall short of those required 'in the laboratory or observatory' (PI 88).

There is a place, then, for the 'asymptotic' use of such words, but this does not support the sceptical case. The sceptical case is that certainty is impossible; and to support this it would have to be shown that when we describe, say, a forthcoming event as certain, this is always incorrect. And this has not been shown. (The assumption that certainty is a necessary condition of *knowledge* is anyway untenable, as we have seen in the last chapter.)

The requirement of 'ruling out other possibilities'

Sceptical arguments often take the form of drawing attention to possibilities that would falsify a claim to know. 'Here is a banana', I state with confidence. How do I know? 'I can see it.' Yet the thing might not really be a banana, but merely a wax imitation of one. But if I cannot rule out this and various other possibilities, can I really know that the object before me is a banana?

To illustrate this predicament, Barry Stroud has used the example of an airman who is trained to identify a variety of aeroplanes, but on the basis of imperfect information.[7] He learns, say, that a plane with features x, y and z belongs to type F and becomes thoroughly competent in recognizing these features. There is also, however, a very small number of planes of type G, which also have the features x, y and z; but 'the trainees were never told about them because it would have made the recognition of F's too difficult' (op. cit. 67). In these circumstances, could the man be said to *know,* on the basis of x, y and z, that the plane he sees is an F? According to Stroud, 'we immediately see' that the answer is negative (68). The man is precluded from having this knowledge because he is not in a position to rule out the other possibility – that the plane is of type G.

But is it true that 'we immediately see' this? Is that how we would respond in such a case? This would depend (as argued in the last chapter) on the situation we are in. If, knowing about the planes of type G, we were trying to *find out* whether a given plane is an F or a G, and if this were very important to us, then we might indeed hesitate to regard the man as having knowledge. Again, if we told him about the existence of Gs, he might perhaps be taken aback, and no longer claim to know that the plane in view is an F. But in other situations we would still say that he knows this. This is especially so in cases where *we* take the plane to be an F. Suppose that, in such a case, I am wondering

---

7   B. Stroud, *The Significance of Philosophical Scepticism* (Clarendon 1984).

whether to inform the man that an F has just passed overhead, mistakenly thinking he is not at his observation post. You, knowing that he is, tell me not to bother. 'There's no need to tell him, he knows already.' In this situation, it is correct to ascribe knowledge to the man, in spite of the complication about the evidence; and it would be incorrect to say that he 'merely believes', for this would imply, falsely, that he was not certain.

Stroud's discussion of this matter is characterized by his concern to do justice to the facts of ordinary language. Having claimed that 'we recognise that [the airman] does not know it is an F', he concedes that 'for all practical purposes we can accept his saying that he knows', and that 'he can perhaps be said to know-for-all-practical-purposes' (68–9). The truth, apparently, is that the man does not really know, though in practical situations we may reasonably speak as if he did. But this is not right. In the situation I described it would be correct, and not merely roughly correct, or correct 'for practical purposes', to say that the man knows; and incorrect to deny it.

Having concluded that it is 'a condition of knowing that the plane is an F on the basis of x, y, z, that one knows it is not a G', Stroud applies the point to the sceptical philosopher's position versus the facts of ordinary language.

> Facts about the way we speak and the procedures we follow in everyday life do not show that the sceptical philosopher has misunderstood or distorted the nature of knowledge if this conception of our everyday practices and procedures is correct. (69)

By 'this conception' Stroud means that of which the airman case is an illustration. But this brings us to a difficulty about the general style of arguments of the kind used by Stroud. Suppose his claim about the airman were correct – that we really would not describe him as having knowledge: what would this show about knowledge in general? It could not show that in other cases too we would refuse to say that a person has knowledge unless the requirement of 'ruling out other possibilities' were satisfied. For this is simply not how the word 'know' is used. This requirement would not, for example, be recognized in the case of my knowing that this is a banana. Hence, if it *were* correct to deny that the airman has knowledge, this might merely show that the airman example is not a suitable model for the ascription of knowledge in general.

Why, we may ask, should the sceptic need to resort to such unusual examples to support his claims? In that example it was supposed that we are given information, which the airman lacks, about the other planes; and here we might perhaps be tempted, with Stroud, to deny that the man has knowledge. But in the example of the banana, no such information, or lack of information, was involved. There is no reason to suppose that the epistemic position in *this* example can be clarified by assimilating it to an unusual and rather complicated case.

The consequential knowledge requirement

Consider a person who knows that p, and is aware that p entails q. Must he know that q? It seems obvious that he must.

S knows that p.
S knows that p entails q.

_____

S knows that q.

I know that today is the 15th May and that on the 15th May I must deliver my script. How can I fail to know that today I must deliver my script?

Let us call this the 'consequential knowledge principle' (CKP).[8] The CKP leads to conclusions which would make the concept of knowledge untenable. For, given any value of p, there will always be some values of q that are entailed by p, but which S would not claim to know. But then, it seems, S should admit, in virtue of *modus tollens*, that the first or second premise must be false. And assuming the second is not in question, it is the first that must give way: S must admit that he does not know that p. Thus a principle which at first sight seems correct and innocuous imposes on the ascription of knowledge a requirement that cannot be met.

John knows that (p) his car is in the car-park; and this entails (as John is aware) that (q) it has not been stolen. But does John *know* it hasn't been stolen?[9] Would we ascribe this knowledge to him? Yes, if his reason for holding that p is that he can see the car there now; for the

8   This is the principle that Robert Nozick refers to as 'closure', in accordance with his way of discussing it (*Philosophical Explanations* (Harvard 1981)). Like myself, Nozick draws attention to its role in sceptical argument and proceeds to reject it; but his way of doing so is very different from mine, which follows. This is connected with the fact that, unlike myself in the last chapter, he accepts both that knowledge entails belief and that 'Gettier' cases are not admissible as knowledge.

9   I shall take 'stolen' to mean stolen-and-not-returned. The car-park example is adapted from E.H. Wolgast, *Paradoxes of Knowledge* (Cornell 1977), 34.

same reason will enable him to know that q. But if his reason is that (o) he left the car there an hour ago, then he is probably not in a position to know that q. In this case he could be said to lack evidence for q, in spite of the fact that p entails q. Should we conclude that he doesn't know that p either? This is what we must conclude if we follow the CKP. The alternative is to reject the CKP.

It might be thought that the CKP is essential to the concepts of knowledge and inference. Here is a person who knows that p, and is aware that p entails q. What better reason could one have for claiming to know that q? The truth is, however, that p may not count as a reason for q, even where it is clear that p entails q. In our example, o is a good reason for p, but p is not a good reason for q. 'How do you know that (p) your car is in the car-park?' – 'Because (o) I left it there an hour ago.' – 'How do you know that (q) it hasn't been stolen?' Here it would be absurd to answer 'Because it is in the car-park', if my reason for the latter were o. Some other reason for q must be produced – for example, that I can see the car there now, or that the car-park is well guarded. (A suitable reason need not *entail* q, as p does.) But what if I have no such other reason? Contrary to the CKP, I would still be expected to say I know that p – even though I was not prepared to say I know that q.

In such a case, the truth of q, and of various other propositions entailed by p, is *taken for granted* in inferring p from o: it is part of the 'logical background' of this inference. In inferring p from o, we ignore or discount the possibility that q, and other propositions entailed by p, may be false. In such cases, q is usually the negation of a proposition with negative import – one that says or implies that things are not normal (e.g. the car has been stolen). And in taking for granted that q, we take for granted that things are normal. But to take q for granted is not to have or claim knowledge that q.

A: I know that p.
B: How do you know?
A: Because o.
B: But aren't you taking for granted that q? (You understand that if q is false – e.g. if the car *has* been stolen – this will interfere between o and p, so that p will be false in spite of o.)
A: Yes, I am taking it for granted that q. But this is something that would normally be taken for granted in claiming to know that p on the basis of o.
B: But how do you *know* that q?
A: I am not claiming to know that q.

Should B now tell A that he ought not to claim knowledge that p? But A's opening statement was justified by normal standards. In that situation he would be expected to answer 'yes' to the question whether he knows where the car is, and he might be accused of falsehood if he answered 'no'.

In inferring p from o, A, as we have seen, takes for granted that q. It might be suggested that when this is spelled out, A's knowledge is seen to be *hypothetical*: what he really knows is not that p, but that *if* q, then p. If this were correct, then the conflict between A's knowledge and the CKP would disappear.

Would this be a way of avoiding scepticism while retaining the CKP? No; the result would be merely a new version of scepticism: *categorical* knowledge would remain impossible. This would be so even with direct perceptual knowledge, though here the CKP might have to be filled out in more fanciful ways. Thus, according to Unger, someone who 'knows that there are rocks' would have to know 'the following quite exotic thing: there is no evil scientist deceiving him into falsely believing that there are rocks' (op. cit.).

It is a confusion, however, to treat the logical role of 'taking for granted' in the sense of a hypothetical proposition. The example I gave should be distinguished from cases in which A has *reason* to think that the car may have been stolen. In such a case he might indeed answer: '... if it hasn't been stolen' or '... assuming it hasn't been stolen'. But this answer would be incorrect if he had no such reason, for it would imply that he did have such a reason. 'Do you know where your car is?' – 'In the car-park, assuming it hasn't been stolen.' This qualification would be correct if there were reasons for thinking it might haven been stolen; but not otherwise.

Defenders of the CKP would need to explain how it is that we are misled into ascribing knowledge, to ourselves and others, as commonly as we do. Are we really unjustified in doing so? According to one defender of the CKP, we are justified in one way but not in another: it is the *raising* of doubt about q that makes the difference. 'Prior to the doubts having been raised, both p and q are justified; after the doubts have been raised, neither p nor q are justified.'[10] On this view, the ordinary ascriptions of knowledge would be justified, but this justification could always be undermined by the raising of sceptical doubts. The existence of knowledge would be as precarious as that of a

10   P.D. Klein, *Certainty* (Harvester 1981), 36.

soap bubble: one prick by the 'raising of doubt', and the bubble of knowledge collapses.

But is it correct to say that after the raising of doubt about q, the assertion of p is no longer justified? It may be so if the doubt is a real one – if there is reason to doubt that q. If reasons for doubting that q are given, then they will have to be set against those for holding that p. However, even if no such reasons are given, there may be a *presumption* that the person raising the doubt has reasons: the mere raising of the question may be a reason for me to doubt that q and, consequently, that p. But what if the doubt is of the sceptical kind, if the 'reasons' are nothing more than the logical possibility that q may be false? In that case I will not have learned anything I did not know before. I knew, of course, of the possibility of cars being stolen, and of all sorts of other, more or less likely, possibilities. But these were already accommodated in my claim to know that p. The raising of *this* kind of doubt should make no difference to my epistemic position.

But may it not do so, in fact? Suppose I am persuaded, rightly or wrongly, by the sceptical argument, agreeing that my inability to know that q prevents me from knowing that p. And suppose I now refuse to say I know that p. In that case I would no longer be held to know that p. Thus it seems as if ordinary ascriptions of knowledge are, after all, hostage to the raising of sceptical doubts and the application of the CKP. But can I really refuse to say I know that p? Suppose that, just after I have allowed myself to be persuaded by the sceptical argument, my wife telephones and asks whether I know where the car is. In that case I would, and would need to, answer 'yes'. Reference to the sceptical argument and its effect on me would not be a justification for refusing to say I know. My admission, while under the influence of the sceptical argument, that I do not know, would not be a *stable* denial of knowledge: it would be countermanded immediately in replying to my wife's question. (It is the denial of knowledge, and not the affirmation of it, that collapses like a bubble.)

In philosophical discussions it is usual to treat knowledge as a matter of *entitlement*. The question is asked whether someone is entitled to *claim* knowledge, whether he should be *credited* with having it, etc. We may also speak of one's duty in speaking to others who have an interest in p. But this duty is twofold. One ought not to say one knows if one's grounds are inadequate; but equally, one *ought* to say one knows if they *are* adequate. It would be wrong of me to say I know what time the train will leave if I have only a vague idea; but I would be equally at fault if, having just checked at the station, I were to deny that I know – if I answered 'no' to an enquirer with an interest in catching the train. In the second case, no less than the first, I would be guilty of falsehood. Yet in this case, again, it would be easy to think of consequential propositions that I could not know to be true.

In some cases, again, the possession of knowledge is a matter of *admission* rather than claim or entitlement. Someone involved in a public scandal may be reluctant to admit that he knew what was going on; and it may be pointed out to him, in court or in the newspapers, that he has or had a duty to disclose this knowledge, that he is lying if he says he didn't know, etc. But here again there will be propositions of type q, which the person concerned would not be said to know. He knew, let us say, that (p) the goods he delivered were contaminated, though he was not in a position to know that (q) no one had replaced them with clean goods prior to despatch. But this failure of consequential knowledge would not absolve him from the duty of admitting knowledge that p. Here, as in the case of the train enquiry, the path of duty leads to rejection of the CKP.

It may be thought that rejection of the CKP must overturn all our notions of valid argument. Here are situations in which, in the most obvious way, p entails q, and S is aware of this. What, it may be asked, is left of the notions of argument and inference if he cannot infer q from p in such cases? What does 'p entails q' mean, if one cannot do this? The truth is that entailment and inference are not linked as closely as one might think. Entailment is ascribed to propositions, while inference (inferring) is ascribed to people. The relation between entailment and inference is prohibitive but not necessarily permissive. Someone who knows that p entails q is prohibited from asserting both p and not-q. Thus if I say the car is in the car-park, I cannot also say it has been removed. But whether I can *infer* q from p depends on the nature of p and q and on the circumstances. To take a different example, 'The car is in the car-park' entails that the car is not on the moon; but it does not follow that anyone is in a position to *infer* the second from the first.

The onus of proof and the second-order knowledge requirement

So far I have considered the CKP in relation to propositions that we may reasonably assume to be true, in accordance with the normal state of affairs. Can we deal similarly with sceptical hypotheses of a more general kind – for example, that the world will end tomorrow, or that we are misled by a Cartesian demon?

In these cases, application of the CKP would again lead to sceptical conclusions. If the world ended tomorrow, then all our knowledge-claims about the time after tomorrow would be false. Does it follow that we cannot have such knowledge? Only if we accept, in accordance with CKP, that such knowledge entails knowing that the world will not end tomorrow. Now it is true that one may hesitate or refuse to say that one know this; but if the CKP is rejected, this refusal will not prevent one from having knowledge about the time after tomorrow.

There is a difference, however, between this and the car-park example. In the latter case we could speak of *normal* conditions, but this is not so in the cases now before us. It makes no sense to say that 'normally' the world will not end tomorrow, or that 'normally' we are not misled by a Cartesian demon. Again, although the person in our example was not in a position to know that his car had not been stolen, he or somebody else might be in a position to know this. But can anyone know that the world will not end tomorrow?

It is sometimes thought that in this matter the sceptical and anti-sceptical positions are parallel: just as the sceptic can put forward a hypothesis which would undermine our knowledge-claims, so his opponent must put forward a contrary hypothesis which would sustain them. 'To meet the ... challenge of scepticism, we must provide some argument to show that the sceptical hypothesis is false and the beliefs of common sense are correct'.[11] But this requirement, again, goes beyond what we normally mean by knowledge. Normally, if such and such particular conditions are satisfied, we say that a person knows that p. It is not required, in addition to these, that he can provide a second-order argument to show that 'the beliefs of common sense are correct' or even that he can make sense of the question. The 'hypothesis' that they are correct is not part of what we mean when we express knowledge or ascribe it to others. This is not to deny the point with which I began, that if the world ended tomorrow, then our knowledge-claims about the time after tomorrow would be false. But to meet this point we need only assume that the world will not end tomorrow, in which case those knowledge-claims will *not* be false. It is not necessary for us, in addition, to 'provide some argument' to show that the belief that the world will not end tomorrow is correct.

But, it may be asked, have we any reason to believe that world will not end tomorrow? It would indeed be hard to produce reasons either for or against this proposition. Does this not mean that the proposition

---

Keith Lehrer, in G. S. Pappas and M. Swain, eds, *Essays on Knowledge and Justification* (Cornell 1978), 361. (In 'Scepticism on Twin Earth', *Ratio* 1984, I consider this kind of claim from the point of view of an inhabitant of Twin Earth.)

is doubtful? And if that is so, must not the knowledge-claims about the time after tomorrow likewise be dragged into doubt? This argument depends on an abnormal use of 'doubt'. Doubt is the appropriate reaction to a proposition for which the evidence is inadequate, or outweighed by other evidence known to the doubter; but in the case of the world going on as before, there is no evidence one way or the other. (Past experience cannot help us here.)

The lack of evidence for doubting that the world will go on tomorrow is matched by an absence of suitable behaviour. In both respects the sceptical doubt may be contrasted with doubts that have really existed about this matter. In the tenth century some Christians believed, on doctrinal evidence, that the world would end in the year 1000, and this did affect their behaviour. But, as sceptics themselves have often pointed out, no suitable behaviour is to be expected in the case of their sceptical doubts. This is sometimes explained by saying that such behaviour would be inconvenient or psychologically difficult; but that is not the real reason. The real reason is that the lack of support for genuine doubting carries over into a lack of grounds for doubting behaviour. The tenth century Christians did not lack such support, and neither did they lack grounds for appropriate behaviour.

Scepticism and ordinary language

In this chapter I have considered arguments tending to show that knowledge is impossible, because of certain requirements that cannot be met. But cannot the sceptic's case be put in a more cautious form? Perhaps he will say, not that we cannot have knowledge, but merely that we do not have it.

This, however, is not really a tenable option for the sceptic. Let us take a straightforward case in which (1) p is true, (2) S claims, on suitable grounds, to know that p, and (3) S's position in relation to p is not affected by 'Gettier' complications. That there are such cases is not in doubt; what is denied is that they are really cases of knowledge. But how can this be denied? Only by imposing requirements on the application of this concept, such as those I have discussed, that *could not* be met – that would make the possession of knowledge impossible.

There are well-established reasons for denying that a person *in fact* possesses knowledge. One such reason is that he is unable to speak or behave in accordance with the supposed knowledge; another is that p is false; and yet another the discovery that he is merely guessing. But these normal ways of showing that a person does not know cannot be generalized so as to lead to philosophical scepticism. For we need only suppose that there are cases – some cases – in which the adverse conditions are *not* present, and this will return us to the common sense position: that knowledge is sometimes present and sometimes lacking; we are sometimes right and sometimes wrong in attributing it; etc. It is only with the introduction of *impossible* conditions that philosophical scepticism can arise.

Such conditions are sometimes introduced with an explicit renunciation of the standards of ordinary language or 'common sense'. C.I. Lewis, admitting that it would not be common sense to argue about Cartesian doubts, said his aim was not to do justice to common sense, 'but to arrive at an accurate analysis of knowledge'.[12] But what is here the standard of accuracy? Why should an analysis that diverges from the normal use of this word be regarded as accurate? A philosopher who redefines 'knowledge' is changing the subject. The discussion is supposed to be about *knowledge*, but this will not be so if the word is redefined: in that case we shall be discussing 'knowledge' – a word with a similar sound but a different meaning from that of the ordinary one. We thought we were going to be faced with a *sceptical* challenge, concerning knowledge; but if the challenge is merely about 'knowledge', then it does not deserve the name of scepticism.

It has also been claimed that sceptical denials of knowledge, though not appropriate for 'the *ordinary* case', may well be justified 'in the extraordinary case in which men are engaged in intellectual speculation'.[13] But what advantages for intellectual speculation can accrue from the sceptic's denials? It might be thought that the introduction, for this purpose, of stricter requirements than the ordinary ones, is justified in the same kind of way as the use of strict definitions in geometry. The word 'circle', for example, is used in geometry in a more rigorous way than in ordinary language. Could not the same be said of the sceptic's redefinition of 'knowledge'? These cases are not alike. We may say of an ordinary use of the word 'circle' – for example, in describing a pond as 'circular' – that it *approximates* to the geometrical ideal. But the sceptic is not saying, similarly, that ordinary knowledge approximates to a sceptical ideal. The point of scepticism is to contradict what we normally say, but that is not the point of geometry. The idealizations of geometry enable us to think in new ways, both theoretical and practical, about spatial relations; but no such

---

12   C.I. Lewis, *An Analysis of Knowledge and Valuation* (La Salle 1946). The passage is quoted with approval by Stroud, op. cit., 65.
13   Lehrer, op. cit. 353. Also see his *Knowledge* (OUP 1979), 114, 119.

horizons are opened up by defining 'knowledge' in such a way as to make the word inapplicable.

In using the words 'knowledge', 'certainty', 'doubt', etc., we take part in a 'language-game'. It is sometimes thought that the use of words is governed by standards that are internal to language-games, in a way that is comparable to the function of rules in games. But this comparison must not be taken too far.[14] Suppose that in a game of Monopoly I owe you £1000. This is unfortunate for me, but still – 'it's only a game'. Now the fact that it is only a game does not make it *false* that I owe you £1000; I do owe you this money, in the appropriate sense of the phrase; but in another sense I do not. It might be thought that the 'rules' for the use of epistemic language are likewise internal to a language-game, which might be either the ordinary one or that of intellectual enquiry.

But this is not a good analogy. There is a sense of 'money' which is 'real' or 'serious' compared with the make-believe that is internal to a game. But there is no real or serious sense of 'knowledge' which it has in contrast to its ordinary sense. In this case the contrast would have to be, not between make-believe and reality, but between reality and some kind of 'super-reality'. It would be comparable to claiming that what we describe as 'owing £1000' in ordinary life is not really owing £1000; that (according to a more accurate analysis of this expression, etc.) it is not really possible for one person to owe £1000 to another. This might suit some people, but it would not be true.[15]

14   See O. Hanfling, 'Does Language need Rules?, *Phil. Quarterly* 1980.
15   This chapter is a much-revised version of 'How is Scepticism Possible?', *Philosophy* 1987.

Part II

The philosophy of 'what we say'

Challenge and rejection

8 Drawing the curtain of words

> We need only draw the curtain of words, to behold the fairest tree of knowledge, whose fruit is excellent, and within the reach of our hand'.
>
> (Berkeley)

'Disputes merely verbal'

A constant objection to linguistic philosophy has been that it neglects to concern itself with the realities behind language, giving preference to 'merely verbal' questions over questions of substance.

The distinction between language and reality is prominent in the work of the seventeenth and eighteenth century writers Locke, Berkeley and Hume, where we are repeatedly warned not to treat questions about words as if they were of primary importance. I shall try to show that, in spite of their protestations to the contrary, the arguments of these writers are often dependent on claims about meaning. Sometimes the claims are explicit, but even where this is not so, questions of meaning may be essential in evaluating those arguments.

One of Locke's examples of a 'merely verbal' dispute was the question 'whether a bat be a bird, or no'.[1] Such a question, he said, may be merely 'about the signification of one or both these words', in which case it would be a waste of time to argue about it. 'When carefully examined', he claimed, 'the greatest part of the disputes in the world are ... merely verbal, and about the signification of words'; so that if only 'the terms they are made in were defined ... those disputes would

---

1 *An Essay Concerning Human Understanding*, ed. P.H. Nidditch (OUP 1975), 3.11.7.

... end of themselves and immediately vanish'.[2] He admonished the reader to 'think on things' rather than words, and questioned 'whether language, as it has been employed, has contributed more to the improvement or hindrance of knowledge amongst mankind' (3.11.4).

Nevertheless, claims about the use and meaning of words have an important role in the *Essay,* and it is about words that we need to think when these claims are put to us. This is so, for example, in Locke's moral philosophy, which is based on claims about the uses of 'good' and 'evil'.

> That we call *Good,* which *is apt to cause or increase Pleasure, or diminish Pain in us* .... And on the contrary we name that *Evil,* which *is apt to produce or increase any Pain or diminish any pleasure in us.* (2.20.2; cf. 2.28.5ff)

Claims about the uses of words are also put forward in the famous discussion of personal identity. One of the questions raised there is whether being a man depends on bodily form or on the possession of reason. According to Locke it is bodily form, and not the possession of reason, that is decisive. He supports this view by an argument from *what we would say* in the relevant cases. 'Whoever should see a creature of his own shape and make, though it had no more reason all its life, than a cat or a parrot, would call him still a man'; and conversely, one would *not* call a cat or parrot a man even if one heard the animal 'discourse, reason and philosophize' (2.27.8).

Another appeal to what we would say occurs in the thought experiment, in the same chapter, in which we are asked to suppose that 'the soul of a prince, carrying with it the consciousness of the prince's past life, enter and inform the body of a cobbler' (2.27.15). In that case, would personal identity be according to identity of consciousness or identity of body? Locke maintains that there is an essential difference between 'person' and 'man', the identity of the former going with consciousness and that of the latter with body. 'Everyone sees that [the cobbler] would be the same person with the prince, accountable only for the prince's actions. But who would say it was the same man?'

In this passage 'see' occurs as well as 'say'. (We 'see' that the

---

2   A similar passage occurs in 3.9.16, where he describes how he was able to resolve a dispute among physicians, about whether 'any Liquor passes through the filaments of the nerves'. This he did by suggesting that they should first establish what was meant by 'liquor', whereupon the dispute melted away.

cobbler would be the same person, but would not 'say' he was the same man.) But in this context 'see' and 'say' amount to the same. To claim that we would *see* that the cobbler is the same person (though not the same man) is to claim that this is what we would *say* about him.

It might be objected that seeing is logically prior to saying: it is *because* we see he is the same person that we would say he is the same person. But what does 'see' mean in this context? It does not mean visual perception, as in a case, say, of recognizing someone. In such a case, seeing (in the visual sense) would indeed be prior to saying. I have to look at the person concerned to recognize who it is, and this enables me to *say* who it is. But no such seeing is called for in the case of the prince and the cobbler. We are not expected actually to observe such a case, and it would make no difference if we did. What Locke wants us to see is that the cobbler would be 'the same person with the prince'; but 'seeing' that this is so is no different from 'seeing' that this is what we would *say* about him.

In the lines immediately following, however, Locke repudiates the appeal to what we would say. 'I know', he writes, 'that in the ordinary way of speaking, the same person, and the same man, stand for one and the same thing'; but to arrive at the truth of the matter 'we must fix the [relevant] *ideas* ... in our minds', rather than attending to the ordinary way of speaking. If we take this advice, we shall find two *different* ideas in respect of 'man' and 'person'; and this would determine us, in the case of the cobbler and the prince, to affirm an identity of person while denying an identity of man.

But the 'ordinary way of speaking' cannot be set aside in this way. If it is true, as Locke concedes, that 'same person' and 'same man' have the same meaning in the ordinary way of speaking, then why should we accept that our *ideas* of man and person are different? There is no other way of considering whether they are different than by reference to the ordinary way of speaking. And if it appeared that we would *not*, for example, describe the cobbler as being the same person as the prince, then Locke could not save his thesis by retreating to ideas as distinct from words.

Hume was another philosopher who warned the reader against mistaking 'disputes of words' for matters 'of the deepest importance and concern'.[3] He was emphatic about this in his discussion of 'liberty and necessity', which he introduced with warnings about the use of ambiguous expressions, where 'the disputants affix different ideas to

---

3   David Hume, *Enquiries* (Clarendon 1975), 312.

the terms employed in the controversy' (80). This had been so especially, he thought, in the dispute he was about to discuss. According to Hume, this dispute is unreal. He will show

> that all men have ever agreed in the doctrine both of necessity and of liberty, according to any reasonable sense, which can be put on these terms; and that the whole controversy has hitherto turned merely upon words. (81)

But in taking his stand on 'any reasonable sense' of the terms concerned, Hume seems himself to regard the question of liberty and necessity as essentially one of meanings. This is confirmed when, in due course, he puts forward a definition of the term 'liberty'.

> For what is meant by liberty, when applied to voluntary actions? We cannot surely mean ... that one [action] does not follow with a certain degree of uniformity from the other .... By liberty, then, we can only mean *a power of acting, according to the determinations of the will*; that is, if we choose to remain at rest, we may; if we choose to move, we also may. (95)

Liberty, in this proper sense, is 'universally allowed to belong to every one who is not a prisoner and in chains'; and its existence is compatible with the fact that the will is itself necessitated by 'motives, inclinations, and circumstances', etc.

Although much of Hume's argument on this topic is not conducted, like the above, in explicitly semantic terms, it emerges that this is essentially how he sees the problem: it is, he thinks, due to confusions about the meanings of 'necessity' and 'liberty', and its solution lies in defining these words correctly. It follows that a critic of Hume would be likely to dispute his definitions (they are certainly open to question), so that the dispute would indeed turn out to be 'of words'. What does not follow is that it would be *merely* about words – as if this were no more than a superficial way of discussing the question.

In the opening pages of his discussion Hume distinguishes between 'questions which lie entirely beyond the reach of human capacity, such as those concerning the origin of worlds ...' and questions regarding 'any subject of common life and experience', including the subject at hand. In the case of the latter, he writes,

> nothing, one would think, could preserve the dispute so long undecided but some ambiguous expressions, which keep the

antagonists still at a distance, and hinder them from grappling with each other. (81)

Now it is true that the dispute has remained 'long undecided' and remains so to this day. But the ambiguities involved in it are not such as can be easily cleared up – even if the subject is one of 'common life and experience'. Hume's opening comments may lead us to think that the matter can be disposed of in a few words, by resolving ambiguities; but the length and complexity of his own discussion, not to mention those that have appeared before and since, prove that this is not so.

'Ideas bare and naked'

Locke's resort to 'ideas' as opposed to words, in the argument about 'man' and 'person' and elsewhere, is connected with a theory *about* words. According to this, 'the use ... of words, is to be sensible marks of ideas; and the ideas they stand for, are their proper and immediate signification' (*Essay* 3.2.1). Ideas are the primary elements of knowledge and understanding and it is to them, therefore, rather than to their 'sensible marks', that we need to turn if we are to gain true understanding. 'Common use regulates the meaning of words pretty well for common conversation', but it is 'not sufficient to adjust them to philosophical discourses', for no one can determine 'to what ideas anyone shall annex' the words concerned (3.9.8). In the preface to the *Essay* Locke advised the reader how to combat the looseness of ordinary language. When he uses any particular word, the reader should 'have in his mind a determined Idea, which he makes it the sign of, and to which he should keep it steadily annexed during that present discourse' (p. 13). Failing this, 'there can be expected nothing but obscurity and confusion'.

But how is Locke's theory of meaning itself to be evaluated? Is it right to say that when, for example, I describe the object before me as a tree, I am really using this word to signify an idea in my mind? Here we cannot set aside the criterion of 'common use'. Is this in fact how the word 'tree' is used? If not, why should we accept that this (an idea in the mind) is what the word signifies?

It might be objected that in posing these questions I have assumed a normal meaning for the word 'idea', whereas Locke seems to have used it as a term of art. But this takes us to a notorious difficulty about the word 'idea' itself: What did Locke mean by it? Locke could not answer *this* question by advising the reader to attend to the idea to which he annexes the word 'idea'. It is true that if 'idea' was meant as a term of art, then we cannot expect it to conform to the criterion of ordinary language. Nevertheless it is by means of ordinary language that his use of that term would have to be explained. If this cannot be done, then his meaning must remain obscure.

This difficulty is not peculiar to Locke's use of 'idea'. The language in which empiricists from Locke onwards have expressed their theories of knowledge and reality has been a continuing obstacle to understanding them. They include such words as 'idea', 'sensation', 'impression' and, more recently, 'sense-datum'. This difficulty is *essentially* about words and cannot be treated otherwise. An early and penetrating critic of the empiricists' uses of words was Thomas Reid, who argued that their claims were vitiated by misuses of language, including such key words as 'idea'. Having described ordinary uses of this word, he said that writers such as Locke had given it a special sense, in which it embodied 'a mere fiction of philosophers'.[4]

According to Locke, as we saw, words signify ideas, the latter being the immediate objects of thought. He advised the reader to keep his mind on ideas, thus avoiding the looseness of words not properly backed by ideas. In Berkeley's writings we find a more radical stance. He will try, he tells us, not merely to keep the relevant ideas before his mind but, as far as possible, avoid words altogether. 'Whatever ideas I consider, I shall take them bare and naked into my view'.[5] This approach, he said, would enable him 'to get clear of all controversies *purely verbal*'. It would also protect him from error:

> So long as I confine my thoughts to my own ideas divested of words, I do not see how I can easily be mistaken. The objects I consider, I clearly and adequately know. I cannot be deceived in thinking I have an idea which I have not. (§22)

He advised everyone in quest of enlightenment to do likewise. To obtain a clear view of his own ideas, the reader should 'separate from them all that dress and encumbrance of words which so much contribute to blind the judgement . . .. We need only draw the curtain of words, to behold the fairest tree of knowledge, whose fruit is excellent, and within the reach of our hand' (§24).

How did Berkeley think he could communicate his ideas to the

---

4   Thomas Reid, *Essays on the Intellectual Powers of Man* (MIT 1969), 16–20.
5   *The Principles of Human Knowledge*, Introduction §21, in G. Berkeley, *Philosophical Works*, ed. M.R. Ayers (Dent 1993).

reader? Here psychology must take over from logic. What was needed was not merely that the relevant *words* be put to the reader, but that they would have the effect of producing the right wordless entities (ideas) in his mind. His final appeal to the reader, before embarking on the main text of the *Principles*, was that he should

> make my words the occasion of his own thinking, and endeavour to attain the same train of thoughts in reading, that I had in writing them. By this means it will be easy for him to discover the truth or falsity of what I say. (§25)

This may seem at first sight no more than a piece of wholesome advice to the reader to think the arguments through for himself. But how is he to assess Berkeley's arguments if not in the form stated by him *in words*? It is, as Berkeley himself puts it, the truth or falsity of *what he says* ('what I say') that is to be considered. Again, if Berkeley's words provoke a 'train of thoughts' in the reader, how can he 'discover truth or falsity' in these if they are not in a verbal form? The thought *that p* – where 'p' stands for a verbal expression – can be described as true or false; but wordless entities (thoughts or ideas divested of words) cannot. Let us take, for example, the opening statement of the *Principles*. (This is the first passage we encounter after the introductory advice.) 'It is evident', we are told here, that 'the objects of human knowledge' are ideas of three kinds (PHK §1). Now it is true that reading this statement may provoke a train of thoughts or ideas in one's mind; but how is one to 'discover the truth or falsity' of what is here stated? Only by reflecting on that *statement*: it cannot be attempted by considering wordless entities, in the mind or elsewhere.

Berkeley's stance on the priority of ideas over words was, as we have seen, more radical than Locke's, and this was connected with the radical nature of his metaphysics, where the divergence from ordinary ways of speaking is blatant and pervasive. This divergence is highlighted by Berkeley himself in an exchange with an imaginary objector. Having expounded his philosophy, whereby objects in the (so-called) material world are really ideas in the mind, Berkeley considers the objection: 'It sounds very harsh to say we eat and drink ideas, and are clothed with ideas .... Would not a man be deservedly laughed at, who should talk after this manner?' Berkeley replies: 'He would so; [but] in such things we ought to *think with the learned, and speak with the vulgar* (PHK §§38, 51). In this dictum two contrasts are made: the learned are preferred to the vulgar and thinking is preferred to speaking (ideas are preferred to words). The reader who sticks to ideas will find that Berkeley's views are correct, in spite of seeming ridiculous when compared with what we ordinarily say.

In expounding his philosophy, Berkeley would, of necessity, rely on 'those inaccurate modes of speech which use has made inevitable', but he would trust the reader to gather what he really had in mind, supposing that this could be achieved by the communication of ideas as opposed to words. To try to alter the existing language for the more accurate expression of his views would be futile.

> It is impossible, even in the most rigid philosophical reasonings, so far to alter the bent and genius of the tongue we speak, as never to give a handle for cavillers to pretend difficulties and inconsistencies. (PHK §52)

He was even prepared, in a notebook, to resort to a kind of subterfuge in the service of truth. Here he resolved that when presenting his argument he would, contrary to what he really believed, 'allow existence to colours in the dark', his reason being that ''tis prudent to correct mens mistakes without altering their language. This makes truth glide into their souls insensibly'.[6] Not wishing to disturb readers by 'altering their language', he would go along with a falsehood in the hope that this would instil truth at the deeper level of ideas.

He also, however, tried to explain the distinction between the learned and the vulgar *within* the domain of words, giving an example to illustrate how the two modes of speech can exist together.

> They who ... are convinced of the truth of the Copernican system, do nevertheless say that the sun rises, the sun sets, or comes to the meridian: and if they affected a contrary style in common talk, it would without doubt appear very ridiculous. (PHK §51)

The ordinary way of speaking and the more accurate Copernican one can exist together; and similarly, according to Berkeley, 'the common use of language would receive no manner of alteration or disturbance from the admission of [his] tenets'.

But this is not a valid analogy. The Copernican philosopher does not need to embarrass himself (like Berkeley) with 'inaccurate modes of speech': he can explain his system perfectly well without that and

---

6   G. Berkeley, *Philosophical Commentaries*, in *Philosophical Works*, op. cit., 324.

indeed within the resources of ordinary language. (And neither does he need to resort to naked ideas as opposed to words.) On the other hand, the difference between the 'learned' and 'vulgar' descriptions in the case of the sun is not one of more and less accuracy, for there is no lack of accuracy when, in ordinary discourse, we speak of the sun rising and setting – unless, say, inaccurate times were given for these events.

What is really at issue between Berkeley and his ordinary language opponent is not a question of accuracy: it is a question of sense versus nonsense. According to the normal use of language, the statement that we eat and drink ideas is unintelligible; but this is not so with statements made under the Copernican system. It is true, as Berkeley says, that Copernican descriptions might 'appear ridiculous' if used in a wrong context, though this would not make them incoherent or untrue. But the charge against the talk of eating and drinking ideas is not that it would be out of place in a wrong context, but that it is, simply, incoherent.

The clash between Berkeley's views and ordinary language is more accurately expressed in another passage, where he says that when we speak of houses, mountains and other objects as existing when not perceived, this 'involves a manifest contradiction' (PHK §4). Here we see that the issue is essentially about what it makes sense to say. In ordinary language – according to 'the bent and genius of the tongue we speak' – it is *not* a 'manifest contradiction' to speak of the unperceived existence of houses, mountains, etc., whereas it *is* nonsense to say that we eat and drink ideas. But according to Berkeley, the reverse is true. The dispute, which is central to Berkeley's philosophy, is essentially about language: it is Berkeley's *language* that the objector finds unintelligible and it is the objector's *language* that Berkeley denounces as involving 'a manifest contradiction'. Such a dispute cannot be resolved by abandoning language and retreating to 'ideas divested of words'.

Hume and the quest for meanings

The view that ideas are more fundamental than words also found expression in another way, which was especially characteristic of Hume. According to Locke, as we saw, words have meaning by standing for ideas; and from this it would follow that a word without a corresponding idea must be meaningless. In Hume's account, the relevant ideas must come from a suitable 'impression', originally imprinted on the mind in the course of sense experience. If no such impression can be identified, then the word lacks a corresponding idea and is therefore meaningless. He used this criterion of meaning in his critique of 'philosophical terms', such as 'substance' and 'essence'. Suspecting that such a term has 'no idea annexed to it', he will ask 'from what impression that [putative] idea is derived'. And if no impression can be produced, he will 'conclude that the term is altogether insignificant'.[7]

Hume does not always conduct his quest for meanings in terms of 'ideas' and 'impressions'. Thus, in trying to find the meaning of 'vice', he looks for 'a matter of fact or real existence' corresponding to the word. But in all these discussions the assumption is that the meaning of a word depends on the existence of some corresponding entity. Hume's approach, in his quest for meanings, is empirical: he thinks they are to be found, if at all, by observation. Thus, in seeking the meaning of 'necessary connexion' as applied to cause and effect, he 'turns [his] eye to two objects supposed to be placed in that relation' and carefully examines them. He can perceive that they are 'contiguous in time and place', and that the one 'precedes the other', but he is 'unable to discover any third relation' and thereby discover the meaning of 'necessary connexion'.[8] Perhaps, after all, this expression has no meaning?

> One event follows another; but we never can observe any tie between them .... The necessary conclusion *seems* to be that we have no idea of [causal] connexion or power at all, and that these words are absolutely without any meaning ... (*Enquiries* 74; cf *Treatise* 161–2)

Happily it turns out, after further research, that a suitable *idea* can be located, so that these words are not without meaning. We had merely been looking in the wrong place.

Another example of the same kind occurs in Hume's moral philosophy, where he tries to define 'vice'. Here again we are invited to proceed in the manner of an empirical investigation.

> Take any action allowed to be vicious: wilful murder, for instance. Examine it in all lights, and see if you can find that matter of fact, or real existence, which you call *vice* .... The vice entirely escapes you, as long as you consider the object. You can never find it, till

---

7   David Hume, *An Abstract* (Archon 1965), 11; cf. *Enquiries*, op. cit., 22.
8   David Hume, *A Treatise of Human Nature* (Clarendon 1888), 155.

you turn your reflexion into your own breast and find a sentiment of disapprobation .... . So that when you pronounce any action or character to be vicious, you mean nothing, but that from the constitution of your nature you have feeling or sentiment of blame from the contemplation of it. (*Treatise* 468–9)

Here the elusive entity – the 'matter of fact or real existence' – that is needed to bestow meaning turns out to be a 'sentiment'; and this, according to Hume, constitutes the meaning of 'vice'.

But are questions of meaning really to be settled in such a way, by looking for matters of fact or real existence? What if one of Hume's readers reported that when he examined the action, he *was* able to find the vice in it and not, or not only, in his own breast? Hume seems to have assumed that the experience of others would match his own. Was this not rash? One might think that a proper scientific approach would be to conduct interviews with a representative sample of people, to discover whether, or to what extent, Hume's own experience was typical of mankind. We may be sure, however, that if Hume had received contrary reports, he would not have accepted them as such. His claim about the meaning of 'vice' was not really based on observation (of one person – himself), but on a priori grounds: he did not think that vice could conceivably be a property of actions (of 'objects' external to the mind).

There is a similar difficulty about the introspective experiment in which Hume attempts to track down 'the self'. Some philosophers, he writes, 'imagine we are every moment intimately conscious of what we call our SELF' (*Treatise* 251). But, he reports,

for my part, when I enter most intimately into what I call *myself*, I always stumble on some particular perception or other, of heat or cold, light or shade, love or hatred, pain or pleasure. I can never catch *myself* at any time .... (252)

From this experiment he concludes that there is no such entity as the self as distinct from particular 'perceptions', so that 'mankind ... are nothing but a bundle ... of perceptions'.

But is this a proper way of dealing with the question of 'what we call our Self'? Suppose, again, that one of Hume's readers reported that when he conducted the experiment, he *was* able to catch his self. Would Hume have regarded this as evidence against his theory? Perhaps he would have asked his correspondent to explain what he meant by 'his self'. Suppose the latter said that whenever he conducted the experiment, he experienced a very peculiar sensation accompanying all his other 'perceptions', and this was what he took the self to be. Hume, we may suppose, would not have been deterred by this, because such a sensation, however peculiar, would be merely another 'particular perception', and he had already decided that the self could not be merely that. But then, what *would* Hume be prepared to allow as a positive finding? What could one conceivably 'stumble on', according to him, other than particular perceptions? The truth is that Hume's experiment was a pretence: its 'result' had already been determined by constraints which made it inconceivable that he or anybody else would ever 'catch' the entity in question.

Hume typically describes his quests for meaning in personal terms: he reports his own experience, or predicts what the reader will find if he tries the experiment for himself. These are not merely figures of speech: his conception of language is such that the meaning of a word is a matter of personal discovery. If he can locate an idea or other entity corresponding to the words 'vice' or 'self', then that is what the word will mean *for him*. Hume assumes that the experiences of others will match his own, but there is no guarantee that it will. But this is not how questions of meaning are normally settled. This is done, not by appeals to personal experience, but by reference to objective conditions governing the use of a word among members of a language community. It is, in any case, by this criterion that Hume's definitions must be evaluated. If he is right about 'vice', then a correct answer to 'Why do you describe action A as "vicious"?' will be 'Because I have a feeling or sentiment of blame from the contemplation of it'. And to test this claim, we must consider whether it is true to the actual use of 'vicious'.

As we have seen, Hume, like Locke and Berkeley before him, regarded words as being of secondary importance. Like Locke, he warned readers against 'merely verbal' disputes; and like Locke and Berkeley, he looked to realities behind the words to determine what, if anything, particular words mean. This led him to conduct quasi-scientific observations to locate suitable meaning-bestowing entities. In this way he concluded – 'discovered' – that what we mean, say, by 'vice' is something in ourselves and not in objects. He made a similar claim about what is meant by 'necessity' as applied to cause and effect: this necessity, he tells us, is 'nothing but an internal impression in the mind' (*Treatise* 165). But, in the light of all this, what are we to make of the first definition of 'cause' that we find towards the end of his discussion?

We may define a CAUSE to be 'An object precedent and contiguous to another, and where all the objects resembling the former are placed in like relations of precedency and contiguity to those objects, that resemble the latter.' (*Treatise* 170)

Someone who reads this definition without the surrounding discussion might think that Hume had emancipated himself from the empiricist theory of meaning. What he has done, it seems, is not to identify a meaning-bestowing entity as required by the theory (thereby confirming that 'cause' is not meaningless), but to give a statement of the *circumstances* under which we describe one thing as the cause of another. What matters, according to the above definition, is not the occurrence of an 'impression', but the way in which the object described as 'a cause' is related to a pattern of events in the past and future. The question answered by the definition is not the empiricist's 'What is the idea that "cause" signifies?', but 'How must an object be related to others in order to be described as "a cause"'?

It is in this sense, moreover, that Hume's definition is discussed and assessed in the literature on causation. Do we really use 'cause' in accordance with that definition? What kinds of reasons do we give for describing one thing as the cause of another? Do we not apply this word to cases from which the regularity stipulated by Hume is lacking? Or refuse to apply it in spite of that regularity being present? In such enquiries careful reflection is called for, but this is not directed to finding a meaning-bestowing entity internal (or external) to the mind.

Popper: facts, not words

As we have seen, the views of Locke, Berkeley and Hume about the secondary importance of words are open to a number of objections. I have argued that since philosophers must use words to communicate their views, questions about what they mean by those words, and whether they are are using them correctly, must sometimes arise and may be crucial; that important claims about meaning are to be found even in the works of those who deny the importance of questions of meaning; and that even if a philosopher's arguments are not based on 'what we say', and even if he repudiates this criterion, his conclusions may still be challenged by reference to it.

These and similar points can also be made against philosophers of recent times, a notable example being Karl Popper. In his auto-biography Popper tells us that when he was only 15 he reached a view about this matter which stood him in good stead throughout his career. He formulated that view as follows:

> Never let yourself be goaded into taking seriously problems about words and their meanings. What must be taken seriously are questions of fact, and assertions about facts: theories and hypotheses; the problems they solve; and the problems they raise.[9]

Popper's position is akin to Berkeley's: both are resolved to 'draw the curtain of words', but whereas Berkeley would draw it in order to reveal the ideas behind the words, Popper's preference is for 'facts' and 'theories'. In Berkeley's case we cannot make sense of the invitation to 'discover the truth or falsity of what I say' if words are to be set aside; and so it is with Popper's preference for 'assertions about facts'. Assertions are made in words; how then can 'problems about words and their meanings' be set aside? If someone makes an assertion or puts forward a theory and there is a problem about its meaning, then this must be settled before we can decide whether to accept that assertion or theory.

Was Popper's own philosophy free of claims about meaning? One of his most prominent contributions was the demarcation betwen science and 'pseudo-science'. 'It became clear to me', he wrote, 'that what makes a theory, or a statement, scientific was its power to rule out, or exclude, the occurrence of some possible events ...' (ibid. 41). A scientific theory must be 'falsifiable': it must be possible for it 'to be refuted by experience'.[10]

Was Popper's demarcation one of facts or one of meanings? Was he talking about science or the word 'science'? These questions are similar to those which arose about the definitions of courage, knowledge, etc. in Plato's dialogues. The truth is that the questions 'What is science?' and 'What do we mean by "science"?' cannot be separated. The question, in either form, cannot itself be treated as a scientific one; it belongs to the *philosophy* and not the *domain* of science; it is a question of meaning and not a question about scientific facts or theories.

Popper's low opinion of the importance of questions of meaning may have made it easier for him to use words in objectionable ways in his own writings. A relevant example occurs in his discussions of the

9   K. Popper, *Unended Quest* (Fontana 1976), 19.
10   K. Popper, *The Logic of Scientific Discovery* (Hutchinson 1979), 41.

limits of human knowledge. Here he introduced the term 'conjectural knowledge', which he contrasted with 'final, demonstrable knowledge' (*Unended Quest* 149). But a critic has pointed out that 'conjectural knowledge' does not make sense. 'To say that something is known … implies that it is true, and known to be true …. To say of something that it is conjectural, on the other hand, implies that it is not known to be true'.[11]

A philosopher may say he is not interested in questions of meaning, but this will not prevent critics from questioning the meaning of what he has written. And if he is serious about his business, the philosopher must be prepared to face such questions when they are raised – or, better, anticipate them before they are raised. He cannot immunize himself by declaring that he is not interested in questions of meaning.

Language and reality in ethics

In Chapter 1 I argued that Socrates' quest for definitions should be regarded as belonging to linguistic philosophy – the investigation of 'what we say'. Now the fact that this quest was largely concerned with moral qualities is of special interest, for it is sometimes thought that, in moral philosophy especially, the linguistic approach can be of only marginal value. How, one might ask, can a consideration of language help to solve moral problems? How can it teach us what is right and wrong and what we ought to do? 'In contemporary ethics', writes a critic of linguistic philosophy, 'what is held to be at issue is not what is or should be the meaning of "good" or "right", but what things are good or right'.[12] Such critics may concede that there is a role for linguistic philosophy in 'meta-ethics' as opposed to 'substantive ethics'. An example of the former is R.M. Hare's *The Language of Morals*, in which he tried to show that moral language has certain formal properties: a moral statement is distinguished as such by being 'prescriptive' and 'universalizable', in a sense explained in the book.[13] But according to Cohen, 'linguistic discussions such as these touch only the linguistic or conceptual framework …. If anyone wishes to discuss what kinds of duty, freedom or privilege deserve respect, he has to … discuss duty, for example, not "duty"' (op. cit. 14–15).

11   D. Stove, *Popper and After* (Pergamon 1982), 14.
12   L.J. Cohen, *Dialogue of Reason* (Clarendon 1986), 16.
13   R.M. Hare, *The Language of Morals* (OUP 1952).

But as far as philosophical discussion is concerned, these distinctions are no more real than those between bravery and the word 'bravery', etc., as discussed in Chapter 1. To ask whether a particular kind of duty deserves respect is no different from asking whether the phrase 'deserves respect' is applicable to it – whether it is describable as 'deserving respect'. It is true, however, that little may be gained by putting the question in this verbal form. For if it is difficult to decide whether a given duty deserves respect, then the same difficulty will arise when trying to answer the question in the verbal form.

In other contexts, however, verbal questions can produce more important and interesting results. This is so when claims made by moral philosophers seem to *contravene* the criterion of 'what we say'. Let us take, for example, Mill's claim that 'actions are right in proportion as they tend to promote happiness', etc.[14] A suitable objection to this would be that it is not true to the ordinary use of 'right'. Thus it might be pointed out that in such and such a case (breaking a promise, for example), we might not describe an action as right even if it tended to promote the greatest happiness. A defender of the principle might then qualify it to make it more conformable to the ordinary use of 'right', perhaps by a version of rule-utilitarianism; and so the discussion would proceed.

But is this a proper way of representing the issue? Perhaps Mill would say that his principle is not about the meaning of 'right', but about what actions *are* right. He might argue that even if most people *described* the breaking of a particular promise as wrong, it would not follow that it really is wrong. Now it is true that what most people say may not be decisive in such matters. If most people favour the death penalty, it does not follow that the death penalty is right; and if most people said that a particular promise ought to be kept, it would not follow that it really ought to be kept.

This reply does not, however, address the essential objection. The objection is not that certain actions would be described as wrong in spite of conforming to Mill's principle; it is that they *might* be so described. Such cases may be matters of opinion, with 'no right answer'; but according to Mill, a right answer would be deducible from his principle. If that principle were correct, then 'ought to be done' would follow logically from 'tending to promote the greatest happiness' and it would be a logical contradiction to say, for example, that one ought to keep a particular promise even when this would not

14   J.S. Mill, *Utilitarianism* (Collins 1962).

tend to promote the greatest happiness. And this entailment is not recognized in the ordinary use of 'right' and 'ought'.

In Mill's 'proof' of the principle we find an explicit argument about language. Here he is concerned to show that the only objects of desire are pleasure and the absence of pain (op. cit. 292). Having conceded that we 'do desire things which, in common language, are decidedly distinguished from happiness ..., for example, virtue' (289), he tries to show that 'in strictness of language' these are not really distinct. We have here, he says, 'a question of fact and experience', to be determined by 'practised self-consciousness and self-observation, assisted by observation of others'; and this evidence 'will declare that desiring a thing and finding it pleasant are ... two different modes of naming the same psychological fact' (292–3).

Mill's approach to this question of meaning is similar to Hume's method of trying to establish the meanings of 'necessary connection', 'self', and 'vice', as discussed in a previous section. For both it is a matter of discovering and inspecting the meaning-bestowing entities behind the words; and Mill's hope is that the reader's self-observation will disclose a suitable psychological fact to confirm his own findings.[15] But, as in Hume's case, we must ask: What would Mill say if a reader reported that his findings were different?

The proper way to settle such questions of meaning is by reference to what is acceptable and unacceptable when the words in question are exchanged among speakers of the language. Are the uses of 'desiring a thing' and 'finding a thing pleasant' the same (or similar)? Could one be exchanged for the other in all or most contexts? The method is similar to that by which we translate from one language to another. Does 'desire' mean the same as 'désirer'? It depends on whether, or the extent to which, their uses are the same.

Another question that has been of great importance in ethics is plainly and explicitly about language. This is the question, raised by Hume, whether a statement about what ought or ought not to be done can be validly deduced from premises using only the copulations 'is' and 'is not' (*Treatise* 469). According to a widely held opinion, the correct answer is 'no'. But is this confirmed by the actual use of the language? Would it make sense, for example, to describe an action as 'murder', without agreeing that it *ought not* to be done? If not, then the widely held opinion cannot be right. Perhaps it will be replied that

---

15 What Mill meant by 'observation of others' is not clear. Are we meant to observe the behaviour of others? (How would this help?) Or should we question them?

'This is murder' is not really (or not merely) an 'is' statement but, so to speak, an 'ought' statement in disguise. But this is also a claim about language, and to be judged accordingly. Again, it is not difficult to think of a set of (pure) 'is' statements from which 'This is murder' would follow; and this too is a matter of language.[16]

Ethics and ontology

A constant subject of criticism in this book is the idea that words have meaning by standing for entities in the 'real world'. In the present chapter I have criticized Locke, Berkeley and Hume, who advise the reader to avoid 'disputes merely verbal', and to 'draw the curtain of words' so as to get at the realities behind the curtain.[17] The idea that words stand for corresponding entities is especially plausible in the case of proper names, but it has been held to apply to all kinds of words, as in this passage from Russell:

> When we examine common words, we find that, broadly speaking, proper names stand for particulars, while other substantives, adjectives, prepositions and verbs stand for universals. The word 'now' stands for a particular, namely the present moment ....[18]

In recent moral philosophy the relevant entities in the case of moral words are sometimes referred to as 'values', and the question has arisen whether there really are such entities. If there are not, then, it is thought, the status of our moral language is brought into question; but to address this question the philosopher must enquire about the existence of the relevant entities – in this case 'values' – as distinct from language. Such an argument is to be found in the work of John Mackie. His question, he says, is one of ontology and not language; it calls for 'factual rather than conceptual analysis'.[19] Contrary to what such analysis would show, 'there are no objective values' (15), and from this he concludes: 'It is precisely for this reason that linguistic and conceptual analysis is not enough' (35).

---

16   For further discussion, see O. Hanfling, ' "Is", "Ought" and the Voluntaristic Fallacy', *Philosophy* 1997.

17   Berkeley did not in fact accept Locke's theory of meaning, claiming that 'words may be significant, although they do not stand for ideas' (*Alciphron* 7.5; also PHK introduction §20). He did, however, regard ideas as the primary components of knowledge.

18   B. Russell, *The Problems of Philosophy* (OUP 1912), 93.

19   J.L. Mackie, *Ethics: Inventing Right and Wrong* (Penguin 1977), 19.

According to Mackie, 'a claim to objectivity [is] ingrained in our language and thought, [but] it is not self-validating' (35). In moral discourse we use such words as 'know', 'fact' and 'true', as when we say 'He knew that what he did was wrong' and 'It's true that I ought to do X, but ...'. Such expressions may be important when it comes to blame and punishment: whether the agent *knew* he was doing wrong may make all the difference. According to Mackie, however, these uses of language are erroneous, the truth being that 'value statements cannot be either true or false' (25). When we use such language we think that values, such as 'moral goodness ..., rightness and wrongness, duty, obligation', etc. 'are part of the fabric of the world' (15); but this is not so. Mackie's 'error theory' is that 'although most people in making moral judgements claim, among other things, to be pointing to something [objective], these claims are all false' (35). The truth, according to him, is that right and wrong are inventions on our part: 'Morality is not to be discovered but to be made' (106).

How should we understand the ontological commitments that Mackie ascribes to ordinary users of moral language? He speaks of them, as we have seen, in terms of 'the fabric of the world'. But how is this to be understood? What is the fabric of the world? One might reply by reference to the materials of which it is made, such as rocks, metals, water, etc.; or, at a more analytic level, chemicals and molecules. But the idea that values could find a place in this company is bizarre and there is no reason to suppose that this is what people are committed to by their use of moral language, or that 'linguistic analysis' would reveal such a commitment. Here, as in the case of free will (discussed in Chapter 5, and other cases to be discussed in later chapters) the opponent of linguistic philosophy helps himself by foisting implausible metaphysical claims and theories on speakers of ordinary language. Having saddled them with such commitments, he points out that they are indeed unacceptable and concludes from this that a philosophy based on ordinary language is itself unreliable.

On the other hand, what are we to make of Mackie's preference for 'factual' over 'conceptual' analysis? The expression suggests an empirical investigation to discover whether values can be found among the components of the world. But this question is not amenable to such treatment, and neither has Mackie arrived at his negative verdict by such research. This is because the question is, contrary to what he says, conceptual and not factual. It is from his knowledge of the relevant *language* that Mackie – like everybody else – knows that it is absurd (a 'category-mistake') to think that values might be part of the fabric of the world.

In support of his denial of 'objective values', Mackie uses an 'argument from relativity'. Here he draws attention to the differences existing between one society and another about what is right and wrong, and comments that 'radical differences between first order moral judgements make it difficult to treat those judgements as apprehensions of objective truths' (36). Such differences, as Mackie points out, are not like differences about the truth of empirical statements. In the latter case we can say that there is a truth of the matter which can be established, circumstances allowing, by observation; but this is not so in the case of moral differences. Here we might indeed conclude that there is no truth of the matter – no 'objective value', in that sense.

But these differences have nothing to do with ontology. There is no conceivable ontology of 'values' which, if it obtained, would provide the required objectivity and unanimity of moral views. What is needed to understand such problems is not an investigation of ontology, but a study of moral language and the ways of life in which it is embedded. On the other hand, the use of 'know' and 'true' in moral discourse, as in the examples given above, is not undermined by the existence of differences between societies. The statement 'He knew he was doing something wrong' would be perfectly correct in suitable circumstances, and it might indeed be unavoidable if we wished to describe exactly what happened.

Mackie's 'error theory' is typical of philosophers criticized in this book, who hold that there is something wrong with the language we speak, as when Berkeley excused himself for having to make do, in expounding his philosophy, with 'those inaccurate modes of speech which use has made inevitable'. But the language we speak cannot, as such, be described as accurate or inaccurate; it is only what someone *says* by means of language that can be so described. Thus the statement 'He knew that what he did was wrong' would be erroneous if he did *not* know this, or if what he did was not really wrong.

The 'error theory' has been well criticized by Simon Blackburn. What, he asks, would an *error-free* moral language be like? And why did Mackie himself not use such a language in his further discussions of ethical topics? Again, if morality is a thing of our creation, did we also choose to fall into the error that moral language contains?[20] According to Blackburn, these difficulties are avoided by his own

20   S. Blackburn, 'Errors and the Phenomenology of Value' in T. Honderich, ed., *Morality and Objectivity* (Routledge 1985), 1–3.

'projectivist' theory. Values, he suggests, 'are projections of our own sentiments (emotions, reactions, attitudes, commendations)' on to the world (op. cit. 180); and this need not involve any error. We are to 'regard ourselves as having *constructed* a notion of moral truth [and] if we have done so, then we can happily say that moral judgements are true or false, only not think that we have sold out to realism when we do so' (196). His aim is to show that we have 'the right to treat [moral] commitments *as if* they had truth-conditions' – as if moral statements could really be true or false (224).

But the 'as if' of projectivism is no less paradoxical than Mackie's error theory. If we know that moral statements do not really have truth-conditions, why should we pretend that they have? And what can it mean to speak of our notion of truth as having been 'constructed' by us? The difficulties are the same whether we embrace an error theory or a non-error theory, and they are reflected in the obscurity of the metaphors used: 'constructing', 'inventing', 'projecting' and the rest. (Blackburn explains the last as being 'what Hume referred to when he talks of "gilding and staining all natural objects with the colours borrowed from internal sentiment", or of the mind "spreading itself on the world"' (171). But this merely reminds us that Hume's philosophy is infected with similar obscurities.)

Given the assumption that language – in this case moral language – needs justification by reference to a corresponding reality, the philosopher is put in a difficult position. He must, it seems, either postulate a realm of queer entities ('values') or resort to the obscure and paradoxical notions of 'projecting', 'inventing' and the error theory. But the assumption that moral language, or any other, needs justification in this way, is false. Questions of justification are in order when applied to statements made *in* the language, but not to language itself. And the question 'How can moral statements have truth-values?' is not to be answered by reference to ontology, but by considering how 'true' and 'false' are actually used in moral discourse. It is, in short, a conceptual, linguistic question of the kind on which Mackie and others have tried to turn their backs.

9 Language remade

Ancient cities and orderly towns

> Our language can be seen as an ancient city: a maze of little streets and squares, of old and new houses with additions from various periods.
>
> (Wittgenstein[1])

> Ancient cities which have gradually grown from mere villages into large towns are usually ill-proportioned, compared with those orderly towns which planners lay out as they fancy on level ground …. You would say it is chance, rather than the will of men using reason, that placed them so.
>
> (Descartes[2])

As we have seen, philosophers have objected to the criterion of 'what we say' for various reasons. It has been argued that a method which confines itself to remarks about language is not dealing with the realities behind language. Another objection (to be discussed in Chapters 11–13) has been that, in the modern world especially, empirical science cannot be set aside in the treatment of philosophical problems. A third objection concerns the *ordinariness* of ordinary language. This point was expressed by Russell when he complained about those who 'are persuaded that common speech is good enough, not only for daily life, but also for philosophy'; whereas he believed it to be 'full of vagueness and inaccuracy'.[3] It might be thought, as far as the last objection is concerned, that what is needed is a *better* language – one that would avoid the deficiencies of common speech. This improvement might be conceived in more than one way: a systematic replacement of ordinary language by a better one; or the redefinition of

1 *Philosophical Investigations* (Blackwell 1958), 18.
2 *Philosophical Writings of Descartes*, transl. J. Cottingham (CUP 1985), I/116.
3 Bertrand Russell, *My Philosophical Development* (Unwin 1959), 178; hereafter 'MPD'.

particular words to remove their 'vagueness'. These alternatives will be considered in turn.

A 'logically perfect' language

In a letter dated 1629, Descartes expressed an ancient aspiration of Rationalism: that all human thought might be reduced to a mathematical form, so that it would all 'be arranged in an order like the natural order of the numbers'. If the secret of such a system could be discovered, the benefits would be immense. Learning it would be as easy as naming 'every one of the infinite series of numbers' and this would make it suitable to be 'understood by the whole human race'. But the 'greatest advantage of such a language' would be

> the assistance it would give to men's judgement, representing matters so clearly that it would be almost impossible to go wrong ... it would make peasants better judges of the truth about the world than philosophers are now.[4]

The key to constructing such a language lay in the reduction of thoughts to their simple elements; and if only 'someone were to explain correctly what are the simple ideas ... out of which all human thoughts are compounded', then the envisaged language might become a reality. But though he thought it 'possible to invent such a language', he did not 'hope ever to see [it] in use'. For that to happen, 'the order of nature would have to change ... and that is too much to suggest outside of fairyland'.

Russell, three centuries later, envisaged a 'logically perfect language', which would be based on 'simple objects' and thereby avoid the vagueness of ordinary language. In the logically perfect language there would be

> one word and no more for every simple object, and everything that is not simple will be expressed by a combination of words .... A language of that sort will be completely analytic, and will show at a glance the logical structure of the facts asserted or denied.[5]

---

4 Descartes, *Philosophical Letters*, transl. A. Kenny (OUP 1970), 5–6. Similar views were expressed by Leibniz among others.
5 *Russell's Logical Atomism*, ed. D. Pears (Fontana 1972), 52–3, cf. 158–9.

If language 'had been invented by scientifically trained observers for purposes of philosophy and logic', then this is how it would have been.[6] 'Actual languages', by contrast, 'are not logically perfect in this sense, and they cannot possibly be, if they are to serve the purposes of daily life'. On the other hand, 'a logically perfect language, if it could be constructed, would not only be intolerably prolix, but, as regards its vocabulary, would be very largely private to one speaker' (op. cit. 193).

A difficulty about these proposals is that they were not to be regarded as practical possibilities. Russell described his in counter-factual terms, while Descartes spoke of his as belonging to 'fairyland'. Suppose, however, that some such language were invented. How would it work, say, in the treatment of problems of philosophy? Let us take Russell's *Problems of Philosophy* as an example. Here we find discussions of empirical and a priori knowledge, sense-data and physical objects, the problem of induction, mind and matter, space and time, universals and truth. Would the envisaged 'logically perfect language' have been better for the discussion of these problems than the ordinary English used by Russell in his book? Suppose it had been shown that universals exist as 'simple objects'. Then this would be reflected in the hypothesized perfect language by the inclusion of 'one word and no more' for each universal; and perhaps this would be a perspicuous way of representing the truth about universals, once it had been established. But the work of *establishing* that truth must have been done prior to that. And similar points can be made about the various other problems of philosophy discussed by Russell in that book and elsewhere.

There is a similar difficulty about the assumptions *underlying* Russell's and Descartes' proposals. Descartes assumed that human thoughts, and perhaps the corresponding reality, were such as to lend themselves to numerical ordering; while Russell took for granted (a) that the world contains 'simple objects' in the required sense, and (b) that the idea of a 'private' language makes sense. But all of these assumptions and claims are, to say the least, questionable; and the arguments in their favour, such as they are, would have to be conducted in the *existing* language. The same is true of Russell's claim that we are in danger of making fallacious 'inferences from the nature of language to the nature of the world' – 'fallacious, because they depend upon the logical defects of language'; whereas a logical perfect language would

---

6   *The Analysis of Mind* (Allen & Unwin 1921), 193.

prevent such errors.[7] This claim, again, is made in the existing language, and it is hard to see how it could be otherwise.

'Logic's ruler': Frege on the defects of language

Russell's views about the defects of ordinary language were inspired by the work of Frege, and it is to Frege that we must turn for the most important contributions in this area. According to Frege, the logician's task was 'to break the power of the word over the human mind, uncovering illusions' due to the nature of existing languages. What was needed was not 'to investigate language', for 'languages are not made to match logic's ruler'.[8] 'Logic should be the judge of languages'; and he invented a new system, the *Begriffsschrift* or 'conceptual notation', which was meant to conform better to this criterion than existing languages. Frege's system has been widely adopted, with modifications, as a standard way of displaying logical relations and I do not wish to question its originality or importance. My concern is with his underlying conception of logic versus ordinary language.

In the preface to the *Begriffsschrift*, Frege compared the relation between it and ordinary language with that between the microscope and the eye. In the circumstances of ordinary life, he acknowledged, the eye has 'a great superiority over the microscope', but 'as soon as scientific purposes place great demands on sharpness of resolution, the eye turns out to be inadequate. The microscope, on the other hand, is perfectly suited for just such purposes'.[9] In a slightly later explanation he spoke of 'a certain softness and instability' of ordinary language, which has both advantages and disadvantages. This time he compared the usefulness of ordinary language with that of the hand, and went on to point out that there is also a place for 'artificial hands' in the form of 'tools for particular purposes', which enable us to 'work with more accuracy than the hand can provide'. Ordinary language, he claimed, 'is inadequate in a similar way. We need a system of symbols from which every ambiguity is banned, which has a strict logical form ...' (CN 86).

---

7   *Logic and Knowledge*, ed. R.C. Marsh (Allen & Unwin 1956), 338.
8   G. Frege, *Philosophical and Mathematical Correspondence* (Blackwell 1980), 67–8; hereafter 'PMC'.
9   G. Frege, transl. T.W. Bynum, *Conceptual Notation and Related Articles* (OUP 1972), 104–5; hereafter 'CN'.

These are attractive and plausible comparisons, but they are not as straightforward as they may seem. With the microscope we are introduced to a new world which would otherwise be hidden from us (and was hidden until the invention of this instrument). But logic cannot be hidden from us in this way.[10] The fact that 'q' follows from the combination of 'If p, then q' with 'p' is a not a matter of discovery: it is one that is recognized, and always has been recognized, in everyday reasoning. This does not mean, of course, that the symbolic way of representing it has always been there; but it does mean that when this representation is put before us, we can *recognize* it as a correct way of displaying that logical relation. Again, it is true that logic may be 'hidden' in the sense that people may be unable to follow a complicated proof, or may arrive at wrong answers owing to fallacious reasoning. But here again, the remedy must be found, if it is found at all, by appealing to logical truths that *are* recognized by the people concerned; and the same will be true of logical truths formulated in Frege's notation. A logical notation must be *recognizable* as a representation of what we understand by 'logic'.

The analogy of the hand and the tool may seem more successful, for a new notation can indeed be described as a *useful tool* for working out logical puzzles, and ordinary language may be deficient in this respect. (Similarly, we might say that the arabic system of numerals is a 'better tool' than others for working out problems of arithmetic.) However, Frege's aim was not merely to provide a useful tool in this sense. If this had been his aim, it would not have posed a challenge to ordinary language philosophy. A tool can be described as an *extension* of the hand; but what Frege proposed was to correct, and not merely to extend, the existing language. According to him, 'a great part of the work of a philosopher consists – or at least ought to consist – in a struggle against language'.[11]

Frege's wording here is close to the later Wittgenstein's description of philosophy as 'a struggle against the bewitchment of our understanding' by language, and his talk of language 'setting traps for us', as discussed in Chapter 3. But their views about how to conduct

---

10   A similar point was made by Wittgenstein about philosophy itself: 'Philosophy simply puts everything before us ... What is hidden is of no interest to us.' (PI 126). Here he rejected both the assimilation of philosophy to empirical science and his own earlier view that language 'disguises thought' and that we use it 'without having any idea how each word has meaning or what its meaning is' (*Tractatus* 4.002).

11   G. Frege, *Posthumous Writings* (Blackwell 1979), 270; hereafter 'PW'.

the struggle were very different. According to Frege, the defects of language could be remedied by inventing a more adequate language or notation, but Wittgenstein regarded this as a futile undertaking. The questions that trouble us in philosophy, he maintained, must be discussed in the existing language; they cannot be transferred to an artificial, supposedly more adequate one.[12] The aspiration of 'logical perfection', as conceived both by Frege and himself in his earlier work, was itself one of the pitfalls to be avoided. Another difference between the two thinkers is that whereas the illusions discussed by Wittgenstein are real and important, this is not so in the case of Frege, as I hope to show.

'A distinction between *subject* and *predicate*', declared Frege in the opening sections of the *Begriffsschrift*, 'does *not occur* in my way of representing a judgment'. Such a distinction exists in ordinary language, but here the logician should 'see his task as that of freeing us from the fetters of language' (PW 143). The subject-predicate language is misleading, he argued, because two sentences which differ markedly in appearance may have the very same 'conceptual content', giving rise to the same inferences (CN 113). This is so, for example, in the case of 'The Greeks defeated the Persians' and 'The Persians were defeated by the Greeks'. One might be inclined to say that while the first sentence is *about the Greeks*, the second is *about the Persians*, but really there is nothing of substance to choose between them: the same logical consequences would follow from both. In Frege's new notation there is to be 'nothing that corresponds' to the superficial difference between such sentences:

> the only thing [to be] considered in a judgement is that which influences its *possible consequences*. Everything necessary for a correct inference is fully expressed . . .; *nothing is left to guessing*. (CN 113)

Now it is true that the two sentences in the example mean virtually the same, and it may also be true that the notation proposed by Frege, in which 'a distinction of subject and predicate finds no place' will be more convenient for certain purposes. What is not true, however, is that

---

12 This also applies to philosophizing about language itself. 'When I talk about language (words, sentences, etc.), I must speak the language of everyday. Is this language somehow too coarse ... for what [I] want to say? *Then how is another to be constructed?*' (PI 120).

the existence of this distinction in ordinary language is an impediment to logical understanding, or that it gives scope for 'guessing'. Given those two sentences, no one would suppose that one would, in using them, be making two different claims, from which different consequences might follow. This equivalence of meaning and logical consequences belongs to an *ordinary* understanding of the two sentences.

It is just because this is so that Frege can count on the reader's assent to what he says about the equivalence of these sentences. If the point were *not* clear – if readers could not see that the sentences are equivalent – then they would not accept what Frege says, and this might lead them to reject *Frege's notation*, in which the sentences are presented as equivalent, as defective. Thus the notation, so far from being corrective of ordinary language, would be dependent on the latter for its validation. It would be acceptable if it accorded with the logic of ordinary language, but not if it contravened it.

The same is true of other examples used by Frege. Some of these concern ambiguity, which he regarded as a serious defect of the existing language (CN 84). The expression 'the horse', he points out, may or may not denote a 'single creature': it would do so in 'The horse is in the meadow' but not in 'The horse is a herbivorous animal'. But this distinction, again, is clear in ordinary language, and no one who understands English would be left guessing whether these sentences are about an individual or a species. In another example, he draws attention to the difference between 'lifeboat' and 'deathbed' as regards 'the logical relations of their constituents' – a difference which, he says, is 'left to guesswork' in ordinary language (PW 13). But, as has been pointed out, 'a competent speaker of English does not have to *guess* that "lifeboat" means "a boat for saving lives" and that "deathbed" does not mean "a bed for saving deaths"'.[13]

Even so, it may be that some distinctions observed in ordinary language could be displayed in more perspicuous ways in Frege's notation. But what shall we say when the two systems are in conflict? An example of this kind is Frege's claim that certain kinds of sentences are really, contrary to appearances, about *concepts*.[14] Thus, although 'it is true that at first sight the proposition "All whales are mammals"

---

13   G.P. Baker and P.M.S. Hacker, *Frege: Logical Excavations* (Blackwell 1984), 70.

14   The role of this claim in Frege's overall philosophy, with its main aim of reducing arithmetic to logic, will not be expounded here. For two recent studies, see A. Kenny, *Frege* (Penguin 1995) and M. Beaney, *Frege: Making Sense* (Duckworth 1996).

seems to be not about concepts but about animals', this is not really so (FA §47). His reason is that 'if we ask which animal we are speaking of, we are unable to point to any one in particular'. Now it is true, but again undisputed and obvious, that 'all whales' does not name a particular whale or group of whales, but this does not prove that the statement is about concepts and not about whales.

There is, indeed, something to be said for the view that 'All whales are mammals' is about concepts, though not for the reason given by Frege. The relevant reason is that the statement could be regarded as true by definition, so that in making it one would be making a conceptual point. The property of being a mammal is, we may say, *analytic* to the concept of whales. This still does not prove that the statement is about the concept and *not* about whales; but in any case, Frege's claim and reasoning were not confined to analytic truths. (They would apply equally to, say, 'All whales live on plankton'.)[15]

If Frege's claims are in conflict with the criterion of ordinary language, why should we accept them? Is there some other, more fundamental criterion to which we should defer? This brings us to an important aspect of Frege's philosophy, which I have not yet discussed. According to him, it is in 'pure thought' and not in language that 'logic's ruler' is located, so that, once we penetrate beyond the level of language, 'thinking will emerge as that which has priority' (PW 270). His 'conceptual notation' (*Begriffschrift*) was subtitled 'A formalized language of pure thought ...' (CN 101).[16]

Ordinary language, according to Frege, is a necessary but imperfect 'vehicle for the expression of thoughts', which must be treated with caution, for there is a 'deep gulf that separates the level of language from that of thought' (PW 259). Language 'is a human creation', subject to a variety of influences and variations; it was 'not constructed from a logical blueprint' (PW 269). We have to resort to language to communicate with one another, but 'we must always rely on other people's understanding' of what we are trying to say in this imperfect medium. In one of his articles he explained that what he had done was 'not trying to give a definition, but only hints'. (Here he thought that 'a feeling for the German language' might help (PW 94).)

---

15   In another passage he claimed that to say 'The King's carriage is drawn by four horses' would be to 'assign the number four to the concept "horse that draws the King's carriage" ' (FA §59).

16   This aspect of Frege's thought, and its historical background, are well brought out by Baker and Hacker, op. cit. 67ff.

He also recognized, however, that the task of reforming the existing language must be carried out *in* that language. 'One might think that language would first have to be freed from all logical imperfections before it was employed' in the investigation of logic; 'but of course [this work] can itself be done only by using this tool' (PW 266). The entanglement with language was, he thought, a necessary part of the human condition. 'For us men the connection of a thought with "some sentence or other" is a necessity' (PW 269); but there might 'exist beings that can grasp the same thought as we do without needing to clothe it in a form that can be perceived by the senses' (PW 269).

But in trying to resort to a 'level of thought' as distinct from language, we encounter difficulties of the kind discussed in the last chapter with regard to Berkeley. The latter, as we saw (page 134), advised readers to 'draw the curtain of words' so as to 'behold the fairest tree of knowledge, whose fruit is excellent . . .'. He resolved, for his part, to 'confine [his] thoughts to [his] own ideas', avoiding 'all that dress and encumbrance of words, which so much contribute to blind the judgement'. But, as I have argued, if thought were really separate from words in this way, then the communication and discussion of thoughts would be impossible. Similarly, if it were supposed that Frege's claims could be saved by retreating from language to a realm of 'pure thought', what would become of the possibility of critical evaluation? Suppose there were a dispute about the logical equivalence between 'A defeated B' and 'B was defeated by A', with Smith pointing out that, so far as logical consequences are concerned, they are treated as equivalent in ordinary language. Could Jones reply that they might, nevertheless, be non-equivalent at the level of thought? What would this mean?

Frege's aim, as we have seen, was to create 'a formalized language of pure thought'. 'If language were logically more perfect', he speculated in another passage, then 'we might read [logic] off from the language' (PW 252); but, language being imperfect, it was up to the logician to produce 'a more perfect instrument'. But here we face another problem. How are we to tell whether a given language is more perfect or less perfect, if the standard of perfection is at the language-transcendent level of 'pure thought'? Suppose one person affirmed, and another denied, that Frege's system comes close to being logically perfect. How could the question be resolved or even discussed?

My comparison of Frege with Berkeley may seem surprising and even perverse, given the former's insistence on the *objectivity* of thoughts. 'Thought' and 'thinking', according to Frege, are not to be understood in the empiricists' sense of a train of images, ideas and the like, which would be private to the thinker. To those who found that his 'conceptual notation does not correctly represent mental processes', he would reply that 'this was not its purpose at all'. The thoughts that the notation was meant to represent 'are not mental entities, and thinking is not an inner generation of such entities but a grasping of thoughts which are already present objectively' (PMC 67). A thought, unlike an idea, 'does not belong specially to the person who thinks it'; otherwise, he argued, there could be no contradiction between one person's thought and another's; 'each thought would be enclosed in its own private world' and discussion would be impossible (PW 133). But this is not so: 'a thought is something impersonal' (PW 133), so that *the same* thought can be discussed by different individuals and expressed in different languages (PW 6).

But, we must ask, how are such thoughts to be identified if not through their expression in language? Yet according to Frege, as we have seen, language is but an imperfect vehicle of thought. It has the advantage of being 'perceptible' – we can hear or read what others say – but thought itself is not perceptible. And while we 'may hope that we can use [language] as a bridge from the perceptible to the imperceptible', we must not suppose that the timeless truths which exist at the level of thought can be properly mirrored in the contingent and shifting materials of language (cf. PW 259).

Frege's position is, if anything, more difficult than Berkeley's. If I follow Berkeley's advice, then I shall know at least where to look for the 'fair tree of knowledge': it is to be found among my ideas and images. But Berkeley's advice would be repudiated by Frege, who warns us repeatedly against the error of confusing logical with psychological investigation. In this he was right; but what, according to him, is the alternative? Where is logic's ruler to be found? If the psychological and linguistic avenues are both rejected, what remains?

Regimented notation as 'a source of insight'

Leaving aside attempts to penetrate to the level of pure thought, let us consider another kind of advantage that is often claimed for such notations as Frege's: that of enabling us to present logical relations more perspicuously than can be done in ordinary language. The defect of language, in this case, is not that it fails to match logic's ruler, but that it can be inconvenient and cumbersome for some logical purposes.

That a symbolic notation can have this advantage can hardly be questioned; but such advantages can be exaggerated and misunderstood. Let us take an example from Russell. According to him, existential statements such as 'Men exist' and 'There are people in Timbuctoo' do not, as we might perhaps suppose, 'say anything about the actual individual[s] but only about the class [of men, or people in Timbuctoo]'.[17] He thought this could be made clearer by using such formulations as 'There is an x such that x is a man' and '(x is a man) is possible'. According to Russell, 'it is exceedingly difficult to make this point clear as long as one adheres to ordinary language .... The only way you can really state it correctly is by inventing a new language *ad hoc*'.

Russell's claim about what such statements are really about is open to question, but let us consider whether he is right in saying that his point could not be made in ordinary language but only by means of a new, invented language. 'There is an x such that x is a man' – or in symbolic form, '(Ex) (mx)': do these formulations really present Russell's claim more clearly than could be done in ordinary language (using the word 'class', etc.)? This is hardly plausible. But if Russell really could not 'state the point correctly' in ordinary language, then how could we understand it? Is the statement in the new language translatable into the old? If it is, then the point *can* be stated in the old. If not, then we could not tell what the point is.

This is not to deny that a new notation may be useful in getting one to see a point that *can* be made in ordinary language, though not as perspicuously as in the new notation. In this way a 'regimented notation', as Quine has put it, may be 'a source of syntactical insights'. He draws attention to insights that might be gained, for example, by the use of parentheses to distinguish between '(p and q) or r' and 'p and (q or r)'. Such insights, he points out, could 'perfectly well have been vouchsafed us even if we had had no acquaintance with the method of parentheses; but they are likelier insights for the parenthesis-minded'.[18]

So far, we may understand Quine to be drawing attention, properly enough, to the usefulness of such notations, which may vary with different people. But he goes further when he imputes to ordinary language defects that are to be *rectified* by a 'regimented notation', so that 'chaos reduces to order' (op. cit. 76). One of his examples is the sentence 'I do not know every poem'. Would this mean that I don't know any of the poems, or that I don't know all of them? According to

---

17 *Logic and Knowledge*, op. cit., 233–4.
18 W.V. Quine, 'Logic as a Source of Syntactical Insights' in D. Davidson and G. Harman eds., *The Logic of Grammar* (Dickenson 1975), 75–6.

Quine, the distinction is 'obscure in ordinary English', but it is 'brought into sharp relief by modern logical notation' with the use of parentheses (76). In another passage he considers the sentence 'I saw a man and you saw him', pointing out that this is 'by no means equivalent to "I saw a man and you saw a man"'. Here again he concedes that the point is 'clear enough, once enunciated, without appeal to subtleties of mathematical logic'; but he thinks the latter 'is likeliest to suggest the point' (77).

But this is a curious account of what is clear and what is obscure. How can a normal speaker of English fail to see that 'I don't know every poem' means 'I don't know all the poems' and not 'I don't know any of the poems'? If the second were meant, then the second would be stated. The distinction is clear and obvious, is easily expressed in ordinary English and could not possibly be made clearer by mathematical logic or other artificial devices. Similarly, if one could not see the difference between 'I saw a man and you saw him' and 'I saw a man and you saw a man', then one's knowledge of English must be deficient, so that what would be needed would be a lesson in English and not a training in mathematical logic.

The same is true of a kind of example that is often cited to bring out the usefulness of Frege's system: that of 'multiple generality'. An example given by Dummett is 'Everybody envies somebody'.[19] Now the first thing that may strike one about this is that such statements are far from usual; and the same is true of various examples that have been put forward with the same purpose. The fact that such examples are uncommon in actual discourse must diminish, even if it does not negate, their effectiveness in demonstrating the advantages of an artificial notation.

It is true, however, that the sentence 'Everybody envies somebody' might actually be used, say, in a discussion of human psychology – where, perhaps, the question has been raised whether some human failings are universal. But would the occurrence of multiple generality (the combination of 'every' with 'some') in that sentence give rise to difficulties of understanding in such a discussion? It is said by supporters of Frege that the word 'somebody' in such sentences is ambiguous, so that the sentence could mean either 'Everybody envies somebody or other' or 'There is one person who is envied by everybody'. But the second interpretation is no more plausible than those offered by Quine in his examples. However, even if the second

19   Michael Dummett, *Frege: Philosophy of Language* (Duckworth 1981), 9–12.

interpretation could be made plausible, it would still need to be shown that the ambiguity cannot be explained, or can be explained only with great difficulty, in ordinary language. Misunderstandings due to ambiguity do, of course, occur in ordinary language, a common case being that of ambiguous words. But such misunderstandings can be, and usually are, cleared up by explaining, in the existing language, what was meant. And there is no reason to suppose that this could not be done in the cases just discussed.

A similar point may be made about the distinction between existential sentences and others, such as 'Men exist' versus 'Men are rational'. It is sometimes pointed out that such sentences have the same grammatical form and this has been regarded as a source of confusion in philosophical thinking. The use of logical notation is supposed to prevent such confusion because it removes the appearance of similarity. In such a notation 'men exist' might be written

(Ex) (mx),

while 'men are rational' would be written

(x) (mx⊃rx).

But the distinction between the two kinds of sentences was perceived long before the invention of this way of displaying it. Kant, indeed, regarded it as obvious that 'being' is 'not a real predicate'.[20] But even if he were wrong about regarding the distinction as obvious, the work of clarifying it must be prior to the introduction of logical notation; the latter would merely reflect an understanding that had been arrived at already.[21] It is not even true that the form 'men exist' is the usual one for asserting existence in ordinary English. The usual form is that beginning with 'There is ...' or 'There are ...', as when we say that there are such creatures as yetis or that there was such a person as King Arthur. These (ordinary) ways of asserting existence have not the least resemblance to sentences such as 'Men are rational'.

It is only when we turn to puzzle sentences such as appear in logic textbooks that artificial notations come into their own. An example

20   I. Kant, *Critique of Pure Reason* (Macmillan 1964), A 598.
21   Cf. Irving Copi, 'Language Analysis', in Richard Rorty, ed., *The Linguistic Turn* (University of Chicago 1967), 129–31.

introduced by Quine is 'Some whom none dislike do not appreciate themselves' (op. cit. 78). Now it is true that an artificial notation may be useful in sorting out the meaning of such a sentence; but Quine's description of that sentence as 'an ordinary verbal example' must make us wonder what he means by 'ordinary'.

As I said, it would be wrong, and indeed foolish, to deny that formal devices can ever be useful in the presentation of claims and arguments, though the extent to which this is so will vary with different people. But there is no justification for Quine's talk about the 'chaos' of ordinary language and the resort to an artificial notation to produce 'order'. His treatment of familiar distinctions as obscure is a pretence and he has not shown that ordinary language is inadequate for philosophical purposes or in need of augmentation by artificial systems.

Redefining our words: what we mean and what we ought to mean

So far I have considered attempts to replace ordinary language by artificial systems supposedly more suitable for scientific purposes. But such attempts have also been made on particular words, where 'strict definitions' have been offered in place of the 'vagueness' of ordinary language. We saw in Chapters 6 and 7 how such motives have influenced discussions of the concept of knowledge, where, to use Moore's words again, the quest for 'unity' and 'system' has been pursued 'at the expense of truth'.

One of the pitfalls of this approach is that the distinction between redefinitions and substantive claims may be left unclear. Let us consider a claim made by Frege about 'definition' and 'concept' themselves. 'A definition of a concept', wrote Frege, 'must be complete; it must unambiguously determine, as regards any object, whether or not it falls under the concept'; and 'a concept that is not sharply defined' is not really a concept.[22] It would seem to follow that concepts are only rarely to be found in ordinary language. But was Frege using 'concept' and 'definition' with their ordinary meanings? Perhaps what he intended was to introduce artificial definitions for these words, for the purpose of scientific discussion. But if this were so, should the distinction not have been made clear?

---

22 *Philosophical Writings of Gottlob Frege*, ed. P. Geach and M. Black (Blackwell 1980), 139.

In any case, Frege could not avoid *using* the ordinary concepts (of concept, definition and others) in expounding his ideas. Let us use his analogy of the eye and the microscope to illustrate this point. Reading Frege's account of that analogy, one might have the impression that it is about two instruments, one provided by nature and the other by human ingenuity, each being suitable for a different purpose – rather as the miscroscope and the telescope are suitable for different purposes. But this would be to overlook the fact that the eye is needed in all cases. It is not as if we could, so to speak, put away our eyes when using the microscope. The latter is an extension of the eye (of our visual powers) and not a replacement for it. Similarly, the use of technical language in logic and philosophy does not mean that ordinary language can be put away.

Another example in which the status of a definition is left unclear is that of Mill's definition of 'happiness': 'By happiness is intended pleasure, and the absence of pain'.[23] Is Mill claiming that this is what is ordinarily meant by 'happiness'? Or is he *proposing* to use it with this meaning? Either course is likely to provoke objections, but perhaps the ambiguity of Mill's statement may help to make it more palatable to the reader.

A further kind of vacillation between claim and redefinition is to be found in the work of Nelson Goodman. In his *Languages of Art*, Goodman claimed that a performance of a work such as Beethoven's Fifth would not really be a performance of that work if any part of it were played wrongly: a single wrong note would be enough to prevent it from being a 'genuine instance' of the work. Most readers found this unacceptable and indeed astonishing. But in a later work Goodman protested that he had been misunderstood: his claim, he said, had not been about 'everyday speech', but about 'the exigencies of technical discourse'.[24] He conceded that these exigencies 'need not govern our everyday speech'.

> I am no more recommending that in ordinary discourse we refuse to say that a pianist who misses a note has performed a Chopin polonaise, than that we refuse to call a whale a fish, the earth spherical, or a grayish pink human white.

These comparisons are meant, presumably, to illustrate how

---

23 J.S. Mill, *Utilitarianism* (Collins 1979), 257.
24 N. Goodman, *Problems and Projects* (Bobbs 1972), 135.

something may not really be an X, in spite of the fact that we call it an X in ordinary speech. But are those examples really comparable with the case at issue? If Goodman had written that the whale is not really a fish, that the earth is not really spherical, or that the skin of white people is not white but grayish pink, no one would have batted an eyelid. But a great many eyelids were batted when readers came upon his claim about musical performances. And it is not hard to see where the difference lies. There are good reasons for denying that the whale is a fish, the earth spherical and human skin white. They are based, respectively, on biology, measurement and comparisons of colour. But there is no such reason to deny that a performance of Beethoven's Fifth with one note missed is really a performance of Beethoven's Fifth.

In further discussion, Goodman used the example of a triangle. 'The performance with a wrong note is not strictly a performance of the work in question, any more than ... a diagram on the blackboard is strictly a triangle.' But this comparison is again inappropriate. There *is* a technical discourse, a well-established and fruitful way of talking about triangles, in which the figure on the board would not count as strictly a triangle; and it would be understood that this is being invoked when someone denies that the figure is really a triangle. (Otherwise the denial would not be acceptable.) But there is no such established technical discourse in the case of the musical performance, and the advantage of Goodman's redefinition remains unexplained.

The idea that ordinary language is inadequate for philosophical purposes is also to be found in the work of Mill, who spoke of the 'loose mode of classing and denominating objects', which 'has rendered the vocabulary of mental and moral philosophy unfit for the purposes of accurate thinking'. 'The problem for the philosopher', he said, is 'how best to alleviate [the] imperfections' of the language we have. He drew attention to a feature that came later to be known as 'family resemblance'. 'Names creep on', he wrote,

> from subject to subject, until ... the word comes to denote a number of things not only independently of any common attribute, but which have actually no attribute in common; or none but what is shared by other things to which the name is capriciously refused.

Quoting Alexander Bain, he pointed out that the word 'stone' is 'applied to mineral and rocky materials, to the kernels of fruit, to the accumulations in the gall-bladder ...; while it is refused to polished minerals [called gems]...'. According to Mill, this 'creeping on' of words is a 'perversion of ... language from its purpose', rendering it 'unfit for the purposes of accurate thinking'.[25]

But how would Mill restore language to its purpose of 'accurate thinking'? An example occurs in his discussion of cause and effect. Here he describes how, ordinarily, 'the fact which is dignified with the name of cause' is selected from the whole 'set of antecedents which determined' the event in question. The selection is made, according to Mill, in a 'capricious manner ...', according to the purpose of our immediate discourse'; whereas 'the real Cause is the whole of these antecedents; and we have, philosophically speaking, no right to give the name cause to one of them exclusively of the others' (op. cit. 214–15).

But, we may ask, how can this claim promote accurate thinking? If our question is (say) 'What is a cause?', how can it help the enquiry if we begin by redefining the word 'cause'? If we do so, and exclude the ordinary 'cause' as unfit for philosophical thinking, then we leave the original question untouched.

A rather different, more sensitive attitude to redefinition is to be found in Ayer's essay 'On the Analysis of Moral Judgements'. Like Mackie (as discussed in Chapter 8), Ayer was concerned about whether there are moral facts. If there are, he wrote, they must be 'a queer sort of fact'. But Ayer was not prepared to dismiss the appeal to ordinary language, as Mackie was. Though he 'still wished to hold' the view he had taken in his youthful *Language, Truth and Logic*, he now admitted that this view was 'in an obvious sense incorrect'.

> For, as the English language is currently used – and what else, it may be asked, is here in question? – it is by no means improper to refer to ethical utterances as statements; when someone characterizes an action by the use of an ethical predicate, it is quite good usage to say that he is thereby describing it; when someone wishes to assent to an ethical verdict, it is perfectly legitimate for him to say that it is true, or that it is a fact ...

---

25   J.S. Mill, *A System of Logic* (Longman 1961), 24. The comparison with Wittgenstein's account of family resemblance concepts is striking, and so is the difference between the two thinkers regarding the significance of such examples. For Mill they illustrate the inadequacy of ordinary language for philosophical purposes; for Wittgenstein, the inadequacy of philosophical theories to explain language. For further discussion, see O. Hanfling, *Wittgenstein's Later Philosophy* (Macmillan 1989), ch. 4.

Nevertheless, he continued, 'when one considers how these ethical statements are actually used, it may be found that they function so very differently from other types of statements that it is advisable to put them into a separate category altogether ...'. And yet, after all, 'if someone still wishes to say that [they] are statements of fact, only it is a queer sort of fact, he is welcome to do so'.[26]

This passage brings out the irrational cravings that may be at work in a philosopher's deliberations. He still 'wishes' to hold the view he had earlier put forward, even though it is 'in an obvious sense incorrect'. He is determined to give due importance to the criterion of 'what we say' ('What else, it may be asked, is here in question?') and will not dismiss this in favour of some language-transcendent 'factual analysis', as Mackie did. Hence he will not claim that it is *wrong* to speak of moral facts, but only that if we do so we should notice that they are different from other kinds of facts – and therefore 'queer'.

Ayer's position is, as I said, more sensitive to the importance of ordinary language than that of other writers; but should we agree with him that moral facts are queer? They may seem so if we take *empirical* facts as the standard of normality; and this is something we might be inclined to do if we look at moral facts through Logical Positivist spectacles. But for people with normal vision they are not queer.[27]

As in his debate with Austin (discussed in Chapter 2), Ayer tried to pass the question off as 'purely verbal':

> it is simply a question of how widely or loosely we want to use the word 'fact'. My own view is that it is preferable so to use it as to exclude ethical judgements, but it must not be inferred from this that I am treating them with disrespect. The only relevant consideration is that of clarity. (233)

But, we may wonder, how would Ayer's preference lead to greater clarity? Suppose Ayer heard me say: 'It's true [or a fact] that what I did was wrong; I didn't know it then but I do now.' Could Ayer advise me

---

26 A.J. Ayer, *Philosophical Essays* (Macmillan 1965), 231–2.
27 That Ayer is handicapped by such spectacles is evident from his ensuing argument. He asks us to imagine that someone had committed a murder and to consider the facts of such a case. But by 'the facts' he means *empirical* facts – 'where and when and how the killing was effected', etc. – such as 'are verified or confuted, as the case may be, by observation' (234). Now it is true that moral facts are not accommodated by this criterion, any more than by Mackie's requirements; but this is no reason for denying that they are facts or for regarding them as queer.

to abstain from such language so as to achieve greater clarity? Given a suitable situation, my statement would be perfectly clear. Again, suppose Ayer had done something wrong and I pointed this out to him, erroneously thinking he did not realize it was wrong. And suppose that Ayer wanted to correct my error. He could do so easily by replying 'I knew it was wrong'. Would he try to avoid this language? What for? 'I knew' would be a correct response in this situation and none could be clearer.

The redefinition of words so as to evade objections from ordinary language was a regular practice among philosophers of the Vienna Circle, sometimes with amusing results. The following 'Advice to the Reader' was placed by Carnap at the front of his monograph *The Unity of Science*:

> *Nonsense* (or *pseudo*-expression) is intended to carry none of its usual abusive connotation. Technical use = whatever cannot be verified in experience.[28]

If Carnap had read *Pickwick Papers*, he might have noticed that this wording is almost identical with that with which Mr Blotton was supposed to extricate himself from an embarrassing situation: he was to say that when he called Mr Pickwick a humbug, he had not meant the word with its usual connotations.

Carnap could hardly have claimed that his usage would promote 'accurate thinking'. The fact is that 'nonsense' *has* an abusive connotation, while 'not verifiable in experience' does not; hence the replacement of one expression for the other can only confuse an innocent reader. Even if he tries to heed Carnap's 'Advice', he will wonder why the substitution has been made.

This and similar redefinitions were the subject of an article by C.L. Stevenson, who tried to diagnose the motives behind them.[29] Stevenson compared the verificationists' treatment of 'meaning' to the claim, made by some nineteenth century critics, that Alexander Pope was not a poet. This, he said, followed from their definition of 'poet', but the definition was itself motivated by an unfavourable attitude to the writings of Pope and others. He diagnosed a similar motive in the verificationists' treatment of 'meaning'. It followed from their definition of this word that 'science alone will receive this

28   R. Carnap, *The Unity of Science*, transl. Max Black (Kegan Paul 1934), 30.
29   C.L. Stevenson, 'Persuasive Definitions', *Mind* 1938.

laudatory title [of being meaningful], and metaphysics the correspondingly derogatory one of "nonsense" '.

Now according to Stevenson, the aim of such definitions is persuasive. The nineteenth century critics, he wrote, were using 'poet' in a 'narrow sense', which

> had the function of stressing, in the reader's attention, certain features common to most poetry, but lacking in Pope's. Perhaps they meant to say this: 'We have long been blind to fundamental differences between Pope's work and that of a Shakespeare or Milton. It is because of this blindness alone that we have been content to give Pope a laudatory title. Let us note the difference, then, and deprive him of the title.'

The claim of the verificationists, he said, would 'easily bear the same interpretation':

> Perhaps they meant to say: 'We have long been blind to the fundamental differences between the use of sentences in science and their use in metaphysics. It is because of this blindness that we have been content to dignify metaphysics with such titles as "meaningful". Let us define meaning, then, in a way that will at once stress these fundamental differences, and deprive metaphysics of its title.'

It might be thought that the positions of Carnap and Ayer could be made to appear more reasonable by presenting them in this light. But how are we to understand the idea that we can, say, deprive Pope of the title of 'poet' by redefining the word 'poet'? If we were persuaded that Pope's work was lacking in qualities essential for poetry, then we would have reason to deprive him of this title. But a proposal to redefine the word 'poet' could not affect the question one way or the other. Similarly, a proposal to redefine the word 'meaning' cannot affect the question whether such and such statements are meaningful. Let us grant the assumption (unlikely though it is) that people had been unaware of the difference between scientific and metaphysical statements. Then the proper way to cure this 'blindness' would be to point out the difference; and nothing would be gained by stipulating new meanings for 'meaning', 'nonsense', etc. Such proposals could not affect the question whether metaphysical statements are really meaningless.

Truth versus 'convenience': the theory of descriptions

I have quoted a number of writers to illustrate the pitfalls of redefining words for philosophical purposes. (1) The philosopher who uses such words as 'concept', 'definition', 'cause', 'fact' and 'meaning' with new meanings turns his back on important questions about these matters. (2) The treatment of philosophy as a 'technical discourse', comparable with mathematics and science, is inappropriate and misleading. (3) In redefining familiar words, philosophers often leave the distinction between 'true' and 'stipulated' definitions unclear. Frege's definitions of 'definition' and 'concept', for example, are implausible as true definitions, and this suggests that he meant to stipulate new definitions. Yet this is not how the matter appears in his text. (4) Ayer's discussions, similarly, are marred by vacillation between substantial claims and 'merely verbal' recommendations to use words in new ways.

Such confusions are also to be found in Russell's attitude to the theory of descriptions. In his presentation of the theory, he made a claim about what one is really saying if one states, for example, that the present King of France is bald.

> When you state that the present King of France is bald you say 'There is a *c* such that *c* is now King of France and *c* is bald' and the denial is ... 'Either there is not a *c* such that *c* is now King of France, or, if there is such a *c*, then *c* is not bald.'[30]

In later life Russell published an overview of his life's work, and here he took the opportunity of replying to one of the principal critics of his theory. 'Mr Strawson', he wrote,

> admits that the sentence [about the King of France] is significant and not true, but not that it is false .... For my part, I find it more convenient to define the word 'false' so that every sentence is either true or false. This is a purely verbal question; and although I have no wish to claim the support of common usage, I do not think he can claim it either.[31]

It now appears that Russell's intention was not to give a true account of such statements, but merely one that, for his part, he 'finds more

---

30   B. Russell, *Logic and Knowledge*, op. cit., 251.

31   B. Russell, *My Philosophical Development*, op. cit., 179.

convenient'. He will, as a matter of personal convenience, redefine the word 'false' so that all statements can be arranged in two columns rather than three. But this is not how the matter was presented originally.

Was Russell aware that in disposing of the dispute in this way he was renouncing the objective of truth? Did he think that truth does not matter in philosophy? If so, his way of dealing with the dispute invites the same comment as that which Austin made on Ayer's claim that the issues between them were 'purely verbal' (see Chapter 2). On that view, said Austin, every dispute could be dismissed as 'purely verbal'.

> For if, when one person says whatever it may be, another person may simply 'prefer to say' something else, they will *always* be arguing only about words .... How could *anything* be a question of truth or falsehood, if anyone can always say whatever he likes?[32]

In philosophy, as in science, there is a place for such criteria as convenience, elegance and the like. A theory based on epicycles may be true to the facts of planetary motion, but if there is a simpler and equally true alternative, then it is to be preferred; and in philosophy, likewise, a simple and elegant account is preferable to a complicated and clumsy one, if there is a choice. But the overriding criterion must be that of truth; without this, such advantages as convenience and simplicity are pointless.

The theory of descriptions has been regarded as a prime example of what divides ordinary language philosophers from their opponents. Quine speaks in this connection of 'the steadfast laymanship' of 'philosophers ... influenced by Wittgenstein, [who] deplore ... departures from ordinary usage';[33] and Russell himself referred to 'a fundamental divergence between myself and many philosophers with whom Mr Strawson appears to be in general agreement' (MPD 178). He went on speak of the 'vagueness and inaccuracy of common speech', which made it unsuitable for philosophy. But Russell is not in a position to claim the advantage of accuracy for his theory. Accuracy is connected with truth: an inaccurate statement or theory is one that falls short of the truth. And Russell, as we saw, renounced the criterion of truth in favour of that of 'convenience'.

Yet, after all, what is the gain in convenience supposed to be? To describe the statement about the King of France as false is no more

---

32 J.L. Austin, *Philosophical Papers* (Clarendon 1961), 59–60.
33 W.V. Quine, *Word and Object* (MIT Press 1960), 261; hereafter 'WO'.

convenient than to describe it as neither true nor false. There is no inconvenience in saying 'neither true nor false', as there is in the representation of epicycles. According to Quine, the convenience of Russell's theory lies in showing us how to 'circumvent the problematic parts of ordinary usage'. The 'initial problems', he writes, are 'the inconvenience of truth-value gaps and the paradoxes of talking of what does not exist'. But in what way are these *initial* problems? The problem about truth-value gaps comes into being only *after* we try to foist the law of bivalence on the language we speak, trying to subject it to the straitjacket of truth-functional logic and similar artificial requirements.

The problem about 'what does not exist' is likewise artificial. According to Quine, the problem is created by our tendency to regard 'nothing', 'everything' and 'something' as proper names. But the idea of regarding 'nothing' as a proper name would be thought ridiculous by any ordinary speaker of English. The problem cited by Quine is one that may arise (as it did for Russell) after studying certain philosophers, but it is not there *initially*. Perhaps, after the problem has been introduced, it would be helpful to the 'parenthetically minded' to provide a notation with parentheses and other devices. But it cannot be helpful, at any stage, to make *false claims* about the truth-values of statements or to redefine the word 'false' or to fudge the distinction between truth and convenience.

There is room in philosophy for the use of technical terminology. It is convenient and justifiable to use 'type' and 'token' to mean a certain ontological status, if it is clear that these words are being used in a technical sense and no contentious questions are being begged in using them thus. The word 'perceive' is often used, in philosophy, to include all the senses and not only sight, and it would be foolish to object that this is contrary to ordinary usage. Writers who use the word in this way are not claiming that this is what 'perceive' really means or that new insights are expressed by using the word in this way; the advantage is merely that of using one word instead of several. But there is no such advantage in Russell's preferred definition of 'false', or in the redefinitions put forward by Goodman and Mill and Ayer; and neither are their redefinitions innocent of contentious claims.

The craving for answers

Having dismissed the appeal to ordinary language, Russell threw in, for good measure, the remark that Strawson could not 'claim the support of common usage' any more than he could. Presumably he was thinking of the description of the sentence about the King of France as 'neither true nor false'. In a later essay Strawson conceded that, given the choice between 'false' and 'neither true nor false', 'ordinary usage does not deliver a clear verdict for one party or the other'.[34]

How, we may wonder, would an ordinary present-day speaker of English respond to the statement that the King of France is bald, if the statement were made, say, in the course of a discussion about baldness? We can be confident that he would reject it, but not about the terms in which he would do so, for these might vary with different speakers and in different situations. (Various examples were given by Strawson in his later essay.)

Does it follow, as Russell claimed, that his opponent could not 'claim the support of common usage' any more than he could? No; to support the view that 'neither true nor false', rather than 'false', is the right answer, it is not necessary to claim that this verdict would be given in ordinary discourse. It is enough to point out that 'false' is *not necessarily* the verdict that would be given. (And neither, of course, is 'true'.) The point is not that we would say 'neither true nor false'; it is that we need not say either 'true' or 'false'. The essential difference between Russell's theory and ordinary language is not that the former delivers one verdict ('false'), while the latter delivers another ('neither true nor false'); it is that whereas the former delivers a verdict, the latter abstains from doing so. (The conclusion 'neither true nor false' is *deduced* from this abstention.) From the point of view of a Russellian philosopher, the deficiencies of ordinary language are worse, and the need for remedy greater, than they might first appear. It is not merely that instead of the neat 'false', ordinary language delivers the less neat 'neither true nor false'; its 'failure' is that of not delivering any clear verdict at all. And it is in this respect that Russell's theory is contrary to ordinary language and goes beyond 'what we say'.

Russell, as we saw, spoke of the 'vagueness' of ordinary language; and the failure to deliver verdicts in this and other matters might be regarded as a kind of vagueness. But whether such vagueness is a *defect* of ordinary language, such as would justify its renunciation from philosophical debate, is another question. The assumption that an artificial 'right answer' is to be preferred to the non-verdict of

---

34 P.F. Strawson, 'Identifying Reference and Truth Values', *Theoria* 1964, 104.

ordinary language cannot be justified on the ground of 'convenience'.[35]

It is not unusual for philosophers to seek, and sometimes to stipulate, answers to questions on which ordinary language delivers no verdict. Let us consider Kripke's ingenious puzzle about the young Frenchman who says 'Londres est jolie' on the basis of what he was taught, in French, at school. Later he visits London and learns English, picking up the word 'London' without being told that it means the same as 'Londres'. He finds that London is not pretty and is heard to say so in English, while continuing to give his original opinion when speaking French. (He can do both, because he doesn't realize that Londres and London are the same city.) The question is now posed: What does he *really* believe? That London is pretty, or that it isn't? To say he believes both that London is pretty and that London is not pretty would be self-contradictory. Yet both beliefs are ascribed to him on perfectly good grounds.

What is the right answer? Does he believe that London is pretty or that it is not? The case has unusual features and we should not expect to find a straightforward answer by reference to ordinary language. What we might say, in accordance with ordinary language, is this: there is reason to say he believes London is pretty and reason to say he believes London is not pretty. And this verdict would not be paradoxical or self-contradictory. In this case 'reasons for and against' would not mean that we are ignorant of a truth that still awaits discovery: it is not as if there were a truth of the matter, beyond the facts already described, so that further evidence might perhaps lead us to the 'real' answer. Having described the example, we have given the whole truth.

To some readers this treatment will seem an evasion rather than a serious attempt to solve the problem. But there is no reason to assume that the quest for a solution, beyond the one I have given and transcending the facts of ordinary language, is justified – though the craving for such solutions is a pervasive feature of human thought.

The same point arises in other areas of philosophy. What is the 'true' answer to Hobbes's question about the ship of Theseus? If all the

---

35   In the essay from which I have quoted, Strawson was more tolerant than I of Russell's position. Having considered arguments for it versus the 'truth-value gap theory', he concluded: 'It no longer seems to me important to come down on one side or the other in this dispute' (135). Strawson's refusal to come down itself leaves us with a truth-value gap – this time concerning the question 'Is the truth-value gap theory true or false?'

planks of the ship were gradually replaced by new ones, would it still be the same ship? But what if someone had kept the old, damaged planks and in due course assembled them into a ship? Would *that* be the same ship, and not the other? Yes, insists Hobbes, 'as long as the matter remains the same'. But why should this be accepted? What is gained by adding this verdict, going beyond the original description of the case, which was perfectly clear? The safe and proper verdict may be that in one way the first is the same ship, and in another way the second. Here, as Wittgenstein wrote in another context, 'we come up against a remarkable and characteristic phenomenon in philosophical investigations: the difficulty – I might say – is not to find a solution, but to recognize as a solution something that looks as if it were merely a preliminary step. "We have already said everything. – Not anything that follows from this, but *this itself* is the solution!" The difficulty here is: to stop' (*Zettel* 314).

10 Grice

'True, even if misleading'

'The ordinary notion of perceiving'

As we have seen, and will see further, the philosophy of 'what we say' has been challenged in various ways. A curious feature of some of these ways is that they are themselves based on arguments from what we say. (This is so in the case of sceptical arguments, as I tried to show in Chapter 7, where I spoke of the ordinary concept of knowledge as having 'suicidal tendencies'.) A particularly interesting case in this connection is that of H.P. Grice, who belonged to the generation of Oxford philosophers with which the ordinary language approach is usually associated. In an article on 'Postwar Oxford Philosophy' he expressed his (qualified) sympathy with this approach and, especially, for what he called 'conceptual analysis'.[1] The appeal to 'what we would say' is prominent in Grice's work, as we shall see; yet he arrived at conclusions that are clearly and admittedly contrary to what we would say. His way of defending these conclusions has been a powerful influence in the widespread rejection of that philosophy.

Grice's position was first set out in an article on the causal theory of perception. Here he began by making it clear that his aim would be 'to elucidate or characterize the ordinary notion of perceiving ...', and not to 'replace it by some concept more appropriate to an ideal or scientific language'[2]; thus distancing himself from thinkers of the kind discussed in my last chapter ('Language remade'). Nevertheless, one of the main

---

1 H.P. Grice, *Studies in the Way of Words* (Harvard 1989); hereafter 'WW', 171–80. (Grice's views about conceptual analysis were, however, criticized by me in Chapter 4.) In Chapter 11 we shall see the appeal to 'what we would say' at work in an article written by Grice together with Strawson.

2 'The Causal Theory of Perception', in G.J. Warnock, ed., *The Philosophy of Perception* (OUP 1967), 85–6; hereafter 'CTP'.

aims of Grice's article was to defend the causal theory against objections from ordinary language.

The argument begins with a statement of the theory in terms of 'sense-data': roughly, that the perception of a physical object consists in the causation, by the perceived object, of a suitable sense-datum in the perceiver's mind. Grice recognized that 'sense-datum' is a 'technical term' and was therefore to be avoided. He thought he could do this by stating the theory in terms of 'standard locutions' such as 'It looks blue to me', 'It looks (feels) to me as if there were a ϕ so-and-so', 'I seem to see something ϕ', etc. (CTP 87). He referred to statements of this kind as 'L-statements'. Expressed in such terms as these, the theory would be saying that if, for example, I perceive a red pillar box, then the latter causes me to 'seem to see something' red.

But such formulations immediately lead to a further difficulty, as Grice pointed out. The difficulty is that it would be wrong, in ordinary speech, to say 'It seems red to me' if one could see perfectly well that the object is red. As Grice put it, such statements are governed by a 'doubt or denial' condition (88): roughly, that one would use them only in cases in which there is doubt ('It looks red, but I'm not sure') or in which things are not what they seem ('It looked red to him, but it wasn't'); but not when the object really is red and there is no doubt about it. Nevertheless, according to the causal theory, 'I plainly see a red object' would entail 'I seem to see a red object'. (The difficulty is similar to that discussed in Chapter 6, about the claim that knowing entails believing.)

How does Grice propose to make room for this claim in spite of the objection from 'what we say'? He draws attention to the fact that a statement may be misleading and true nevertheless. In this way, he argues, it may be the case that L-statements are true in all cases of perception, even though it would be misleading to make them.

Let us assume, for now, that this is indeed the reason for our refusal to make or assent to the relevant L-statements – that Grice's explanation is correct. The fact remains that we *do not* assent to them in cases in which, according to the entailment thesis, we should. The basic difficulty for the entailment thesis is not that L-statements imply doubt or denial, but simply that, in straightforward cases, the entailment to L-statements is not recognized. Grice's position may be compared to that of an imaginary philosopher who claims that, for any value of S, (1) S committed a theft entails (2) S did a good deed. To the objection that, given a case of (1), we would not necessarily assent to (2), the philosopher replies that this is because of the misleading implication of (2): one would be unlikely to state (2) if S had committed a theft and therefore to state (2) would be to imply that he had not done so. Now it is indeed likely that (2) would be misleading, given the truth of (1); but this does not remove the difficulty of non-assent.

How, in general, is the existence of such entailments established in ordinary language? One way, just illustrated, is to consider whether someone who had accepted the first proposition would be expected to assent to the second. Let us call this 'the method of assent'. Another method, often more useful in discussion, is that of contradiction. (The two methods correspond to *modus ponens* and *modus tollens*.) By way of illustration, let us take another condition associated with perceiving: that of truth. According to this, 'S perceives that p' (or 'S perceives an X') is true only if 'p' is true (or an X is truly there).[3] Now this claim can readily be confirmed by my two methods. The method of contradiction occurs in such examples as: 'I see that John is in the room.' – 'No you don't; he isn't in the room.' The first speaker must now be prepared either to withdraw ('I must have been mistaken') or to deny the contradiction ('Yes, he is'). And turning to the method of assent: 'I see that John is in the room.' – 'So according to you John *is* in the room.' (Or simply: 'So John is in the room.') The first speaker must be prepared to assent to these statements if he is to stand by his opening statement; to answer 'Yes' if questioned, etc. The same conditions apply when attributing perception to others (or to oneself in the past). Thus if someone said 'She saw an elephant', he would be expected to react likewise in the cases of contradiction ('No, she didn't; there was no elephant there') and assent ('So according to you there was an elephant there').[4]

Grice himself used such arguments in his defence of the causal theory. In one of his examples he supposed that it looked to him as if there were a certain sort of pillar before him when there was indeed such a pillar there. Would this be a case of seeing the pillar? Not necessarily, he argued.

> If, unknown to me, there was a mirror interposed between myself and the pillar, which reflected a numerically different though similar pillar, it would certainly be incorrect to say that I saw the first pillar, and correct to say that I saw the second. (CTP 104)

---

3   This condition needs to be qualified to allow for the perception of remote stars that are no longer in existence by the time their light reaches us.

4   This again needs to be qualified, to allow for the case of Macbeth seeing a dagger, etc.

Thus, according to Grice, the statement 'I see the first pillar' would be *contradicted* by pointing out that there was a mirror interposed, etc.

In another example, he supposed that 'it looks to X as if there is a clock on the shelf' and there really is one there. Would it follow that X *sees* the clock? What if X's cortex were being artificially stimulated in such a way that the clock would seem to him to be there anyway? In that case, said Grice, 'we should be inclined to say that X did not see the clock' (103). Here again the method of contradiction is being invoked. 'X sees the clock.' – 'No, he doesn't; his cortex is being stimulated', etc.[5]

Whether this is really what we would say (or would be 'inclined to say') in these far-fetched examples is open to question, but it is clear that Grice's argument here depends on 'what we would say' – in this case, the method of contradiction. But when we apply this method to the claim about L-statements, the result is negative. 'I see that John is in the room.' – 'No you don't; it doesn't seem to you as if John is there.' Would such a response make sense? Perhaps it would, in unusual circumstances. But in the absence of these, the first speaker would be puzzled and would not see the response as a contradiction of what he had said. Perhaps he would reply: 'How do you mean? I didn't say it seemed to me', etc. Similar difficulties would arise in the case of assent. 'I see that John is there.' – 'So it seems to you as if . . .' Such a comment, again, would provoke a puzzled reaction. 'How do you mean? I said I see him, not that it seems to me, etc.'. Or perhaps: 'Oh, you mean he isn't really there?' One might indeed explain the meaning of L-statements by reference to doubt or denial: 'This is what you say if you are not quite sure', etc.

This is not to deny that perceptual statements may be compatible with corresponding L-statements in special situations. Grice, a master of ingenious examples, asks us to suppose that he suffers from occasional attacks of an imaginary 'Smith's Disease', the effect of which is that red objects would, on those occasions, look as if they had a different colour (CTP 96). The example, which I shall not spell out, is meant to show that an L-statement might provoke assent even when an object is perceived in full view. But even if this would be so in cases of Smith's Disease, it is not so in straightforward cases of perception. And Grice's aim, as he says at the outset, is 'to give a *general* analysis of

---

5 These arguments are supposed to show that, for genuine cases of perception, a *causal* condition must be satisfied: there must be a suitable causal connection between the object and the perceiver.

perceptual statements'; he will claim that the relevant L-statements are 'true whenever a perceptual statement is true' (88).

A similar weakness affects Grice's example, in a later discussion, about the relation between doing and trying. As Grice observed, we would not normally say 'A *tried* to x' unless we thought that A 'was or might have been prevented from doing x, or might have done x only with difficulty'; and yet some philosophers have claimed that doing x *entails* trying to do x. Now according to Grice, this claim might be correct in spite of the point about 'what we would say', since 'He tried to do x' might be *true* even though it would be misleading to state it.[6]

He produced an ingenious example to support this view. We are to suppose that he (Grice) had seen Mrs Smith presenting a cheque for payment at a bank, after which he left. On his return home, his wife asks whom he had seen that morning and he replies 'I saw Mrs Smith cashing a cheque'. In these circumstances, as Grice observes, it would be inappropriate to say that he saw her *trying* to cash a cheque. Later in the day, however, he meets Miss Jones and mentions to her that he saw Mrs Smith cashing a cheque. But Miss Jones, 'the local know-it-all', replies: 'She can't have been cashing a cheque; she is overdrawn and the bank would not honour her cheque'. They have an argument and finally Grice retorts 'Well, I saw her trying to cash a cheque ... and have no doubt that she succeeded' (WW 17). In this case the statement 'She tried' was both appropriate and true, even though the speaker also took her to have *performed* the action ('she succeeded'). But if 'She tried' was true when said to Miss Jones, would it not also have been true when said to his wife? The reason, then, for not saying it to his wife must be that it would have been misleading, and not that it failed to be true.

But what does this example prove? We can agree that the statement would have been true on both occasions. The fact of the matter, as it turned out, was that there *was doubt* about whether Mrs Smith would succeed; and this would have made the statement 'She tried ...' true, even when Grice was ignorant of Miss Jones's allegation. It would have been true by luck, so to speak. But this does nothing to show that such statements are true in straightforward cases of doing – including that in which there is *no* doubt about Mrs Smith's cashing her cheque.

It is hard to see how, in this case or in that of L-statements, the entailment thesis can survive unless the criterion of ordinary language is abandoned. Conceding that one would not use an L-statement in

6 H.P. Grice, *Studies in the Way of Words* op. cit., 7.

straightforwarded cases of perception, Grice claimed, nevertheless, that to do so 'would have been to have said something linguistically correct and true, even if misleading' (CTP 106). But what can be the standard of 'linguistic correctness', other than the normal use of language? And how, having announced at the start his intention to elucidate the 'ordinary notion' of perception, can Grice hope to achieve this by defending a grossly unordinary use of language? There is a deep ambivalence in his treatment of the matter. His conclusion, as I said, represents a decisive break from ordinary language and yet he is throughout acutely sensitive to the latter, supporting his argument with various examples of 'what we would say', which he discusses with considerable insight.

A note on method

The methods of assent and contradiction, on which I have based my argument, might strike readers as altogether too simple a way of dealing with claims put forward by philosophers. Could we not be led astray by relying on such methods? Do they even provide a stable criterion? It is a familiar fact that people can be induced to assent to all kinds of claims by means of more or less plausible arguments. Consider again the question of free will, as discussed in Chapter 5. It is notorious how readily many people, students and others, will assent to the negative conclusion, given only the sketchiest of arguments. Yet, according to my argument in that chapter, the negative conclusion is false. But even if it were true, one would hardly judge it to be so merely because many or most people are prepared to assent to it. Doesn't this show that my method is hopelessly inadequate?

This objection involves a misunderstanding of the method. The method is based on how the relevant language is used in ordinary conversation, and not on what people would say when faced by claims and arguments of a philosophical kind. Let us consider the role of the two methods in the case of free will. One of the arguments for the negative conclusion was based, as we saw, on the premise that we are not free to choose our desires, beliefs etc.; from which it was thought to follow that when we act on those desires and beliefs the actions themselves cannot be free. According to this argument, 'He acted freely' can be true only if the desires and beliefs on which he acted were themselves freely chosen. But this condition would not be recognized in ordinary conversation. If I said that Smith acted freely in handing over the money, I would not be expected to assent to the proposition that he chose the desires and beliefs on which he acted; and neither could a denial of this proposition be used, in ordinary conversation, to contradict the statement that Smith acted freely. It is true that when confronted with philosophical arguments, people might assent to the conclusion that there is no free will. But this does not affect my claims about what we would and would not assent to in ordinary conversation. Similarly, though it is true that people might be brought by philosophical arguments to agree that perceptual statements entail L-statements, they would not assent to such statements in straightforward situations of perception. And this means, contrary to what Grice was at pains to show, that when philosophers make such claims, they are imposing artificial conditions on the relevant words.

Another objection to my methods might be that what people say in ordinary conversation is often marred by faulty reasoning. There are common fallacies ('affirming the consequent' and various others) that cause people to assent to conclusions that do not really follow and refuse to assent to conclusions that do really follow. But this is not relevant to the issues in question. The philosopher who argues that L-statements are true in straightforward cases of perception is not suggesting that we are *mistaken* in observing the doubt-or-denial condition, which prevents such statements from being made; and neither is the philosopher who denies the existence of free will suggesting that we commit a fallacy when we (and he) describe an action as free in accordance with the normal conditions for using this word. Their arguments are meant to take us, in some sense, beyond this level.

Explaining the difference: (i) 'cancellability'

How could Grice describe L-statements as 'linguistically correct and true' when they would not be so regarded in ordinary discourse? To account for the discrepancy he argued that the condition which prevents the making of L-statements – the doubt-or-denial condition – is not really part of their meaning. L-statements, he argued, can be shorn of their doubt-or-denial implication – the implication is 'cancellable' – and this shows that it is not really part of their meaning.

He illustrated his idea by a number of examples. A tutor, asked to report on his student's work, writes that 'Jones has a beautiful handwriting and his English is grammatical', and nothing else. Such a report would imply that there was nothing else of merit in Jones's work; but according to Grice the implication might be cancelled by an explicit disclaimer on the tutor's part: 'I do not of course mean to imply that he is no good at philosophy' (CTP 92–3). The whole performance, says Grice, 'though it may be extraordinary tutorial behaviour', would be 'intelligible and linguistically impeccable' (93).

In another of Grice's examples a man tells us 'My wife is either in the kitchen or in the bedroom'. In this case, as Grice points out, 'it would normally be implied that [the man] did not know in *which* of the two rooms [his wife] was' and he would not be expected to speak as he did if he did know this. But what if he spoke thus in spite of knowing it? Might his statement not be true all the same? 'The disjunctive statement', according to Grice, might be true even if 'the implied ignorance is in fact not realized'; and this would be so because 'the implication is cancellable'. Having made his disjunctive statement, the man might go on, 'Mind you, I'm not saying that I don't know which'. This, says Grice, 'might be unfriendly ... but would be perfectly intelligible' (93–4).

Now according to Grice, the use of L-statements in cases where the doubt-or-denial condition is not present would similarly be intelligible, because their misleading implications could be cancelled. 'It is surely clear', he writes,

> that if I were now to say 'Nothing is the case which would make it false for me to say that the palm of his hand looks pink to me, though I do not mean to imply that I or anyone else is or might be inclined to deny that, or doubt whether, it is pink', this would be a perfectly intelligible remark .... (99)

He clinches the point by assuring the reader: 'Indeed I am prepared actually to say it'. But here we may ask whether Grice has not stretched the meaning of 'intelligible' to the point of being unintelligible. A natural response to that remark might indeed be that it is unintelligible. (Grice's verdict on the tutor's behaviour – 'intelligible and linguistically impeccable' – would also not be acceptable.)

What may give plausibility to Grice's argument is that in the tutor example (and others like it) the desired conclusion was, at least, *true*; i.e. it was true that what the tutor's report implied was not part of the meaning of the sentences used in it. And it might be thought that if the test of cancellability (the tutor's being able to say 'I do not of course mean to imply') was successful in this case, it would also be so in other cases, including that of L-statements. But this would be a false inference. In the case of the tutor's report the test of cancellability could not be *successful,* because it was not necessary – since in this case the distinction between meaning and mere implication would be obvious anyway. (It is obvious that 'is no good at philosophy' is not part of the *meaning* of 'has a beautiful handwriting'.) But this is not so in the case of L-statements, where the implication of doubt or denial might indeed be regarded, contrary to Grice's view, as belonging to the meaning of those statements.

The implication of doubt or denial in the case of L-statements is due to general conditions of perception and language, in the following way. In the great majority of cases, there is a presumption that things are really as we perceive them to be; and straightforward statements of perception, such as 'I see that p', are tailored for this normal situation. Here the speaker commits himself to the truth of 'p' and, at the same time, tells us how he knows that p. But we also need expressions to be used in those less straightforward cases in which we do not wish to be committed to the truth of 'p'; and this is what L-statements are for. It is essential to these that they can be completed by a disclaimer: 'It looks as if p, even though p is (or may be) false.' This implication is quite general: it is one of meaning. And the fact that L-statements are not acceptable in standard cases of perception remains as an objection to the entailment thesis.

In his example of the student, and various others, Grice illustrated a variety of ways in which a statement might be true even if it were misleading. But he overestimated the importance of this point. Of course the statement 'It looks blue to me', for example, may be misleading in various ways and true nevertheless; and the same may be said about any other statement; but this does not help to resolve the issue about L-statements. The philosopher's claim must be, not merely that L-statements may be true even when they are misleading, but, to quote Grice again, that they are 'true whenever a perceptual statement is true'. And the objector who denies this general claim is not to be answered by pointing out that L-statements – like any others – *may* be true even when they are misleading.

Having observed that a statement may be criticized either for being inappropriate or for being untrue, Grice diagnosed the error of those who objected to certain philosophical claims as mistaking the first of these reasons for the second. But is this a mistake that is likely to occur? Given the example of the student, no one would be tempted to think that 'He has a beautiful handwriting' was false just because it was wrong to say it in those circumstances. In ordinary conversation the occurrence of inappropriate (irrelevant, etc.) remarks is common, and they are criticized accordingly; but we are not inclined to question their truth for this reason. Again, the fact that it would be inappropriate to make a given statement would not prevent us from seeing that it is *entailed* by a statement already made. Suppose the tutor reported: 'I read Smith's work and found it very good'. This would entail that the work was legible. Now it might well be inappropriate for the tutor to state that the work was legible; but this would not prevent him, or anyone, from seeing that this was entailed by what he did say. Similarly, if L-statements really were entailed by statements of perception, then we would not be prevented from seeing this merely because it was inappropriate to utter them.

Explaining the difference: (ii) the 'weaker/stronger' principle

Another way in which Grice tried to account for the discrepancy between his claims and what is acceptable in ordinary discourse was by reference to 'a general principle governing the use of language': that 'one should not make a weaker statement rather than a stronger one unless there is a good reason for doing so' (CTP 94). This principle, in one form or another, has been influential in philosophy since the appearance of Grice's work.

He introduced the principle in his discussion of the man who said 'My wife is either in the kitchen or in the bedroom' although he knew she was in the kitchen. In that case, according to Grice, the statement was misleading because a stronger one could have been made. The statement 'She is in the kitchen' is supposed to be stronger, in the sense that it entails, but is not entailed by, the disjunction. (Whether disjunctions are really entailed in this way is a question to which I shall return.) Similarly, according to Grice, a perceptual statement is stronger than the corresponding L-statement because it entails, but is not entailed by, the L-statement. Hence, to make an L-statement when one is in a position to make the stronger, perceptual statement would be misleading; yet it would not follow that the L-statement was untrue.

The situation is a curious one, if Grice is right. Using 'P' for a perceptual fact (as when S perceives an object) and 'L' for the corresponding L-statement, we may put it thus: The fact that P makes it true that L; but the same fact prevents one from *stating* that L. And this would be the *normal* case, and not one that arises only in special circumstances.

Apparently Grice had the weaker/stronger principle in mind in a later passage in which he lists half a dozen examples which, he thought, might be 'amenable to treatment of the same general kind' as that which he had given to the case of perception (CTP 102). The examples are of various kinds, but they include the widely accepted claims that 'what is actual is also possible' and that 'what is known by me to be the case is also believed by me to be the case' (a claim discussed in Chapter 6). It is often thought that in each of these cases we have a 'stronger' versus a 'weaker' claim, and similarly in the case of 'I see a red object' versus 'It looks red to me'. And to the objector who points out, in each case, that one would not make the latter claim if one were in a position to make the former, the reply is made that this is merely because of the principle adumbrated by Grice. Here again we find an argument from ordinary use – an exercise of ordinary language philosophy – being used to subvert ordinary language philosophy. Grice's principle must be understood as a claim about the ordinary use of language, and yet it is invoked to support claims that are contrary to the ordinary use of language – implying that the true meanings of words (such as 'see' and 'seem') may transcend their actual use.[7]

What is there to be said for Grice's principle in general? Is it really 'a principle governing the use of language' that 'one should not make a weaker statement rather than a stronger one', etc.? If this were so, then it would be wrong for me to say I have some money in my pocket if I knew I had ten pounds in my pocket; wrong to say that Grice was in England if I knew he was in Oxford; wrong to say that so-and-so had a baby if I knew it was a boy. If the claim about L-statements versus straightforward statements of perception depends on such a principle, then it had better be given up without further ado.

Let us consider an illustration in support of the principle which was given by P.F. Strawson. In his *Introduction to Logical Theory,* he spoke of 'a "pragmatic" consideration, a general rule of linguistic conduct', which he attributed to Grice: 'the rule, namely, that one does not make the (logically) lesser, when one could truthfully (and with equal or greater linguistic economy) make the greater, claim'.[8] He gave the example of someone saying 'There is not a single foreign book in this room', when he knows that there are no books in the room at all. The latter proposition entails (is stronger than) the former and therefore it was wrong to state merely the former.

However, it is not the weaker/stronger principle that would make it wrong to do so. This can be seen by considering the similar case of someone saying 'There are no books in the room' when he knows that there is no literature of any kind in the room – or that the room is quite empty. In these cases it would not, except in certain circumstances, be

---

7   In a later writing Grice declared his sympathy for 'the precept that one should be careful not to confuse meaning and use' (WW 4).

8   P.F. Strawson, *Introduction to Logical Theory* (Methuen 1952), 178–9; hereafter 'ILT'.

wrong for him to make the weaker statement when he could make the stronger one.

What is at work in Strawson's example is not the weaker/stronger principle, but a principle similar to Austin's 'No modification without aberration'.[9] Let us call it 'No modification without implication'. To add a modification is to imply that there is a point in doing so; and there would be no point in saying 'foreign books', if plain 'books' would do just as well. The point of adding 'foreign' must be to contrast these books with others that were not foreign; hence the presence of non-foreign books would be implied and to use the modification if none were there would be misleading. (The point of adding 'foreign' may be brought out, in actual conversation, by stressing the word 'foreign' in the sentence.) It was this, and not transgression of the weaker/stronger principle, that made it wrong to say 'foreign book' instead of plain 'book'.

It is true that in some situations it would be wrong to make a weaker statement when a stronger one could be made. If I am aware that my hearer *wants* the fuller information, then – other things being equal – I will be expected to give it if I am able to do so; and if I do not, it will be assumed that I am not able to do so. But in other cases this expectation is not present. In most cases, indeed, the strongest possible statement is *not* what is expected. Asked whether I can see a pillar box, it would be wrong to reply 'I can see a *red* pillar box', or to provide other details known to me, unless there were a point in doing so; and to provide such extra information would imply that there is such a point. But now we have arrived at a principle of conversation which, though true, is more general and less interesting than that advocated by Grice. It is merely this: that we should be as specific as is appropriate in the circumstances.[10]

A more moderate version of Grice's principle has been put forward by Strawson in terms of more and less *information*:

> ... One should not (unless one has some special justification for doing so) deliberately make a *less* informative statement on the

---

9 J.L. Austin, *Philosophical Papers* (Clarendon 1961), 137–8. His discussion was about verbs of action. Austin's remarks were included by Grice in his list of 'suspect examples' of philosophy on page 8 of WW, but, as far as I can see, he made no attempt to refute them.

10 In a later essay by Grice, the weaker/stronger principle is superseded by a set of conversational 'maxims', one of which is that we should not be 'more informative than is required'. This is subsumed under the more general maxim: 'Be relevant' (WW 26–7).

topic of conversational exchange when one has just as good grounds for making a ... *more* informative statement.[11]

This principle would exclude the absurd examples given above (about Grice being in England, etc.), since the mere fact that p entails q would not make it obligatory to state p rather q. What would be needed in addition is that one has 'just as good grounds' for stating p as for stating q. Even so, the principle is not satisfactory. If, in a given conversation, my grounds for saying 'Grice was in England' and 'Grice was in Oxford' were equally good – if both served the purpose of conversational exchange equally well – then it would *not* follow that I ought to prefer the 'more informative' statement: there would be no reason to prefer one statement or the other.

Conversational implicature and truth-functional logic

Grice's views about ordinary language versus 'literal truth' were elaborated in later writings. Here he was especially concerned about the apparent divergence between what we say in ordinary conversation and what is correct according to the truth-functional system of logic. In 'Logic and Conversation' (WW Chapter 2), he drew a contrast between 'formalist' and 'informalist' philosophers. According to the former, he said, 'the formal devices: $\sim$, $\wedge$, v, $\supset$, etc.' have the advantage of providing 'a decision procedure' for 'handling dubiously acceptable patterns of inference', whereas the presence of 'elements of meaning' in the corresponding words of ordinary language, 'which they do not share with the corresponding formal devices, is to be regarded as an imperfection of natural languages'. These elements, according to the 'formalist', are 'undesirable excrescences', for their presence has the result both that the concepts within which they appear cannot be precisely and clearly defined, and that at least some statements involving them cannot, in some circumstances, be assigned a definite truth-value (WW 22–3).

Grice would maintain, however, that the dispute between formalists and informalists was based on an illusion: the 'assumption of the contestants' that the truth-functional expressions diverge in meaning from their ordinary language counterparts was 'a common mistake', which was due to 'inadequate attention to ... the conditions governing

---

11   P.F. Strawson, ' "If" and "$\supset$" ', in R.E. Grandy ed., *Philosophical Grounds of Rationality* (Clarendon 1986), 236.

conversation' (24). Comparing the truth-functional '∧' with its 'natural analogue', 'and', he acknowledged that one 'would not say "He got into bed and took off his trousers" of a man who first took off his trousers and then got into bed' (8). Such examples, he continued, had been used to support the suggestion 'that it is part of the meaning, or part of *one* meaning, of "and" to convey temporal succession'; whereas no such meaning is conveyed by its truth-functional counterpart. In his view, however, the difference would turn out to be merely one of 'conversational implicature'. He illustrated this idea by means of the following example. A and B are talking about C, who had recently started work in a bank. A asks B how C is getting on and B replies: 'Oh quite well, I think; he likes his colleagues, and he hasn't been to prison yet' (24). In this case, says Grice, we can distinguish between what B said and what was implied by his saying it. The statement 'He hasn't been to prison yet' might be perfectly true without the implication ('implicature') being so. The implication was that there was some reason for thinking that A was liable to go to prison; and the statement, though not actually false, should not have been made unless this were so. (The example is similar to that of the tutor's report, as quoted earlier.)

Now it is unlikely that anyone would regard temporal succession as part of the meaning of 'and'; the suggestion would simply not apply to the many uses of this word in non-temporal contexts. But even in suitable contexts, such as Grice's example, it is not the use of 'and' that conveys the corresponding succession, but the order of the conjoined statements; the same meaning would be conveyed if 'and' were omitted. 'He got into bed; he took off his trousers': this means that he did the first and then the second. Similarly, 'I came, I saw, I conquered' means that the events took place in that order (though in this case the order is partly determined by the nature of the events). Hence it is better to present the divergence of meaning as being between sentences and not words; the point being that the sentence in Grice's example, with or without 'and', has temporal succession as part of its meaning, while the same sentence with '∧' inserted would not have this meaning.

It would not be right, however, to maintain that the order of such sentences always indicates a corresponding temporal order. 'She came by car and he came by bicycle': this would not mean that the events occurred in that order. But does this show that the temporal implication, when it is present (as in Grice's example), is not one of meaning but merely one of implicature? If this were so, then the comment 'True, even if misleading' would be appropriate here, as in the cases of the bank employee and tutor's report. 'He went to bed, he took off his trousers': suppose this were said if the actual sequence had been the reverse. Then one would be justified in *refusing* to describe the statement as true; one might indeed contradict it. 'No; first he took off his trousers and then he went to bed.' But such refusal and contradiction would not be appropriate in the cases of the bank employee and the tutor's report.

Hence we are still left with a divergence of meaning between '∧' and its natural counterpart: the latter carries a temporal meaning in cases such as that of the man going bed, but this is not so with '∧': someone who thought that the truth of 'He did A ∧ he did B' could ever be questioned on the ground that he did B before A, would show that he had not understood the meaning of that sign.

Perhaps Grice would argue that the temporal implication is 'cancellable' and therefore not part of the meaning. The cancellation might be attempted thus: 'He went to bed [and] he took off his trousers, but I don't mean to imply that he did them in that order.' But would this be intelligible? One might object that 'He went to bed and he took off his trousers' *means* that he did them in that order. Grice would have to insist that the statement with the cancellation is not unintelligible; but there is no reason why this verdict should be accepted.

A divergence between the natural and artificial systems also appears when we consider the relation between 'p ∧ q' and other truth-functional expressions, such as '∼p'. It follows from the definitions of these expressions that if '∼p' is true, then 'p ∧ q' is false; but this is not so in the case of their natural counterparts. 'The capital of Greece is Athens and the capital of Turkey is Istanbul.' Then it turns out that the capital of Turkey is not Istanbul. Would one say that the conjunctive statement was false? Perhaps. But perhaps the answer would be: partly true and partly false. A defender of Grice's position would have to insist that, properly speaking, the conjunctive statement would be false; but there is no good reason why this ruling should be accepted. Here we come to a divergence between the use of 'true' and 'false' in ordinary language and the use of these words in truth-functional logic. As ordinarily used, 'true' and 'false' are capable of qualification: a statement may be described as 'partly true', 'not wholly false', etc.; but these uses are excluded from the truth-functional system.

What should we say about the truth-functional entailment from 'p ∧ q' to 'p'? This, at least, might seem to correspond with the logic of ordinary language. Someone who has asserted that p and q would indeed be expected to assent to p and q individually. But this still leaves a divergence between the natural and artificial systems. The latter presents the relation between the conjunction and its conjuncts as one of entailment; but 'p' would not be said to *follow* from 'p and q' in natural logic. Someone who asserts that p and q has *already asserted* that p, and not merely something from which p follows. His assent to p would be merely an act of repetition. Here we come to a divergence in the meaning of 'it follows': in truth-functional logic the use of this expression is such that 'p' is said to follow from 'p', but this is not so according to the ordinary concepts of entailment and inference.

Another sort of divergence arises in connection with such conjunctions as 'but' – a word that is even further away than 'and' from the truth-functional sign. When two sentences are joined by 'but', there is an implication of contrast or opposition, but this is so neither with 'and' nor with '∧'. It has been argued, however, that the choice of 'but' or 'and' makes no difference to what is actually being asserted when such sentences are used. According to Grice,

> if, instead of saying 'She is poor but she is honest' I were to say 'She is poor and she is honest', I would assert just what I would have asserted if I had used the original sentence; but there would now be no implication of a contrast between poverty and honesty. (CTP 92)

In his choice of 'poor but honest', Grice took an example which might make his position appear more reasonable than it really is. There is a contrast between 'poor' and 'honest', which is due to their meanings. 'Poor' is a negative, and 'honest' a positive term; it is, generally, bad to be poor and good to be honest. This contrast is confirmed by the use of 'but', but exists prior to that use. Hence one might feel, with Grice, that there would be no important difference between the two assertions – the one with 'but' and the one with 'and'.[12] But this is not so if we take two qualities that are *not*

---

12 Grice also tried the test of cancellability on this example, but with less confidence. He admitted that if one made the 'but' statement and added the rider 'though I do not mean to imply that there is any contrast ...', this would seem 'a puzzling and eccentric thing to have said'; he did not think, however, that 'we should go so far as to say that [the] utterance was *unintelligible*'. But here the choice of example goes against Grice. The cancellation in this case *would* be unintelligible, for the fact that poverty is a negative and honesty a positive quality is not subject to cancellation. The proposed cancellation might perhaps seem reasonable if one took it to mean that poverty and honesty are *not incompatible* – that a person may be both poor and honest. But this would not be relevant to the question about *contrast*.

contrasting, and consider how 'but' and 'and' would work with them. 'She is rich and she is handsome': this would be a straightforward remark; but if the two sentences were joined with 'but', the result would be unintelligible, unless an explanation for the 'but' were added. Here it is clear that the two assertions (the one with 'but' and the one with 'and') could not properly be described as the same.

The point can also be put in terms of truth-values. Suppose the person in Grice's example were, indeed, both poor and honest. Then '... poor but honest' and '... poor and honest' would both be true. But this is not so in the case of my example. Here 'rich and handsome' would be described as 'true', whereas 'rich but handsome' could not be so described (unless an explanation of the 'but' were forthcoming).[13]

Let us turn to disjunction, and the divergence between the truth-functional 'v' and its natural counterpart. One would not, Grice remarked, say 'My wife is either in Oxford or in London' if one knew that she is in Oxford; and this, he said, had 'led to the idea that it is part of the meaning of "or" (or of "either ... or") to convey that the speaker is ignorant of the truth-values of the particular disjuncts' (WW 8–9; compare Strawson ILT 91). This would not be conveyed by the truth-functional 'p v q'; but is the difference one of meaning or merely one of implicature? Grice saw the question as being about the 'strength' of the natural expression as compared with its artificial counterpart. He would criticize the suggestion that

> the word *or* has a single 'strong' sense, which is such that it is part of the meaning of *A or B* to say (or imply) not only (1) that A v B, but also (2) that there is some non-truth-functional reason for accepting that A v B. (WW 44)

The non-truth-functional reason would be that the speaker was 'ignorant of the truth-values of the particular disjuncts'.

---

13 A position similar to Grice's has been defended by Frank Jackson, in F. Jackson, ed., *Conditionals* (OUP 1991). According to him, 'you dissent from "He is poor but happy" just when it is probable that he is either not poor or not happy, not when you dissent from the signalled contrast' (132); and this shows that 'but' is merely a 'signal' and not a contributor to truth-conditions. Here again, however, it is illuminating to try a different example. Suppose one were told 'He is rich but happy' and could not, in the supposed case, see a contrast between being rich and being happy. In that case one would indeed dissent from the statement, even if one believed both conjuncts to be true. Such a statement would not be accepted as true, and this is enough to show, contrary to Jackson's position, that the difference between 'but' and 'and' is a contributor to truth-conditions.

To show that this condition belongs to implicature and not meaning, Grice produced an example in which the condition would be 'cancellable':

> I can say to my children at some stage in a treasure hunt, *The prize is either in the garden or in the attic. I know where I put it, but I'm not going to tell you.* (44–5)

But what can such examples prove? The fact that the ignorance condition is cancellable when a special kind of game is being played would not entail that it is so in general, or that this condition is not part of the meaning of 'either ... or ...'.

Nevertheless Grice was right to question whether the ignorance condition is part of the meaning of this phrase (or of the word 'or'). He pointed out that if this were so, then we might expect the word to carry that meaning in 'a reasonably wide range of linguistic settings', including 'It is not the case that A or B', 'Suppose that A or B', and so on; and this is not so. It is, in any case, unlikely that anyone would regard the ignorance condition as part of the meaning of 'or', as Grice had supposed. However, the main divergence between 'or' and 'v' does not lie here; it lies in the ways in which disjunctive statements are related to their respective disjuncts. Given the truth of 'p', the correct value to fill in for 'p v q' is 'true'; but this is not so in the case of the natural 'p or q'; the inference 'My wife is in Oxford, therefore she is either in Oxford or in London' would not be recognized in natural logic. In the artificial system, the fact that today is Sunday would serve to verify 'Today is Sunday v the moon is made of polystyrene'; but this would not be so if 'v' were replaced by the natural 'or'. Again, the idea that 'Today is Sunday' entails that today is either Sunday or Monday or Tuesday or Wednesday or Thursday or Friday or Saturday would be regarded as absurd; but this would not be so if 'or' were replaced by the truth-functional sign.

It might be thought that the claim that, in ordinary logic, 'p' entails 'p or q' can be defended by reference to such exchanges as the following. Suppose I believe, and say, that my wife is either in Oxford or in London, not knowing which it is; and you reply 'You're right; she's in Oxford'. Here it may seem as if my belief that p or q is confirmed by the discovery that p; and that this can be so only if 'p' entails 'p or q'. Now such arguments cannot, in any case, *prove* that 'p' entails 'p or q', for the fact remains that this entailment is not recognized in the straightforward case in which one simply knows that p and there is no special context of the kind just described. The nature of such 'proofs' appears to be this: In the great majority of cases the entailment would, admittedly, not be recognized; here is a kind of case in which it *would* be recognized; therefore it is also present, somehow, in the other cases. But this, of course, does not follow.

At most, therefore, the example would show that 'p' entails 'p or q' in certain contexts and with suitable fillings for 'p' and 'q'. But does it show even this? When you reply 'You're right, she's in Oxford', you are not thereby saying that *'p or q'* is true, but that *'p'* is true. If you were saying the former, then I would now be in a position to say: 'I thought she was either in Oxford or in London; now I *know* she's either in Oxford or in London.' But this would be absurd if I had just learned that she is in Oxford.[14] A proper comment, in that case, would be: 'I thought (or knew) it was either one or the other; now I know which it is.' Having been apprised of this fact, I am no longer in a position to believe, or to know, that it is either one or the other. 'No longer' does not mean, of course, that I am now more ignorant than before but, on the contrary, that I am less so: because I now know that p, I can no longer be ignorant whether p or q.

The ignorance condition, as I said, is unlikely to be regarded as part of the meaning of 'or', as Grice supposed. This condition is, however, relevant to the difference between 'or' and 'v', for it is this condition that obstructs the inference from 'p' to 'p or q'.[15]

---

14   A similar absurdity occurs in the following story. A sailor in the British navy found that, in spite of his preference for coffee, tea was the only beverage provided. At the approach of Christmas, however, the cook put out a special festive menu. including 'tea or coffee'. When the time came, the sailor asked for coffee. To his disappointment, only tea was offered. In protest, he quoted from the menu: 'tea or coffee'. 'But', was the reply, 'you are getting tea or coffee – namely, tea'. In this case there was a question of choice and not merely belief, but in other respects the cases are similar. The cook thought, erroneously, that by offering one alternative he was confirming the disjunction of that alternative with another. (I owe this story to Peter Lewis. The sailor was his father.)

15   The obstructive role of the ignorance condition is relevant to a paradox which I have adapted from an article by Vann McGee. According to McGee, opinion polls taken just before the American presidential election in 1980 showed the Republican Ronald Reagan to be decisively ahead of the Democrat Jimmy Carter, with the other Republican, John Anderson, a distant third (*Journal of Philosophy* 1985, 462). Now someone apprised of these polls might reason as follows:

   (a)   Reagan will win and Reagan is a Republican; therefore a Republican will win.
   (b)   A Republican will win and Reagan and Anderson are the only Republicans in the race; therefore either Reagan or Anderson will win.
   (c)   Therefore, if it isn't Reagan who wins, it will be Anderson.

   The steps of the argument seem impeccable, but is it true that someone having

Let us contrast the example of the wife with one in which it would be correct to say that a belief that either p or q had been confirmed. Suppose the inspector believes that the murder was done either by X or by Y. After careful investigation it is proved that no other person was there at the time. Here is a case in which a belief that either p or q has been confirmed – not by the discovery that p, but by confirmation of 'either p or q'. (If, later, it turns out that X did the murder, then the inspector might say 'I knew it would be either X or Y', but he could not say 'Now I know it was either X or Y'.)

So far I have discussed cases where one of the disjuncts is true and the other false (corresponding to the second and third lines of the truth table). A further difference between 'v' and its natural counterpart[16] appears in cases where both disjuncts are true (the first line of the truth table). 'Paris is the capital of France v London is the capital of England': according to the definition of 'v' this must be declared true, since both disjuncts are true. But this would not be so if 'v' were replaced by 'or', for then it would be implied that one but not both of the disjuncts are true. (This is especially clear if 'either ... or ...' is used.)

Another divergence to which Grice turned his attention was that between the artificial '⊃' and its natural counterpart 'if ..., then ...'. In dealing with this matter, he took up Strawson's suggestion that the relation between the two expressions is one of stronger and weaker, so that 'if p then q' entails 'p ⊃ q', but not conversely (WW 9; cf. ILT 83). He proposed, accordingly, to enquire whether 'in standard cases to say "if p then q" is to be ... committed, in virtue of meaning ... to both the proposition that p ⊃ q' and the further conditions identified by Strawson as governing the use of 'if ... then ...' (WW 58).

What were these further conditions? According to Strawson, 'the standard or primary use' of 'if p then q' is such as to entail that (A) the proposition that p would be a good reason for accepting that q; and (B)

knowledge of (a) and (b) must infer (c)? Suppose one also knows that Carter, though behind Reagan, is well in front of Anderson. Then the reasonable inference on the basis of the evidence would be that if Reagan doesn't win, Carter will.

The fault lies in inference (b). Someone who has already concluded that (a) 'Reagan will win' is not in a position to infer that (b) 'either Reagan or Anderson will win'; for he cannot make both of these statements together – expressing both certainty and uncertainty at the same time. (An example rather similar to McGee's was used by Grice in connection with the 'wife' case, at CTP 93–4.)

16 Here 'natural counterpart' refers to the English word and not, say, to the Latin 'vel', which conforms, on the point in question, to the artificial sign.

there is doubt or uncertainty about both propositions. (I have re-worded and simplified the conditions.) But these conditions, he said, are not present in the case of the artificial expression, from which it appeared to follow that while 'a statement of the form "if p then q" does entail the corresponding statement of the form "p ⊃ q"', the latter does not entail the former (ILT 83). In response, Grice claimed that these conditions apply to 'p ⊃ q' no less than to the natural expression, and that they belong, in both cases, to implicature rather than meaning.[17]

In support of the first claim, he used as an example 'If Smith is in London, he is attending the meeting'. Such a statement would normally be taken to imply the conditions identified by Strawson, but according to Grice the same would be true if the sign '⊃' were used – as in 'Smith is in London ⊃ Smith is attending the meeting'. But is this really so? One might wonder how to approach this question, since '⊃' is not an English word and a sentence containing it is not an English sentence. However, Grice provided a paraphrase which avoided the artificial sign while still conforming to 'the appropriate truth-table'.

> One of the combinations of truth possibilities for the statements (i) that Smith is in London and (ii) that Smith is attending the meeting is realized, other than the one which consists in the first statement's being true and the second false. (WW 59)

'After one has sorted this out', he commented, 'one still detects the implications' identified by Strawson.

Let us consider this with regard to condition (A) – that the first proposition would be a good reason for accepting the second. Now in the above example the two propositions are connected in a way that makes this plausible in advance. People commonly go to places to attend meetings, and hence 'Smith is in London' *can* be a suitable reason for concluding that he is at the meeting. It is against this background that condition (A) is satisfied, both in Grice's original example and in his 'truth table' paraphrase of it, and it is against such background conditions that 'if ... then ...' is normally used. But no such conditions constrain the use of the artificial sign; and here lies the essential difference, involving condition (A), between it and its natural counterpart. It is indeed usual in textbooks in which the use of '⊃' is

---

17   The two claims were connected via Grice's criterion of 'detachability' (WW 58; cf CTP 91–2). I have not discussed this criterion, because I find it unhelpful and implausible. (For further discussion see Strawson, ' "If" and "⊃" ' op. cit., 240–1.)

explained, to give examples with wildly disconnected propositions, to make the point that connectedness is *not* a condition of the use of this sign.

What is the origin of 'if . . . then . . . ' sentences in our language? They result from our ability to (a) perceive suitable connections and (b) consider possibilities. It is in such contexts that conditional sentences serve their purpose, but such contexts and purposes are not relevant to the use of the artificial sign. We *deny* or *question* statements of the ordinary kind by denying or questioning the implied connection; but this is not so in the case of '⊃' where no such connections are presupposed.[18]

The point about connection is, however, only one aspect of the divergence between '⊃' and 'if . . . then . . . '; and, as in the case of 'or', it is misleading to present this as a matter of stronger and weaker. A conspicuous divergence between '⊃' and the natural expression appears in the third and fourth lines of the truth-table for '⊃'. According to these, the mere falsehood of p would make it true that 'p ⊃ q'; but, as has often been noted, it would be absurd to think that ordinary if-then statements such as 'If he goes to the party, then he will have a good time' could be verified in that way. Again, according to the first and third lines of the truth-table, the mere truth of q would yield the verdict 'true' for 'p ⊃ q', but this is not so in the case of 'if p, then q'.

In a later essay Strawson reviewed arguments for and against the view that there is more to the meaning of 'if p then q' than to that of the artificial expression.[19] Here he thought that the divergences apparent from the truth-table for '⊃' might be accounted for by a principle of 'maximum informativeness'.

---

18 A suitable connection for the use of 'if . . . then . . . ' need not be one of 'being a good reason', as can be seen from the following examples.

  1 'If he comes, I'll tell him'. Wittgenstein described this as 'a *resolution*, a *promise*'. (*Last Writings I* (Blackwell 1982) §7).
  2 'If her aunt could not see why she must go down, Margaret was not going to tell her' (Forster, *Howards End*).
  3 'But if this is so, it merely shows . . . ' (myself, in a previous chapter).

In these cases, however, there are still suitable connections, which the hearer or reader would be expected to recognize; he would not be expected to reply 'What do you mean?', etc.

19 "'If' and "⊃"', op. cit.

The statement that it is false that p or the statement that it is true that q are each of them more informative than the statement that it is not the case that it is true that p and false that q. Each of the first two is more informative than the third in the straightforward sense that it entails the third and is not entailed by it. (ibid. 236–7)

This being so, the principle of maximum informativeness could be invoked to explain the difference of use between the natural and artificial expressions as a matter of implicature and not meaning. The explanation would be that one would not make the less informative statement ('it is not the case that p is true and q is false' – in other words, 'p ⊃ q') if one were in a position to make the more informative one (which might be either 'not-p' or 'q').

I have already argued against the weaker/stronger principle, including the 'informativeness' version of it, in a previous section; but the claim about a 'straightforward' entailment should also be questioned. The claim that (say) 'p is false' entails that 'it is not the case that it is true that p and false that q' is itself valid only within the truth-functional system; outside that it would not be recognized. Thus the fact that Smith is not in London ('Smith is in London' is false) would not be thought to entail that 'It is not the case that it is true that Smith is in London and false that Smith is working'. (And neither would this be entailed, in ordinary language, by the fact that Smith *is* working (q is true).)[20]

Another writer who has tried to bridge the gap between the truth-conditions of the natural and artificial expressions is Frank Jackson.[21] He did so by interposing another form of words between them. According to Jackson, 'the circumstances in which it is natural to assert "If p then q" are those in which it is natural to assert "Either not p or, p and q".' Thus, the circumstances for asserting 'If it rains, the match will be cancelled' are the same as those for asserting 'Either it won't rain, or it will and the match will be cancelled' (ibid. 111). Having suggested that the two kinds of statements have 'the same truth conditions', he claims that 'this hypothesis ... amounts to the Equivalence thesis': namely, that the ordinary conditional 'is

---

20   Strawson explained that his arguments were based on memory of an unpublished paper by Grice (ILT 229, 235). He did not, however, settle for the Gricean view. 'Although I think these arguments are powerful, I do not think they are conclusive' (235). He thought that the contrary view was 'more realistic ... even if it is less beautiful'.

21   In F. Jackson, ed., *Conditionals* op. cit.

equivalent to (p ⊃ q)'. Their truth-conditions, he concludes, are 'the same – they agree in sense or literal content' (123).

Jackson's 'bridging' argument relies (i) on the assumption that 'Either not p or, p and q' is equivalent to its truth-functional counterpart, '∼p ∨ (p ∧ q)', and (ii) on the truth-functional equivalence of '∼p ∨ (p ∧ q)' with 'p ⊃ q'.[22] In this way he can pass from (a) 'If ... then ...' to (b) 'Either not p or, p and q', and thence to (c) '∼p ∨ (p ∧ q)' and (d) 'p ⊃ q', treating each step as one of equivalence. Now whether (a) and the strange-sounding (b) are really equivalent is open to question. Someone who says 'true' to (a) might not know what to say when faced with (b) – even if he has time to think about it. But in any case, the step from (b) to (c) is open to the objections I have already made to the treatment of 'or' and '∨' as equivalent. According to the rules for '∨', someone who writes 'true' for '∼p' must also write 'true' for '∼p ∨ (p ∧ q)'. But, by contrast, someone who says 'It won't rain' does not thereby commit himself to assenting to 'Either it won't rain or it will rain and the match will be cancelled'. This is just another example of the discrepancy between the logic of '∨' and that of the natural 'or'. (Jackson, however, relies explicitly on 'the standard and widely accepted truth-functional treatment of "not", "or" and "and"' (111).)

Conversational implicature and the theory of descriptions

The notions of 'implicature' and 'pragmatics' have been invoked to make Russell's theory of descriptions palatable in spite of its divergence from ordinary language.

> The strategy is to keep the semantics of definite descriptions as simple as possible, which means regarding them as Russell did, and to use ordinary pragmatic principles ... in order to explain surface divergences from the account.[23]

In his presentation of the theory, Russell, as we saw in the last chapter, had claimed:

---

22 Like myself, though for different reasons, Jackson rejects the weaker/stronger principle. Instead, he tries to explain the difference between the natural and artificial expressions by a principle of 'robustness', which affects assertability but not truth-conditions. This principle will not be discussed here.

23 S. Blackburn, *Spreading the Word* (OUP 1984), 310. Blackburn also speaks of what is 'implied pragmatically, or has as a "conversational implicature"...' (308–9).

When you state that the present King of France is bald you say 'There is a c such that c is now King of France and c is bald' and the denial is ... 'Either there is not a c such that c is now King of France, or, if there is such a c, then c is not bald'.[24]

Leaving aside the alleged advantage of 'convenience', discussed in the last chapter, let us consider whether Russell's claim might be regarded as true. If you made such a statement to me, I might put it to you: 'So you are saying there *is* such a person as the King of France', to which you would be expected to assent. Conversely, if I said 'But there is no such person', this would be a way of contradicting your statement and you would be expected to react in a suitable way. (It would not do to reply 'But I didn't say there is such a person.') So far, Russell's claim is confirmed. But what about the second part of it ('the denial is ...')? 'I deny that the King of France is bald.' – 'So you are saying that either there is no such person or, if there is, etc.'. The reply might be: 'No, that is not what I said.'

Let us consider how the statements of others would be reported. If Russell's claim were true, then someone who made the statement about the King of France would be reported as having said that there is such a person. 'She said there is such a person'. But to this one might reply: 'No, she didn't; she merely assumed it.' Let us try the method of contradiction: 'She said the King of France is bald'. – 'But she didn't say there is a King of France.' This would *not* serve to contradict the report of what she said. The second part of Russell's claim (about denial) would also be refuted by such tests.

There are similar objections to Blackburn's treatment of the example 'Have you stopped beating your wife?', which he introduces by way of analogy with Russell's claims. Faced with that question,

the hapless witness does not want to answer 'yes' or 'no'. But in fact 'no' is the correct answer for an innocent witness to give. Stopping doing something entails having at some time done it, and at a later time not to be doing it. If you never beat your wife, then you never stopped doing so. (op. cit. 310)

Blackburn admits that the answer 'No' might, as he puts it, 'mislead the jury', and he suggests a suitable 'signal' to avoid this possibility: to

---

24 'The Philosophy of Logical Atomism' in *Logic and Knowledge*, ed. R.C. Marsh (Allen & Unwin 1956), 251.

say 'No – because I never started'. This is comparable to Grice's cancellations of misleading implicatures. On this view, the answer 'No' would be 'true even if misleading'; and the misleading implicature could be removed by adding a suitable remark. But how can that answer be correct, when it would not be accepted as correct in ordinary conversation? If I have not been beating my wife, I would not be expected to assent to the statement that I have not stopped beating her. Conversely, if I said 'I have not been beating her', the reply 'But you have stopped beating her' would not serve to contradict what I said.

Let us spell out the analogy with Russell's example. There the existence of the King of France is assumed or presupposed in using the description 'The present King of France'. In the wife-beating case, on the other hand, the relevant presupposition is carried by a question ('Have you stopped?'). The corresponding *description* in this case would be 'your beating of your wife' or 'your wife-beating'; and on Russell's view the relevant statements would be analyzable as follows:

> When you state that your wife-beating has stopped you say 'There is a c such that c was your wife-beating and c has stopped' and the denial [the innocent witness's 'no', as recommended by Blackburn] is ... 'Either there was not a c such that c was your wife-beating, or, if there was such a c, then c has not stopped'.

On this view, what the witness would be saying if he answered 'No' would be 'Either I wasn't beating my wife or, if I was, I am still doing it.' But clearly this is not how the witness's 'No' would be reported. As in the use of 'the King of France' the existence of that person would be presupposed, so the use of 'your wife-beating' would presuppose the existence of the wife-beating. Hence the witness who denied that he had stopped beating her would be understood to have accepted that presupposition and to be saying that the beating was still going on.

For the same reason, 'Have you stopped beating her?' would never be a way of asking whether it was true that *either* there had been no beating *or* that the beating, if any, had stopped; just as 'Do you deny that the King of France is bald?' would not be a way of asking whether *either* the King does not exist *or*, if he does, he is not bald. A correct response from Blackburn's 'innocent witness' would be 'What do you mean? I haven't been beating her'. This, admittedly, would fail to satisfy those who insist on 'yes' or 'no', but it would be correct nevertheless.

Conclusion

Grice, as we have seen, regarded 'conversational implicature' as the key to resolving discrepancies between the ordinary use of certain expressions and the meanings and truth-conditions ascribed to them by philosophers. But in this he was mistaken. In the case of the bank employee, the tutor's report and others used by Grice, there is a fact of the matter (that the employee has or has not been to prison, etc.) which is independent of what we say and which can be established by observation; but this is not so with the philosophers' claims, which are essentially about meanings. Such claims can only be decided by reference to the normal use of the words in question.

The cases of the bank employee and the tutor's report depend on particular contexts. In one conversation the implication of saying 'He hasn't been to prison yet' might be p, in another q or r. As Grice pointed out, it 'might be any one of such things as that C [the bank employee] is the sort of person likely to yield to temptation, that C's colleagues are ... unpleasant and treacherous', etc. (WW 24).[25] But the philosophers' claims about L-statements, about trying and about the meanings of words such as 'and' and 'or' are not context-dependent; and neither are the objections to them.

Grice's position, again, invites comparison with that of Berkeley. As we saw in Chapter 8, Berkeley's way of accommodating philosophical truth, as he saw it, together with the ordinary use of language was to 'think with the learned and speak with the vulgar'. Given his views about the priority of thought over language, this was an appropriate way of dealing with that problem. The twentieth century philosopher Grice could not set language aside in this way; his solution was to identify two different standards governing the use of language. The first, suitable for ordinary conversation, is such that a statement may be faulted on grounds of implicature; while, according to the second, which is suitable when doing philosophy or formal logic, a statement could be 'linguistically correct and true, even if misleading' (previously quoted on page 181). In this way, he thought, one could philosophize with the learned while not interfering with ordinary conversation. But this compatibilism is an illusion, in Grice no less than in Berkeley. The objection to the philosophers' claims is not that they are misleading, but that they contravene the existing standards of correct use and inference.

---

25 Grice seems, however, to have overlooked the implication of 'yet', which is not conversation-relative. The difference between not having been to prison and *not yet* having been to prison is one of meaning and not implicature.

11 Quine and the unity of science

Philosophy and science

In Chapter 4 I contrasted our knowledge of 'what we say', in the sense that is relevant to philosophy, with empirical knowledge about language or languages. Here, as in other parts of the book, I have supported the separation of philosophy from empirical science. Now it must be admitted that as far as the word 'philosophy' is concerned, this separation is of fairly recent date. The word was formerly used to include, or even to mean, what is called 'science' nowadays. (It was in this sense that Galileo used the word when, applying for a post in Florence in 1610, 'he insisted on being described as a philosopher, not as a mathematician'.[1]) On the other hand, the words 'science' and 'scientific' have often been used without the empirical connotation.

Nevertheless there is an important distinction between empirical studies and what is called 'philosophy' according to a present usage. Let us take as an example the question 'What is perception?'. This might be understood in a scientific sense, as being, say, about processes of the eye and the brain that are involved in visual perception. But in another, philosophical sense it would be about the *logic* of the concept: about whether, say (as discussed in the last chapter), the truth of 'S saw that p' entails that it *seemed* to S as if p; and this would not be a question for scientific research. In other areas the significance of scientific results may be *questioned* on philosophical grounds. In recent times it has been widely assumed that research into brain processes may help to solve the traditional 'mind/body problem', on the assumption that the mind is nothing other than the brain, that

---

1 Ted Waring, *Cogito* 3/1989, 253. (The word 'science' has also, of course, undergone changes of meaning.)

consciousness is a brain process, and so on. But these assumptions are questionable on philosophical grounds and it has been argued that they do not make sense.[2]

It is sometimes held that the history of philosophy and science has been one in which the former has steadily contracted by transferring its contents to the latter.

> In developing from its older to its modern form, [philosophy] has shed the sciences one by one as they became amenable to systematic empirical study rather than armchair speculation – first physics and chemistry, and then the human sciences (economics, psychology, sociology).[3]

But the truth of this depends on what is meant by 'philosophy'. If what is meant is what was formerly called 'philosophy', then the claim is uncontroversial; but this is not so if 'philosophy' is meant in the sense just illustrated. For in that sense, the questions that were 'shed' never were part of philosophy; and this follows from the fact that they were able to become amenable to empirical study.

A similar point may be made about a remark made in more colourful language by J.L. Austin. 'In the history of human inquiry', he wrote,

> philosophy has the place of the initial central sun, seminal and tumultuous: from time to time it throws off some portion of itself to take station as a science, a planet, cool and well regulated, progressing steadily towards a distant final state.[4]

He thought that linguistic philosophy itself might undergo such a transmigration, becoming, in the next century perhaps, 'a true and comprehensive *science of language*'.

But if by 'philosophy' we understand the kind of enquiry undertaken by Austin himself, then it is not clear how a science of language, or any other science, could be relevant to it. Take, for example, the distinction he drew between 'It was a mistake' and 'It was an accident', as discussed in Chapter 4: this calls for reflection on the use of these expressions and not for scientific research.

---

2   See O. Hanfling, 'Consciousness: "The Last Mystery" ', forthcoming in S. Schroeder, ed., *Wittgenstein and Contemporary Philosophy of Mind* (Macmillan 2000)

3   A.R. Lacey, *A Dictionary of Philosophy* (Routledge Kegan Paul 1976), 159.

4   J.L. Austin, *Philosophical Papers* (Clarendon 1961), 180.

In recent times, however, the exclusion of scientific research from the province of philosophy has been questioned and those who insist on it may be accused of being narrow-minded. Should not the philosopher be open to the possibility, at least, that empirical science may have something to contribute to his questions? In the movement to integrate philosophy with science, W.V. Quine has been one of the most influential figures. His position is often described as 'holistic'. Our system of beliefs, he insists, is a single whole; and the whole of it is subject to the test of experience. Philosophy is no exception: 'as an effort to get clearer on things, [it] is not to be distinguished in essential points of purpose and method from ... science'.[5] He proceeded to introduce 'the proposition that external things are ultimately to be known only through their action on our bodies' (WO 4). Is this a philosophical or a scientific claim? Quine would not allow this separation: the proposition 'should be taken as one among various coordinate truths, in physics and elsewhere'.

Quine's integration of philosophy with science is expounded most explicitly in 'Epistemology Naturalized', where he discusses scepticism about the external world. Here he advocates the replacement of traditional epistemology by psychology, the latter being regarded as a physical science. Quine's reasons are similar to Hume's. The latter, he writes, 'despaired' of justifying our beliefs about the world; and he (Quine) could not do any better himself: 'I do not see that we are farther along today than where Hume left us. The Humean predicament is the human predicament'.[6] The thing to do is to give up attempts at justification and turn instead, as Hume did, to the *psychology* of belief formation: to try to explain how we do in fact arrive at those 'beliefs about the world'.

> Why not just see how this construction really proceeds? Why not settle for psychology? ... Epistemology, or something like it, simply falls into place as a chapter of psychology and hence of natural science. It studies a natural phenomenon, viz., a physical human subject. (EN 75, 82)

The business of this scientific enterprise was to study 'how evidence relates to theory, and in what ways one's theory of [the external world]

---

5   W.V. Quine, *Word and Object* (MIT Press 1960), 3–4.
6   W.V. Quine, 'Epistemology Naturalized' in *Ontological Relativity and Other Essays* (Columbia 1969), 72; hereafter 'EN'.

transcends any available evidence' (EN 83). We are to study how a person 'posits bodies and projects his physics from his data'. Here science is invoked at two levels. The ordinary person is supposed to be engaged in a kind of science in constructing his theory about the external world, and then the philosopher gives a scientific (psychological) account of this theory construction on the part of the ordinary person.[7]

In a later work Quine defended his resort to science as follows. It is science, he wrote, that 'teaches us that the only information that can reach our sensory surfaces from external objects must be limited to two-dimensional optical projections and various impacts of air waves on eardrums [etc.]'; and this being so, 'the sceptical challenge [to belief in an external world] springs from science itself, and in coping with it we are free to use scientific knowledge'.[8]

Now it is true that scientific teachings may give rise to philosophical problems. This was so, as we saw in Chapter 5, in the controversy about the solidity of tables and similar objects. Other examples are the statements of relativity theorists about time, and the discovery that among the objects we see (or appear to see) in the night sky, many have ceased to exist long before their light reaches us. But the fact that these problems spring from scientific findings and theories does not entail that the problems are themselves scientific or that they are to be settled by doing more science. Quine's argument relies on a homoeopathic principle: if the disease is brought on by X, apply more X to cure it. But what matters, in philosophy at least, is the nature and not the source of a problem. If its nature is philosophical, then it is to philosophy and not science that we must look for a cure. To abandon this approach is to leave the problem untreated.

However, Quine's reason for making the switch into science is not merely the homoeopathic one; he also holds that philosophical attempts

---

7   One might wonder whether the activity of the philosopher qua scientist-psychologist is itself to be explained by psychological science. The answer is 'yes'.

[The philosopher's] very epistemological enterprise, and the psychology wherein it is a component chapter, and the whole of natural science wherein psychology is a component book – all this is [his] own construction or projection from stimulations [of his senses] (EN 83).

Thus the input-output model that is supposed to account for human perception and behaviour is also invoked to explain how the philosopher qua scientist-psychologist *arrives* at that model.

8   W.V. Quine, *The Roots of Reference* (Open Court 1974), 2–3.

to deal with 'the sceptical challenge' are futile. But how did Quine arrive at this (philosophical) conclusion? On this question he has little to say, being content to accept Hume's conclusion (about 'the human predicament') as the last word.

One might have thought that Quine would at least consider some objections to this form of scepticism. He might, for instance, have questioned the usual empiricist representation of the human being as a passive observer, receiving 'impressions', 'sense data', 'inputs' and the like. He speaks, as we saw, of 'the stimulation of sensory receptors' and of 'the action on our bodies' of external objects (WO 4). But what about our actions on them? This aspect of the human predicament was frequently stressed by Wittgenstein, for one. Questioning how an idealist might teach his children the word 'chair', he pointed out that this would have to include the action of *fetching* a chair.[9] Quine and other empiricists speak of the physical three-dimensional world as if it were something external to us. But we are ourselves part of that world: we are embodied, we move about in the physical, spatial world and we *interact* with other bodies in various ways. It is by interacting with them – fetching them, lifting them, breaking them, eating them, bumping into them – that we form our ideas of particular bodies and the bodily world in general.

This consideration is, if anything, more urgent for Quine than for the older empiricists. The 'Humean predicament' was in fact not the same as the Quinean one (i.e. 'the human predicament', according to Quine). For Hume, as for Descartes, Locke and others, the frontier between the internal and external worlds is that between the mental and physical worlds. And since the body, being physical, is part of the external world whose existence is called into question by the sceptical challenge, the same will be true of the actions of the body on other physical things. But for Quine, who speaks throughout of the 'physical human subject', the frontier between internal and external is at the surface – the 'sensory surface', as he puts it – of that physical subject: it is a frontier within the physical world and not between that world and another. This makes it all the more surprising that in his discussion of scepticism about the external world, Quine has nothing to say about the *actions* of such subjects on their physical environment.

This is not the place for an extended discussion of scepticism about the external world, but I hope I have shown, at least, that Quine's deviation into science is unjustified and the 'despair' which prompted

9   L. Wittgenstein, *Zettel* (Blackwell 1967), 414.

it premature. There are ways of responding to the sceptical arguments used by Hume and others, but they are philosophical and not scientific.

A shrouded science

Quine's holism concerns not only the distinction between philosophy and science, but also that between scientific theories and the belief systems of ordinary people. Beliefs of the latter kind are to be treated, no less than scientific beliefs, as part of an overall system of science. And the task of the philosopher-scientist-psychologist will be to provide a theory about the theorizing that gives rise to our beliefs about an external world.

We normally think of scientists as engaged in a special kind of enquiry, sometimes with the use of special equipment and often involving unfamiliar concepts and arriving at theories that may be surprising and hard to understand. But according to Quine, we are all involved in physical science merely by believing in a world of external physical things. Our information about such things comes to us, according to Quine, 'only through the effects which they help to induce at our sensory surfaces' (WO 1). These 'surface irritations ... exhaust our clues to an external world' (22), and our talk of desks and other bodily things belongs to the domain of theory. The human subject 'posits bodies and projects his physics from his data' (EN 83). He receives only 'a meagre input' of sensory stimulation and from this there emerges 'a torrential output' of descriptions of 'the three-dimensional external world and its history'. And this output constitutes a physical theory, whose status is essentially the same as that of theories put forward by scientists. The physical scientist, working from observed data, posits a world of atomic particles; and 'the positing of these extraordinary things' is to be compared with 'the positing or acknowledging of ordinary [physical] things' by ordinary people.

In another work he compared the ordinary person's positing of physical things to the positing, by people of another age, of Homeric gods. 'For my part', he continued,

> I do, qua lay physicist, believe in physical objects and not in Homer's gods; and I consider it a scientific error to believe otherwise. But in point of epistemological footing the physical objects and the gods differ only in degree and not in kind.[10]

10   W.V. Quine, *From a Logical Point of View* (Harper 1961), 44; hereafter 'LPV'.

The superiority of 'the myth of physical objects' lay merely in the fact that it had 'proved more efficacious than other myths as a device for working a manageable structure into the flux of experience'. Further advantages of the same kind were to be gained, according to Quine, by the positing of atomic and sub-atomic entities by physicists.

Quine describes himself as an empiricist and, as already noted, his position resembles that of classic empiricists such as Hume. The fundamental epistemological role that Quine ascribes to 'sensory stimulation' was ascribed by the older empiricists to 'sensations' and 'impressions'; and in both cases the question arises how we can proceed, from these inputs, to knowledge about an external world of physical bodies extended in space and time. But there is also an important difference. According to the older empiricists, a person's knowledge and concepts are acquired from, and composed of, that person's experience of sensory qualities. Quine, however, insists that in the acquisition of concepts physical objects must come first. Although such objects 'become known to us only through [their] effects ... on our sensory surfaces', these effects do not belong to 'the primordial conceptual scheme'; so that 'talk of subjective sense qualities comes mainly as a derivative idiom. When one tries to describe a particular sensory quality, he typically resorts to reference to public things' (WO 1). We must learn our language in intersubjective situations in which reference is made to public physical objects and therefore 'it is to these that words apply first and foremost'.

In this respect Quine's position may seem more satisfactory than that of his predecessors. But does it seem so in other respects? What are we to make of the claim that the world of ordinary physical things is 'posited' by us or of the description of our knowledge of that world as a 'theory'? This is not how we normally understand our position. 'There is', Quine conceded, 'a certain verbal perversity in the idea that ordinary talk of physical things is not in large part understood as it stands'; or that evidence for the reality of 'familiar physical things ... needs to be uncovered' (WO 3). But, he complained, some philosophers make too much of these and other 'verbal perversities': they 'overdo this line of thought, treating ordinary language as sacrosanct'. Such philosophers, he said, ignore an important feature of ordinary language itself: 'its disposition to keep evolving'. One way in which this happens is the introduction of 'scientific neologisms', which he described as 'linguistic evolution gone self-conscious'.

It is true that ordinary language changes, in the course of time, in various ways and for various reasons, and it would be foolish for an ordinary language philosopher to object to a word or usage just because it is new. The word 'input', for example, has found its way into ordinary language and there is nothing wrong with it in suitable contexts. But there is more to the 'perversity' of Quine's language than the use of neologisms. To say that physical things may not be real, that 'evidence for their reality needs to be uncovered', and that we do not ('in large part') understand what we are saying when we talk about tables and chairs, is not to use neologisms, scientific or otherwise; it is to make substantive claims. And the objection to them will not be that they involve novel uses of language, but that they are unjustified. Again, the objection to Quine's uses of 'posit', 'theory' and 'physics', and his talk of 'sensory stimulation' in place of ordinary verbs of perception, will not be that they are new, but that they are incorrect and confusing.

How can we make sense of the idea that ordinary people posit bodies? To posit is to *propose* the existence of something; and we are not, and cannot be, in this position with respect to physical objects, given that these are, as Quine put it, 'our conceptual firsts'. According to Quine, we have to 'start in the middle', working back from there to the basic data impinging on our 'sensory surfaces'. 'Retrospectively we may distinguish the components of theory-building' (WO 4–5). But how are we to understand this? If those objects are conceptual firsts – if their existence must be taken for granted before we start our enquiries – then it makes no sense to speak of positing them as theoretical entities.

The positing of entities and processes is typical of scientific theorizing. A cosmologist, reasoning from astronomical observations and accepted laws of nature, may posit the existence of 'black holes' to account for otherwise inexplicable phenomena; and likewise entities of atomic theory are posited to explain the behaviour of matter. Such positing is done consciously and deliberately, on the basis of arguments put forward by the scientists concerned. But the positing of physical objects that Quine ascribes to ordinary people has to be unconscious, given that we are bound to 'start in the middle'. Such 'positing' cannot be positing in the normal sense. An ordinary person might posit the existence of *particular* bodies and such a 'theory' might be confirmed or disconfirmed in a quasi-scientific way. But this is not so with the existence of bodies in general and no such 'theory of the world' can properly be ascribed to ordinary people.

Sometimes Quine attributes the positing in question to our remote ancestors, and makes the comparison between lay and professional physics in these terms. The only difference between the two kinds of physics, he maintains, is that the professional physicist 'audibly posits [his objects] for recognized reasons, whereas the hypothesis of ordinary things is shrouded in prehistory'. The 'immemorial doctrine of ordinary enduring middle-sized physical objects' is an 'archaic and unconscious hypothesis', but 'in point of function and survival value it and the hypothesis of molecules are alike' (11, 22). The original positing having been done by our remote ancestors, there is, perhaps, no need for it to be repeated by each one of us on coming into the world. Perhaps we might think of it as being passed down from generation to generation, rather like some religious doctrine which is now taken for granted but whose origins are shrouded in the past. But even if all this were granted, the problem about doing science unconsciously would arise with our ancestors no less than with us.

The word 'positing', which is prominent in Quine's writings, may be applied to his own scientific philosophy: he *posits* unconscious processes of positing and theory building, in our minds or those of our ancestors. These processes must be unconscious; for we are not, and could not be, conscious of positing what is most familiar to us – the physical world in which we live and of which we are part.

Another difficulty with Quine's account is his treatment of perception in terms of 'surface irritations' and the 'stimulation of sensory receptors' (4, 22). To speak in this way is to imply that perception is an inferential process: we experience an irritation and from this we infer, more or less reliably, that something is the case in the external world. Such inferences are familiar enough: a person may infer from an irritation in his nose that the pollen count is high; a soreness of the eyes may indicate a lack of humidity, and so on. But *perception* is not like this and such language is not appropriate here. When I saw Smith in the office I was not conscious of any relevant 'surface irritation' or 'stimulation' and would be mystified if I were asked to identify one or to relate my perception of Smith to such an event. The distinction between perception and inference is also present in the case of science. The scientist makes inferences, puts forward hypotheses, etc., on the basis of observations; but the latter are not themselves inferences. When a scientist observes, say, a pattern of waves on a screen, he is not *inferring* (on the basis of sensory irritations, or anything else) that the waves are on the screen: he can see that they are. These observations are the basis, and not the product, of inference.

Quine, as we saw, spoke of a discrepancy between the 'meagre input' of sensory stimulation and a 'torrential output' of descriptions of 'a three-dimensional world', etc.; and he thought this called for the positing of an intervening theory. But it is only through a perversion of the language of perception that such a discrepancy appears.

'No statement is immune'

Quine's holism was eloquently expressed in an article in which he criticized the traditional separation of analytic statements from empirical ones. Our beliefs form an interdependent system and all of them, he insisted, 'face the tribunal of sense experience' together.

> The totality of our so-called knowledge or beliefs, from the most casual matters of geography and history to the profoundest laws of atomic physics or even of pure mathematics and logic ... is like a field of force whose boundary conditions are experience. (LPV 41, 42)

We are not to suppose that any beliefs are immune from revision.

> Any statement can be held true come what may, if we make drastic enough adjustments elsewhere in the system .... Conversely, by the same token, no statement is immune to revision. (43)

Now it is obvious that our beliefs are interdependent in various ways, and that the revision of one belief often entails corresponding changes in others. It is also true that one sometimes wants to cling to a belief ('come what may') even though it is in conflict with others in one's system. But Quine's position is far beyond these familiar aspects of belief: his claim is that 'the tribunal of sense experience' must be faced even by those departments of human knowledge, such as 'pure mathematics and logic', which have not usually been regarded as subject to its jurisdiction; and the same would apply to philosophy itself. Although he was not directly concerned, in this article, about the status of philosophy, his argument here has been influential in eroding the distinction between philosophy and empirical science.

Quine illustrated the non-immunity thesis with the case of analytic statements, using 'No bachelors are married' as an example. Let us suppose that my wife tells me that our new neighbour, Mr Smith, is a bachelor. A little later I go to visit Smith and he introduces me to a lady whom he describes as his wife. This will require an adjustment in my beliefs, and more than one possibility is open. The most likely is that I now believe my wife to have been misinformed; another would be that I believe her to have made a mistake; a third, less likely, that Smith made a mistake; a fourth, that he is engaged in some sort of pretence. And these possibilities, in turn, will be rendered more or less likely by other beliefs in my system, and so on. But in Quine's view, there is a further possibility to be considered, which would adjust that system equally well: to reject the statement that no bachelors are married. In that way, the conflict between my wife's report and my experience on visiting Smith would be resolved and the system restored to harmony.

A difficulty for the non-immunity thesis is that it would call into question the very notion of contradiction. If one's belief system were found to contain two contradictory statements, what adjustment would be needed? One could help oneself simply by introducing a statement denying the law of non-contradiction either in general or as applied to the troublesome case. (As Quine himself put it, we could retain any given statement 'by amending certain statements of the kind called logical laws' (LPV 43).) But if we did that, there would be no need to look for 'adjustments elsewhere in the system'; the same single adjustment, applied directly to the troublesome statement, would do the trick every time. It is, however, hard to see how language could exist at all under these conditions. If, for example, 'Smith is a bachelor' could be made coherent, by this expedient, with 'Smith is not a bachelor', then these statements would become meaningless.

Another difficulty concerns the words 'can', in 'can be held to be true' and 'make' in 'make drastic enough adjustments'. Quine speaks as if it were up to us whether to adopt a given belief or regard a given statement as true. But belief is a not a matter of choice. If I believe that Smith is a bachelor, then I cannot choose to believe that Smith is not a bachelor; and the same is true of other beliefs. This is not, as Descartes thought in his 'method of doubt', because the effort might be too great, but because the idea of choosing what to believe does not make sense. The 'cannot' is a logical and not a psychological one.[11]

Let us consider Quine's discussion of analytic statements in more detail. He introduced the traditional view as follows. The truth of a statement, he said,

> depends on both language and extralinguistic fact. The statement 'Brutus killed Caesar' would be false if the world had been different in certain ways, but it would also be false if the word 'killed' happened rather to have the sense of 'begat'. (LPV 36)

But, he went on, if truth is 'analyzable into a linguistic component and a factual component', then 'it seems reasonable that in some

---

11 This is not to deny that one can *suppose* a statement to be true – 'hold it to be true', in that sense – without, however, believing it to be true. For further discussion see O. Hanfling, 'Can there be a Method of Doubt?', *Philosophy* 1984.

statements the factual component should be null; and these are the analytic statements' (36–7). He would argue, however, that it is 'folly to seek a boundary between synthetic statements, which hold contingently on experience, and analytic statements which hold come what may' (43).

Let us consider Quine's way of introducing the traditional distinction. Given his remark that 'it seems reasonable' that in some cases 'the factual component should be null', one might wonder whether the same should not apply to the 'linguistic component'. By a 'linguistic component', Quine means the difference that the meaning of a statement makes to its truth-value. But it would be nonsense to suppose that the meaning could make *no* such difference – that the meaning component might be 'null'. On the traditional view, analytic statements remain true whatever the facts might be ('the factual component is null'). But it would be nonsense to suppose that a statement remains true whatever its *meaning* might be.

In speaking as he does of fact and meaning as 'two components' of truth, Quine obscures the priority of meaning. The meaning of a sentence determines *what* (if anything) is being stated by means of it; and *then* – in the case of synthetic statements – the facts determine whether what is stated is true. If, as Quine supposes, 'killed' had the sense of 'begat', then someone who said 'Brutus killed Caesar' would not be stating what is stated when one uses these words in English; and one statement would be true while the other was false. Two different statements would be involved.

The meaning of a word, and of sentences in which it occurs, *depends* on the relevant analytic truths. Thus if the meaning of 'bachelor' were such as to allow for the falsehood of 'No bachelors are married', then it would not be the same as that of the English 'bachelor', so that different assertions would be made in using it. If, however, the word is used with its normal meaning, then 'No bachelors are married' will be stating an analytic truth.

Instead of speaking, as Quine does, of 'two components' into which 'truth can be analyzed', the traditional distinction can be better explained by reference to how an assertion would be defended: whether it would be done by reference to empirical facts or in terms of the meanings of the words used. Or one might speak, similarly, of what is required in order to *know* whether the assertion is true: whether a knowledge of meaning is sufficient, etc.

What are Quine's reasons for rejecting the traditional distinction? Most of his article is taken up with arguments to show that no satisfactory definition of 'analytic' can be produced. We may try to define it in terms of such words as 'synonymous', 'definition' and 'necessary truth'; but these all belong to the same family as 'analytic', so that if we were asked what we mean by them, we might find ourselves thrown back on the word 'analytic'. But in Quine's view, 'we do not understand the word "analytic"' unless and until we can break out of this circle (cf. LPV 33).

This argument would have some force if 'analytic' and the rest were technical notions that had been introduced by philosophers. In that case one might reasonably hold that if they could not be defined outside the circle of that terminology, then their meanings – or whether they had any – would remain in doubt. According to Quine, the distinction between analytic and synthetic 'is a dogma of empiricists, a metaphysical article of faith' (LPV 37). But is it not recognized in ordinary language? It is true that the words 'analytic' and 'synthetic' were given special meanings by Kant and are not used, in that sense, in ordinary language. But, as Grice and Strawson showed, the distinction expressed by them is well established in ordinary language; and the same is true of 'synonymous'.[12] Thus if 'A bachelor is an unmarried male' is analytic, this might be expressed in ordinary language by saying (explaining to someone, perhaps) that the statement is true 'by definition' – 'unmarried male' being part of the definition of 'bachelor'. And if 'unmarried male of marriageable age' were regarded as the whole meaning of 'bachelor', then it might be said that they are *synonymous* or mean the same.

Such explanations are essential to our language. We need to be able to ask what a given word or phrase means, whether it does or does not mean the same as another, and whether one is entailed by another in virtue of what they mean, as 'unmarried' is entailed by 'bachelor'. The meanings of such expressions as 'means the same as , 'What does it mean?' and 'is part of the meaning of' are expressed in their use, in the work they do in our language, and it is not necessary to produce independent definitions to prove that they have meaning.

The distinction between analytic and synthetic was illustrated by Grice and Strawson in their example of a 3-year-old child. We are asked to imagine someone saying that the child 'understands Russell's Theory of Types'; and in another case, that the child 'is an adult' (op. cit. 131). The authors show how the difference between these statements would emerge in our reactions to them. In both cases one

12 H.P. Grice and P.F. Strawson, 'In Defense of a Dogma', *Philosophical Review* 1956, reprinted in H. Feigl, *New Readings in Philosophical Analysis.*

might begin by suspecting a hyperbolic use of language. But if the speaker insisted that he meant his words literally, then 'it would be appropriate in the first case to say that we did not believe him and in the second case that we did not understand him' – 'that his words have no sense'. In the first case, we can *suppose*, at least, that the child understood the theory; but it would not make sense to suppose that someone were both a child and an adult.

The notion of analytic truth – 'true in virtue of meaning' – is essential to the very concept of *meaning*. But Quine, in a reply to Grice and Strawson, tried to cast doubt on this concept too. 'It is argued', he wrote,

> that if we can speak of a sentence as meaningful, or as having meaning, then there must be a meaning that it has, and this meaning will be identical with or distinct from the meaning that another sentence has. (WO 206)

But this argument, he complained, involves a 'hypostasis' of meanings; and if it were acceptable, then 'we could as well justify the hypostasis of sakes and unicorns on the basis of the idioms "for the sake of" and "is hunting unicorns" '. (WO 207)

But the concepts of meaning, and having the same meaning, do not depend on deductions from language to ontology. That words and sentences have meaning is not inferred 'on the basis of idioms', or anything else; it is part of what is *meant* by 'word' and 'sentence' as these words are used in ordinary English, and no 'hypostasis' is needed to underpin the claim that this is so.

In another passage Quine criticized the idea that analytic statements can be identified as those we would adhere to 'come what may'. He did so in two ways, arguing that (1) supposedly analytic statements may not pass this test, while (2) supposedly synthetic statements *may* pass it. On the first point he again used the example 'No bachelor is married', claiming that 'we would not adhere to [this statement] if we found a married bachelor' (66). This, however, is to ignore Grice and Strawson's point about not understanding. The supposition that we might find a married bachelor is unintelligible in the same way as the supposition that a child might (literally) be an adult. Our reaction to it is not one of disbelief ('such a bachelor would never be found'), but of incomprehension ('What do you mean? We don't understand what you are supposing'). Or again, given the way in which truth and meaning are connected in the case of analytic statements, we might conclude that when Quine speaks of 'finding a married bachelor', he cannot be using these words in accordance with their normal meanings.

It is true, however, that this reaction would not occur with all analytic statements, and Quine was right to argue that we cannot look to such criteria as 'bewilderment' and adherence 'come what may' to establish the desired distinction (67). These criteria would be satisfactory in the cases of 'No bachelors . . .' and the 3-year-old child described as an adult, but they would fail us in the case of less obvious entailments and contradictions. In such cases the reactions of listeners would vary according to their grasp of logic and quickness of thought in such matters.

The distinction can still, however, be maintained by reference to how the relevant statements would be challenged and defended. Suppose it were said that 'An unmarried male is a bachelor' is true by definition. Many people would accept this as correct, not noticing that an unmarried male of five years of age would not be called a bachelor.[13] How would it be shown that they are mistaken? Not by empirical evidence (a survey of bachelors, etc.), but by reference to language – in this case, the use of 'bachelor': we would point out that this word is not applied to children. By contrast the statement 'Bachelors are more wealthy than other men' *would* have to be investigated by empirical methods. This distinction between methods is not affected by the limitations of the 'come what may' and 'bewilderment' criteria.

The distinction between treatments can also arise in the case of a single statement. Take the statement that horses are vegetarians. Is this analytic or synthetic? It could be either. Which it is depends on what a speaker would say in answer to the question 'How do you know?' If his answer begins 'Research has shown . . .', then his meaning is synthetic; but if he refers to a *definition* of 'horse' as 'herbivore' and hence 'vegetarian', then his meaning is analytic.

In another kind of case an *assumption* that a statement is analytic may be upset by empirical discoveries. 'All creatures that give birth to others are females': this might be accepted as analytic. But what if we learned that 'in certain varieties of sea horse, it is the male who gives

---

13 The definition of even such a word as 'bachelor' turns out to be surprisingly complicated. 'Unmarried' needs to be replaced by 'has never been married' to allow for the case of widowers. And further stipulations are needed to exclude men in societies where there is no concept of marriage, and men in our society who live in a stable relationship without being married.

birth to the young'?[14] Would this show that so-called analytic statements are, after all, not immune from revision in the light of experience? No, it would not. If we are prepared to reject the statement when we learn about sea horses, then our description of it as analytic was mistaken. If we had thought more carefully about it, we would have considered what we would say to such counter-examples and would have noticed that we would not exclude them on grounds of meaning. What such examples show is not that the distinction between analytic and synthetic is untenable, but that the identification of analytic statements is not as simple as might be thought.[15]

Another example of the same kind involves an argument put forward by an imaginary pre-Copernican thinker about the meaning of 'motion':

> Consider what it *means* to say that something moves: 'x moves' means 'x changes position relative to the Earth'. Thus, to say that the Earth moves is to say that the Earth changes position relative to itself: which is absurd. Copernicus's position is therefore an abuse of language.[16]

The imagined pre-Copernican thinker regarded his definition as analytic, and yet it was liable to be refuted by science.

But would the pre-Copernican thinker have been right to regard that definition as analytic? What if someone – say Copernicus himself – had pointed out that it is possible to think of the sun as standing still and the earth moving relative to the sun? There is no reason to suppose that this would have been unintelligible to people of that time, even though they might have rejected the idea on other grounds. Of course we cannot be sure how people at the time of Copernicus would have responded to such questions. But if the idea that the Earth moves had really been self-contradictory (like Wittgenstein's 'five o'clock on the sun'), then Copernicus could not have made his claim that the Earth moves round the sun; nor could any empirical observations have enabled him to do.

14　I have taken this example from John Hospers' discussion of analytic statements in *An Introduction to Philosophical Analysis* (Routledge 1990), 131.

15　The disjunctive entry in my dictionary (*New Shorter Oxford*) allows nicely for the case of the sea horse, defining 'female' as '. . . the sex which can bear offspring or produce eggs'. The male sea horse bears the offspring, but it is the female that produces the eggs, placing them in the male's special pouch.

16　P.M. Churchland, *Matter and Consciousness* (MIT 1984), 21.

Another way in which analytic statements may seem vulnerable to empirical refutation is that of non-existence. Phlogiston, once thought to be present in all combustible materials, was defined as being elemental; so that 'phlogiston is an elemental substance' would have been regarded as analytic.[17] Yet this statement had to be given up when, in the course of scientific development, belief in the existence of phlogiston was abandoned.

But such cases, again, do not undermine the traditional distinction. What they show is that apparently categorical statements can be, in a certain sense, hypothetical. In stating that phlogiston is a substance with such and such properties, the existence of such a substance was assumed or presupposed, in the kind of way in which the existence of the King of France would be presupposed in the statement 'The King of France is bald'.[18] With this understood, the traditional distinction between kinds of statements remains valid. Thus, assuming there is a King of France, 'The King of France is bald' would be a matter of empirical fact, while 'The King of France is a monarch' would be analytic; and similarly, assuming that phlogiston exists, 'Phlogiston is present in glass' would be empirical, while 'Phlogiston is an elemental substance' would be analytic.

Let us turn to Quine's argument on the second point: his criticism of the 'come what may' criterion as applied to synthetic statements. Are there not synthetic statements that we would adhere to, come what may? This criterion, as Quine pointed out, 'will apply as well to "There have been black dogs" as to "2 + 2 = 4" and "No bachelor is married" ' (WO 66).

'There have been black dogs' belongs to that rather heterogeneous class that Wittgenstein described as 'framework' propositions. His examples included 'I am sitting on a chair', 'The earth existed 100 years ago' and 'Motor cars don't grow out of the earth'. Such propositions, he said, have a 'peculiar logical role in our system', which he characterized in a number of ways.[19] According to the traditional classification, such propositions would count as synthetic, but it does not follow that they are subject to empirical confirmation. If someone suggested that I might be wrong in believing that there have been black dogs, I would not try to convince him by empirical

---

17 P.M. Churchland, *Scientific Realism and the Plasticity of the Mind* (CUP 1979), 47.
18 This was discussed in Chapters 9 and 10.
19 L. Wittgenstein, *On Certainty* (Blackwell 1969). See especially sections 136, 257, 308, 341, 494.

evidence. My reaction would be one of bewilderment, no less than in the case of the bachelor, the 3-year-old child and '2 + 2 = 4'. In all these cases, one might conclude that the speaker did not understand what he was saying.

But what this shows, again, is not that the traditional distinction is untenable, but only that it does not conform to the criteria of 'bewilderment' and 'come what may'. The fact remains that 'There have been black dogs' is synthetic: it is true in virtue of a contingent fact about dogs and not in virtue of meaning. It would be easy to *suppose* that the statement was false, whereas it would be nonsense to suppose that we might find a married bachelor.

In later writings Quine recognized a class of analytic statements but argued that the distinction between them and synthetic statements was not as radical as might be thought. He now presented the notion of analyticity in the light of his account of language learning.

> The learning of 'A dog is an animal' as I represented it consisted in learning to assent to it, and this hinged ... on our having learned to assent to 'dog' only in circumstances in which we learned also to assent to 'animal'.[20]

In these circumstances, he thought, it would be reasonable to describe the statement as analytic, 'for to learn even to understand it is to learn that it is true'.

On Quine's view, the analyticity of a sentence is relative to contingencies of learning. Thus a sentence is 'analytic if *everybody* learns that it is true by learning its words' (op. cit. 79), but there is no 'radical cleavage between analytic and synthetic sentences'; for while 'there are sentences whose truth is learned in that way by many of us, there are sentences whose truth is learned in that way by few or none of us'. The former, he concludes, are 'more *nearly* analytic than the latter' but they 'do not differ notably from their neighbours' (80). Analyticity is a matter of degree and varies according to circumstances of learning.

Presumably this account would also affect sentences normally regarded as synthetic: they too could turn out to be analytic to a greater or lesser extent. Thus if some people learned 'A dog is brown' by learning 'to assent to "dog" only in circumstances in which [they] learned also to assent to "brown" ', then the statement that dogs are brown would be analytic to that extent. But this statement is not

---

20   W.V. Quine, *The Roots of Reference* (Open Court 1974), 79.

analytic and someone who thought it was, or was so to some extent, would be confused. Analyticity is not a matter of degree and neither is it contingent on circumstances of learning that might vary from person to person. What matters is not what a person 'assents to' when confronted with 'stimuli' in the nursery, but how we, who have mastered the language, treat the sentences in question in our discourse with one another.[21]

21 In the last few paragraphs, and in earlier passages, I have used 'statement' where Quine prefers 'sentence'. Quine frequently speaks of *sentences* as being true or false, analytic or synthetic. But this is a confusing usage. What is true or false is what is stated or asserted *by means* of a sentence. When S asserts that Brutus killed Caesar, his words – in the case of English, the words 'Brutus', 'killed' and 'Caesar' – are the *instrument* of his assertion; and an instrument cannot be described as true or false. The same assertion can be made by means of other words (say in French or German), with the truth-value remaining constant.

12 Scientific realism
Discovering what we really mean

We have seen how, according to Quine's argument, the distinction between a priori and empirical knowledge cannot be sustained, so that the enquiries of the philosopher cannot be insulated from the findings of scientific research. Another development of this kind is the 'scientific realism' of Putnam and Kripke, who claim that what we mean by our words depends on the real nature of things, as revealed by scientific investigation, and is not to be established by a priori reflection on 'what we say'. They also claim that statements regarded as analytic may turn out, in the light of scientific discoveries, to be false.

Although the claims of these writers are mainly about words for 'natural kinds', such as 'gold', 'water' and 'cat', they are thought to have wider implications for philosophical practice and to undermine the philosophy of 'what we say'. According to this, philosophical questions are essentially about meaning, and the meaning of a word is known by anyone who uses it correctly in the contexts in which it is at home. But according to scientific realism, this may not be the last word: the real meanings of words may depend on 'scientific essences' – the real nature of things as revealed by science. Hence, if a philosopher objected, say, to the identification of thoughts with brain processes on the ground that this is contrary to the meanings of the relevant words as displayed in their use, the reply may be made that the use of a word is not a reliable guide to its meaning; and that the true meaning of 'thought' and related words may be such as to allow for the identification of thoughts with brain processes.

Intension and extension

Scientific realism was expounded by Putnam in terms of 'intension' versus 'extension'. If we take for example the word 'lemon', we might think of its meaning in two different ways. There is the class of objects to which the word is applicable, i.e. lemons: this is the extension (or 'reference') of the word; and there is the set of conditions that are accepted as reasons for calling something a lemon: this is the intension. On the 'traditional' view, the meaning of a word is primarily a matter of its intension. It is *because* the word has the intension it has that people apply it to the objects making up the extension. Thus 'intension determines extension'.

The matter is sometimes discussed in terms of what is in the mind or 'in the head' versus what is 'really there'. Thus Putnam rejects the traditional view by denying that 'meanings are in the head'.[1] But a defender of that view does not need to subscribe to this strange assertion. What he would say is that knowing the meaning of a word is the ability to use it in accordance with its intension, so that one would know the meaning of 'lemon' if one knew the relevant properties on the basis of which the word is normally applied. The knowledge of meaning would not depend on whether the objects one describes are really ('extensionally') lemons, but on one's grounds for calling them lemons. To take a different example, a defender of the traditional view would say that a person knows the meaning of the word 'pain', not on condition that the people he describes as being in pain are really in pain, but on condition that these descriptions are based on suitable grounds. But in neither case is there any need to speak of 'meanings in the head' (or in the mind, etc.).

In opposing the traditional view of meaning, Putnam, Kripke and their followers have produced a variety of interesting examples, which may be grouped into two kinds. In the first, a word is applied, in accordance with its intension, to things which are really different in nature. Here we are to say that the word does not have the same meaning throughout, even though this is not known to those using the word. In the second kind of case, the real nature of the objects is the same, but the relevant intensions differ from one time to another. This time we are to say that the meaning remains the same, in spite of changes of intension. In both cases, meaning is determined by the real nature of things and not by intensions. I shall argue that these examples do not entail a separation of meaning from intension and that knowledge of meaning is not a matter of scientific discovery. It will also emerge, if I am right, that the question at stake in these examples is not about intension versus extension, but about rival *in*tensions. If

---

1 Hilary Putnam, *Mind, Language and Reality* (CUP 1975), 223–7; hereafter 'MLR'.

this is correct, then the theory in question is not as far removed as might be thought from the method of 'what we say': it is indeed an example of that method, the dispute being *about* what we would say in the relevant cases. I begin with the first kind of example.

Same intension, difference in objects

'A colony of English-speaking Earthlings is leaving in a spaceship for a distant planet' (MLR 150–1). On board they have a quantity of aluminium and a quantity of another metal, molybdenum, supposed to be indistinguishable from aluminium, except by such 'hidden' characteristics as atomic weight. On arrival at the distant planet no one remembers these characteristics. A guess is made as to which metal is which and it happens to be wrong. As a result, they apply 'aluminium' to their molybdenum and vice versa. What should we say about the meanings of their words in these circumstances? 'It is clear', concludes Putnam, 'that "aluminium" has a different meaning in this community than in ours: in fact, it means molybdenum'. The meaning, if Putnam is right, is determined by what is really there and not by the intensions governing the use of these words.

But is this a case of extension versus intension? Have the intensions remained the same? There is more than one way of understanding the story. Suppose the travellers had forgotten, not merely *what* the hidden characteristics were, but that there were such characteristics. In that case there will have been a *change* of intensions, since these characteristics were part of the intension before the flight. And then the supposed change of meanings would be accounted for by a change of intensions.

On this reading, however, it would be hard to see how they could go on using two different words for the metals – how they could regard them as two different metals when, as far as they were concerned, they would be completely indistinguishable. So let us try the other alternative: they remember that there was a hidden difference, but not what it was. Perhaps the metals had been packed in two boxes at the start of the journey and a careless attendant had chalked 'M' on the one containing aluminium and 'A' on the other. The travellers remember that there was a reason, to do with hidden characteristics, for using two different words, and that is why they go on using them, as described in the example.

Would this be a case of 'same intension, but change of meaning'? According to Putnam, there would have been a change of meaning because of the exchange of metals, with each word now being applied to the other metal. But this is wrong: such a change would not be a change of meaning, but merely one of mistaken identification. The travellers think that the stuff marked 'A' is aluminium, but they are mistaken. They think that if the 'hidden' criteria, whatever they were, were applied to this stuff, the verdict would be 'aluminium', and in this they are wrong. But a mistake in identification does not entail a change of meaning. Such mistakes are common in everyday life and, so far from constituting changes of meaning, they presuppose a *stability* of meaning. Suppose someone describes his furniture as wood, but it is really a plastic imitation of wood. He is mistaken; but to say this is to presuppose that when he says 'wood' he means the word in the *same* sense as when he uses it in reference to genuine wood.

There is, however, a use of 'mean' which may seem more favourable to the extensional view. One might say that when the space travellers say 'aluminium', *they mean* molybdenum. But this would not be saying that *the word* had changed its meaning. The change would be in their state of knowledge and not in the meaning of the word. Suppose an inspector from Earth, who knows what the hidden characteristics are, visits the travellers and tells them about their mistake. The reaction will not be 'We used the word with a different meaning', but 'We thought this stuff was aluminium and we were mistaken'.

In another, famous example we are taken to a planet called 'Twin Earth'. This planet, we are told, is very much like ours and the people there 'even speak English' (MLR 223). There is just one difference. What is called 'water' on Twin Earth 'is not H_2O but a different liquid', whose chemical formula is 'XYZ'. This liquid does not, however, differ from what we call 'water' in any of the properties that would be apparent to ordinary users of the word on either planet. Thus 'XYZ is indistinguishable from water at normal temperatures and pressures. In particular, it tastes like water and it quenches thirst like water.' XYZ is what the lakes and oceans of Twin Earth contain, what comes down when it rains there, etc.

What would we say about the meaning of 'water' when the word is used by Twin Earthians? Putnam argues that in spite of the superficial resemblance between XYZ and H_2O, they are really different substances, and that 'water' would therefore have two different meanings: 'in the sense in which it is used on Twin Earth ... what we call "water" simply isn't water'. Hence 'the Earthian spaceship will report "On Twin Earth the word 'water' means XYZ" ' (MLR 223–4).

But may not the Earthians report their discovery in a different way? Perhaps they will say 'On Twin Earth, *water* has the chemical structure XYZ' – thus implying that 'water' has the same meaning on Twin

Earth as on Earth, in spite of the difference of chemical structure. Whether the Earthians would report this or something else is impossible to say. Perhaps, if they have studied under Putnam, they would report as he says. But if they did, would that entail a separation of meaning from intension? Again the answer is 'No'. If the Earthians' reason for reporting a difference of meaning is that the stuff is not H_2O, then H_2O must be part of their *intension* for 'water'.

Putnam is mistaken in treating the issue as one of intension versus extension: it is really about rival *in*tensions. If the visitors from Earth judge that the ordinary qualities constitute the intension of 'water', then they will not report a difference of meaning; but if they judge chemical structure to be of overriding importance, then they will report as predicted by Putnam. The choice would probably depend on the context in which the word 'water' was to be used. But either way, the issue is not about intension versus extension, but about ordinary versus scientific intensions. Putnam thinks that the latter would always prevail, but while they might do in some contexts, there is no reason to think that it would be so in general.

This can also be seen if we consider the case of another planet, Twin Earth₁. On this planet, as on Twin Earth, there are people just like ourselves, who speak English etc. There is one difference, however. When they use the word 'water', they refer to a thick green sludge with a nasty smell. On noticing this the explorers from Earth report: 'On Twin Earth₁ "water" means something other than what is meant by "water" on Earth: it means a thick green sludge with a nasty smell'. But now suppose that, after some time, they carry out tests on the stuff and discover, to their amazement, that its chemical composition is nothing other than H_2O! This, according to Putnam's view, would require a second report: 'Correction: the Twin Earth₁ "water" means *the same* as our word; we were misled by the superficial qualities of their water.' We may wonder how this report would be received at the base station on Earth. But there is no reason to think that this is how the matter would or should be reported.

In a later work Putnam considered the objection, made by 'some philosophers', that the verdict on the Twin Earth discovery should be 'There are two kinds of water' and not 'that our word "water" does not refer to the Twin Earth liquid'.[2] He thought he could deal with this objection by modifying his example. We are now to suppose that the liquid on Twin Earth is 'not *that* similar to water': it is, in fact, a

---

2   Hilary Putnam, *Reason, Truth and History* (CUP 1981), 23.

mixture of 80 per cent water and 20 per cent grain alcohol, but 'the body chemistry of the Twin Earth people is such' that they cannot tell the difference. In this case we would surely agree with Putnam that 'our word "water" does not refer to the Twin Earth liquid' – or as we might put it, that what they call 'water' isn't really water. Should we not similarly agree in the case in which the liquid turned out to be XYZ and not H_2O?

These examples are not alike. In the XYZ example there is a challenge to the assumption that the 'hidden', scientific intension would prevail over the ordinary one. In the new example, by contrast, it is clear that the liquid described would not conform to the *ordinary* intension. According to this, 'water' means a tasteless, non-intoxicating liquid; and by this is meant, of course, that it is tasteless, etc., for ordinary human earthlings and not that it is so for beings with a different body chemistry, whether on earth or in other parts of the universe. It is because the liquid in the new example does not satisfy the ordinary *intension* of 'water', that we would not describe it as such.

Here, as in other passages, Putnam treats questions of meaning and belief as being about what is in a person's head as against what is there externally to the person. His conclusion about the new Twin Earth example is the 'externalist' one, that

> the statement 'John believes there is a glass of water in front of him' is not just a statement about what goes on in John's head, but is in part a statement about John's environment, and John's relationship to that environment. If it turns out that John is a Twin Earth person, then what John believes when he says 'there is a glass of water on the table' is that there is a glass containing a liquid which *in fact* consists of water and grain alcohol on the table. (ibid. 28)

Let us consider these claims in reverse. The second is true, but not for the reasons given in the first. It is true because in saying the sentence 'there is a glass of water on the table', John would not be expressing a belief *that there is a glass of water on the table*, for this is not what that sentence would mean in John's language. The first claim, however, is false: the statement 'John believes there is a glass of water in front of him' would be *neither* about 'what goes on in John's head' *nor* about his environment. The difference between John's environment (including his body chemistry) would be *responsible* for the difference between his language and ours; but this is not what we would be *stating* if we said 'John believes there is a glass of water in front of him'. The latter would not be (even in part) a statement about John's environment.

Same object, difference of intension

In another kind of example we are to consider words whose intensions have changed, but where the corresponding objects remain the same. The claim of the realist will be that meanings remain the same in spite of changes of intension.

A favourite example is 'gold'. We are asked by Kripke to suppose that scientific discoveries have led us to adopt new criteria (intensions) for gold, so that we now exclude certain specimens from the description 'gold', which would not have been excluded in earlier times. Would this be a change of meaning? No, says Kripke, we would not 'have changed the *meaning* of the term gold'. We would merely have *'discovered* that certain properties were true of gold in addition to the initial identifying marks by which we identified it'; and 'scientific discoveries of species essence do not constitute a "change of meaning" '.[3] The meaning of the word is determined by the nature of the stuff, which remains unchanged.

To illustrate how the meaning – the real meaning – of 'gold' was already present when the word was used in earlier times, Putnam considers the position of Archimedes. When the latter 'asserted that something was gold (χρυσοζ)', writes Putnam,

> he was not just saying that it had the superficial characteristics of gold ...; he was saying that it had the same *hidden structure* (the same 'essence', so to speak) as any local piece of gold (MLR 235).

Although Archimedes did not have the modern scientist's knowledge of hidden structure, it was, on this view, already allowed for in his meaning. According to Putnam, this is borne out by the way in which Archimedes would have reacted to a modern scientific explanation. Given the explanation that 'gold has such and such a molecular structure' and that X, an object he had described as gold (χρυσοζ), did not have this structure, 'is there any doubt that he would have agreed with us that X isn't gold?' (237–8). Assuming the answer to be that there is none, Putnam concludes that the meaning of 'gold' has remained the same throughout – just as the real nature of gold has

---

3 Saul Kripke, *Naming and Necessity* (Blackwell 1980), 118–19, 138; hereafter 'NN'.

remained the same throughout. What happened was merely that the hidden part of the meaning was made known to Archimedes and this led him to recognize that certain objects were not really gold: not really *what he had meant* by this word.

Here again, however, the issue is not about intension versus extension: it is about the hidden versus the known intension (or the hidden part of the intension versus the known part), and Putnam's claim is that the former would, when made known to Archimedes, prevail over the latter.

Are there really such 'hidden' components of meaning, which, when made known, prevail over the known components? Yes; when an ordinary person uses the word 'gold' today, he means to refer to whatever the experts, using tests unknown to him, would pronounce to be gold. Putnam, in an apt phrase, speaks in this connection of a 'division of linguistic labour' (227). This division, to be sure, is more complicated than that between layman and expert; for the meaning of 'expert' depends on the circumstances. In one case it might be a jeweller and in another a scientist; and their verdicts would not necessarily coincide. The scientist might know, qua scientist, that the gold ring he bought at the jeweller's is not 'really' gold, without denying that it is really gold in the jewellers' (and legal) sense. (Putnam tells us (250) that 'pure gold is nearly white'.)

But was Archimedes' 'χρυσοζ' related in this sort of way to the modern scientists' 'gold'? Was his meaning, in that sense, the same as theirs? Whether he would have answered in the way described by Putnam is impossible to tell. Perhaps the latter based his hope on the fact that Archimedes was a scientist. But what if the interview were conducted with some other person, living in a non-scientific community, past or present, in which there was no conception of hidden scientific criteria?[4] It might be said that such a person could be taught about modern science and learn that 'gold has such and such a molecular structure'; and perhaps, if this happened, he would 'agree with us that X isn't gold'. But in that case there would have been, contrary to the realist theory, a *change* in the meaning of 'gold': the meaning would now include the 'hidden' component, whereas it did not do so before. Perhaps it will be said that this change of meaning was always there potentially, since it was always possible that those people would come to 'agree with us' on being suitably instructed. But a potential change of meaning is not part of an existing meaning. If a

---

4   See Quassim Cassam, 'Science and Essence', *Philosophy* Jan. 1986.

word may come to mean something different in the future, it follows that this is not its meaning now.

However, sameness and difference of meaning is not a matter of all or nothing; and here we have an important difference between meaning according to the realist theory and meaning as ordinarily understood. We recognize partial changes of meaning and indeed they are characteristic of the development of language through the ages. Nowadays bronze is not included in the meaning of 'brass', but in the seventeenth century it was. Should we say that 'brass' had a different meaning then? Yes, but only to some extent. There is no absolute answer and the appeal to hidden structures will not provide one. In modern English texts 'χρυσος' is translated as 'gold'. If this is a correct translation, does it follow that the modern word means exactly the same as the ancient one? No; but there is a sufficient overlap of meaning to justify the translation.

Such partial changes of meaning are not allowed for by the realist theory, for according to it, meaning is determined by the thing or stuff referred to; and since these have not changed (gold remains gold and water remains water), the meanings must similarly remain unchanged. Hence, according to the theory, the component of hidden structure must have been present in the ancient meaning – the interview with Archimedes must go as predicted by Putnam – if the translation is to be justified.

In this respect Locke's discussion of gold and other 'natural kinds' was nearer to what we ordinarily understand by 'meaning'. He spoke of 'real essences', which 'may be taken for the very being of any thing, whereby it is, what it is', depending on the 'unknown constitution of things' (*Essay*, 3.3.15). According to Locke, however, we are not to think that the real essence of a thing is what the name for it means. Thus the 'ordinary signification of the name Man ... is our complex idea, usually annexed to it' (3.6.43): it corresponds to the known features of men by which we recognize them as such. Locke describes how and why we may want our words to stand for the real and not merely 'nominal' essences of things, but he thinks this is a vain hope, given that the real essences (of natural kinds) are beyond our knowledge (3.6.49–50). In this account of meaning there is room for partial changes of meaning, when 'the ideas annexed to' a word change, to some extent, in the course of time.

In support of the view that meanings adhere to the real essences of things, Kripke used the example of light, among others.

> Though we may identify light by the characteristic visual
> impressions it produces in us, this seems to be a good example

of fixing a reference [to the real essence of a thing]. We fix what light is by the fact that it is whatever, out in the world, affects our eyes in a certain way.

This 'whatever' turns out to be 'a stream of photons' and it follows, according to Kripke, that *this* is what 'light' really means (NN 129–30).

But this story about 'identifying light' and 'fixing a reference' is a philosopher's myth. No such acts take place in using or learning to use the word 'light', and neither is there reason to suppose that such acts occurred in the distant past. Kripke's account might be more appropriate for entities posited in the context of a scientific theory. The word 'gene' may have been introduced to mean 'the ultimate units of mutation and recombination', etc., whatever these might turn out to be. But the concept of light could not have been introduced in such a way, and neither is it a 'whatever' concept. Light is an object of direct experience, and 'light' a word of ordinary language.

To support his claim that 'light' means 'a stream of photons', Kripke points out that light would exist even if people's eyes were not affected in the relevant way – if 'human beings were blind or their eyes didn't work' (129). Now it is true that light would and does exist even if there is no one there to see it. Light does not disappear when no one is looking and it existed long before sentient beings appeared on earth. But this is not because light is a stream of photons; it is because light is a property of the objective world. Just as 'full many a flower is born to blush unseen', so we may speak of light existing, or having existed, in totally unvisited places. But such statements do not owe their truth to the fact that light is a stream of photons; nor do they entail that this is what we really mean by 'light'.

The treatment of 'light' as a 'whatever' concept is comparable to recent analyses of the language of consciousness in causal or 'functionalist' terms, and similar difficulties arise here. Thus it has been claimed that what we mean by 'pain' or 'anger', for example, is whatever 'is apt to be the cause of certain effects or apt to be the effect of certain causes', where this might turn out to be a state of the brain.[5] But here again the 'whatever' is unjustified. We know from ordinary experience what pain and anger are, and whether they are present; and it is by their ordinary use that the words 'pain' and 'anger' are defined.

---

5 See D.M. Armstrong, 'Early Causal and Functionalist views', in W.G. Lycan, ed., *Mind and Cognition* (Blackwell 1990), 37.

Intension and analytic truth

The intensional view of meaning is connected with the recognition of analytic truths. To know the intension of a given word is to know its meaning, and this enables us to recognize certain statements as true in virtue of meaning. But according to the realist theory, as we have seen, meaning is not determined by intension, and therefore statements regarded as analytic are not really so. Thus

> it is not analytic that all tigers have stripes, nor that some tigers have stripes; it is not analytic that all lemons are yellow, nor that some lemons are yellow; it is not even analytic that tigers are animals or that lemons are fruits. (MLR 205)

According to Kripke, 'such statements are not known a priori, and hence are not analytic; whether a given kind is a species of animal is for empirical investigation' (NN 122–3).

The inclusion of 'lemons are yellow' and 'tigers have stripes' as candidates for analytic truth was, however, misleading. It is true that being yellow and having stripes are commonly associated with (respectively) lemons and tigers; but one would not be particularly surprised to read in guide-book that, say, in parts of South America there are tigers without stripes, or to learn that certain varieties of lemon are, say, green and not yellow. These suppositions would not be regarded as self-contradictory or incoherent. But what are we to make of the claim that 'Tigers are animals' is not analytic? Kripke, having made a similar claim about cats, asks us to consider that 'cats might turn out to be automata, or strange demons ... planted by a magician'. In that case, according to him, we would say, 'not that there turned out to be no cats, but that cats have turned out not to be animals' (NN 122; cf. MLR 243–4).

It is not clear how we are to understand this. Presumably the word 'cats' in the example is intended to mean cats – those small furry animals familiar to us, whose reproductive arrangements are well known and whose insides are known to vets and subject to treatment in the same kind of way as ours. This being so, what could it mean to describe them as 'automata' or 'strange demons', or to suppose that they 'turned out' to have been 'planted by a magician'?

Let us consider a more intelligible supposition. Suppose that a process had been perfected for making 'cats' out of computer-parts and other inorganic materials. Would this show that 'cats are animals' is not analytic? If the behaviour of these creatures were largely indistinguishable from that of ordinary cats, we might well resist the conclusion that they are 'not animals'.[6] According to Putnam and Kripke, they would not be animals because of the difference of 'hidden structure'. But if we agree with this, why should we agree that they are cats? One way or the other, there is no reason to think that what we would say would be contrary to the analytic statement that cats are animals.

Another example used by Kripke is the statement that tigers have four legs. This, he says, is 'part of the concept [intension]' of 'tiger' and yet it does not follow that 'having four legs' is analytic to the meaning of 'tiger'. May it not turn out, he asks, that tigers are really three-legged, that 'explorers who attributed these properties to tigers were deceived by an optical illusion'? (NN 120). In that case no tigers (or no normal tigers) would answer to the existing concept; but does it follow that there would be no tigers? No, replies Kripke: what we would say is that 'tigers in fact have three legs'. This, however, would not entail a change of *meaning*, for in this case again the meaning would depend on the real nature of things; and it would now appear that the intension (or 'concept') had not corresponded to the true meaning of 'tiger'.

But how are we to understand this example? The writings of Kripke and Putnam are full of colourful suppositions in which things 'turn out' to be amazingly different from what we had thought, owing to some optical or other illusion. Now it is often useful, in philosophy, to introduce thought-experiments which are beyond the bounds of empirical possibility; but they should not go beyond the bounds of sense. How can we make sense of the supposition about tigers? If those explorers were deceived by an optical illusion, would we be similarly deceived when we look at tigers in the zoo or on television? Do the television people use trick photography to fool us, perhaps with the intention of supporting Kripke? Again, where would the three legs be situated and how would the animals run? Finally, if illusion were conceivable here, how could we trust our senses at all? And if we could not, how could we have our system of beliefs and concepts at all? If these questions cannot be cleared up, then we are in no position to evaluate Kripke's argument. The argument depends on a claim about 'what we would say': that in the supposed case we would say that 'tigers in fact have three legs'. But in view of the incompleteness of the example, there is no telling what we might say.

---

6 For discussion of such suppositions with regard to persons, see my article 'Machines as Persons?' in David Cockburn, ed., *Human Beings* (CUP 1991).

Rigid designators and 'metaphysical necessity'

As we have seen, the main aim of the realist argument was to show that the meaning of a word is fixed by the real nature of the corresponding things (or stuffs) and not by the word's intension as known to those who use it. Now according to Kripke and Putnam, this relation is of the same kind as that between a proper name and the individual named by it; and to understand their position fully, we must consider it in this light.

According to Kripke a proper name is a 'rigid designator'. It retains its attachment to the individual originally designated by it, regardless of variations in beliefs about that individual by subsequent users of the name. The attachment is sustained by a suitable 'chain of communication', with the name being passed from speaker to speaker, and not by any associated beliefs. Thus if all our beliefs about, say, the prophet Jonah were false, we could still be speaking of the same person to whom this name was originally given (NN 66–7). Similarly, someone who thought of Einstein simply (and falsely) as 'the man who invented the atomic bomb' could be referring to the same individual, when he used this name, as a person with a fuller and more accurate knowledge about Einstein (85).

This account of proper names has implications for identity statements, such as 'Cicero was Tully' and 'Hesperus is Phosphorus'. By 'Hesperus' we mean, on this account, the body to which this name was originally given; and by 'Phosphorus' we mean the body to which *this* name was originally given. But if it turns out that it was one and the same body to which the two names were given, then we cannot suppose that Hesperus were not identical with Phosphorus, for this would be to suppose that a thing were not identical with itself. Hence, it is argued, if 'Hesperus is Phosphorus' is true, then it is *necessarily* true; and in this way necessary truths can be discovered *a posteriori*.

Kripke and Putnam believe that this account of proper names can be extended to names of natural kinds. According to them, such words as 'water' and 'gold' mean what they mean by being related in a 'rigid' way to the corresponding substances and not in virtue of the intensions assigned to the words by those who use them; and statements such as 'Water is H_2O' and 'Gold is the element with atomic number 79' are, if true, necessarily true. Kripke speaks of this necessity as 'metaphysical' (NN 35–6) and it has been claimed that his and similar views have resulted 'in the resurgence of metaphysics as an important branch of philosophical study'.[7]

---

7   S. Schwartz, ed., *Naming, Necessity and Natural Kinds* (Cornell 1979), 34–5.

Sometimes we are invited to think of names of natural kinds in terms of an initial 'introducing event', corresponding to an act of baptism in the case of proper names. Putnam supposes he had been introduced to the word 'electricity' by the electrical pioneer Benjamin Franklin 'as he performed his famous experiment', with Franklin telling him what, as he understood it, electricity consists in. This might result in a very defective understanding of electricity on the learner's part; but it would still be true that when he used the word 'electricity', it would mean electricity. What would make this so, according to Putnam, would not be the (defective) intension, but the causal connection with the introducing event (MLR 200). After that event (which might be long forgotten) the word would retain its meaning through a chain of transmission from one speaker to another. Thus it might have been introduced into a given speaker's vocabulary 'by an introducing event, or by his learning the word from someone who learned it via an introducing event, or by his learning the word from someone linked by a chain of such transmissions to an introducing event' (202).

Again, it might be that 'different speakers use the word "electricity" without there being any discernible "intension" that they all share' (199–200), apart from the minimal understanding of it as 'a physical quantity'. (In more radical versions by other writers this kind of requirement is also discarded.) What matters is the causal nexus by which the uses of 'electricity' are all linked, however indirectly, to the common introducing event that originally established the connection between word and object (202). If the speaker's 'use of the word is connected by [that] sort of causal chain . . ., then we have a clear basis for saying that he uses the word to refer to electricity' (201). Here, as in the case of proper names, name and object are held together by a kind of metaphysical super-glue: once brought together, they remain joined for ever.

Electricity is a useful example from Putnam's point of view. We know that this word was introduced at a particular time as the name of a new phenomenon; and it is also clear that in the case of this word the 'hidden', scientific part of the intension carries much weight. For ordinary people electricity is largely a mystery; it is something that makes things work when plugged in, something produced at power stations, and so on; but beyond this the meaning of the word depends largely on what scientists mean by it. Even so, is it true that whether 'electricity' means the same today as formerly depends on a causal continuity with an introducing event, as opposed to the intensions recognized by speakers then and now? This cannot be maintained if 'meaning' itself is to retain its normal meaning. Suppose that in the course of time 'electricity' came to have the intension that 'water' has now. (We could think of a causal chain, perhaps involving the phrase 'electric current', by which this might happen.) Then a future person consulting an etymological dictionary would discover, and would say, that the word had *changed* its meaning – regardless of any causal chain linking the new meaning with the old.

According to the theory, as I said, necessary truths, in a 'metaphysical' sense, can be discovered *a posteriori* by scientific investigation. An example used by Kripke is the discovery that whales are mammals. The scientist who made the discovery was, he says, in the position of 'discovering that "whales are mammals, not fish" is a necessary truth' (NN 138). But if 'whales are mammals' is a necessary truth, this is because 'mammal' is (now) part of the meaning of 'whale'; it is because 'whales are mammals' is (now) an *analytic* truth, which can be known a priori in accordance with the traditional dichotomies. This was not so in earlier times, from which we may conclude that the word has, to that extent, changed its meaning. This, however, is just what Kripke denies: 'scientific discoveries do not constitute a "change of meaning" ' (138). The meaning, tied to the real, unchanging nature of the objects, remains the same throughout.

Now it is true that scientific discoveries do not 'constitute' a change of meaning, but they can *bring about* such a change; and this is just what we can say in the present case. 'In the year ... it was discovered that whales are mammals and as a result "mammal" became part of the meaning of "whale".' The corresponding necessary (i.e. analytic) truth would be *consequent* on the scientific discovery and not itself an object of scientific discovery.[8]

The realist theory, with its reliance on rigid designators, leaves no room for partial changes of meaning. If there is a suitable chain of

---

8 That these things are separate is suggested in a passage from *Moby Dick*:

> in some quarters it still remains a moot point whether a whale be a fish. In his System of Nature, AD 1776, Linnaeus declares, 'I hereby separate the whales from the fish ... on account of their warm bilocular heart, their lungs, their movable eyelids, their hollow ears, *penem intrantem feminam mammis lactantem*'. .... I submitted all this to my friends Simeon Macey and Charley Coffin, of Nantucket, both messmates of mine in a certain voyage, and they united in the opinion that the reasons set forth were altogether insufficient. Charley profanely hinted they were humbug.
>
> Be it known that, waiving all argument, I take the good old-fashioned ground that the whale is a fish, and call upon holy Jonah to back me.
>
> This fundamental thing settled, the next point is, in what internal respect does the whale differ from other fish?

transmission from the 'introducing event', then the meaning remains unchanged; if the chain is broken, the meaning is lost. Partial changes of meaning are, however, essential to the development of a language. At one time the word 'germ' meant 'that portion of an organic being which is capable of developing into a new individual'; but nowadays it also means 'a micro-organism or microbe, especially one that causes disease'. Let us suppose that the earlier meaning was that originally given to the word. It is not hard to see how the new meaning might have developed out of the old, and to regard the new meaning as *continuous* with the old. But this is not to say that the meaning has remained unchanged. To take another example, 'hardwood', as used in the timber trade, is applied to woods such as balsa, which are far from hard; but it is not difficult to imagine how 'hardwood' may have developed out of 'hard wood'. In this, as in a thousand other cases, meanings change; they are not held rigid by unchanging essences or attachment to an original introducing event.

The meaning of a word may also depend on the context in which it is used. Consider the word 'ear'. Ears are things visible at the side of the head, but they are also the organs of hearing. Now we know that if we block the holes at the sides of the head we cannot hear, and from this we infer that the ear qua organ of hearing is somewhere inside the hole. Should we say, then, that this is the *real* ear – that this is what the word 'ear' really means? No; for it would not be the real ear in the context of describing a person's appearance. In that case the visible ear would be 'the real' ear. (Consider, similarly, the word 'egg' as used (a) in shopping or on a menu and (b) in gynaecology. To describe one of these as 'the real' meaning would betray a misunderstanding of the concept of meaning.)

Knowing what we mean

'In philosophy', wrote Wittgenstein, 'everything lies open to view', and 'what is hidden . . . is of no interest to us' (PI 126). The philosophy of 'what we say' is about the meanings of words and these 'lie open to view', given that the meaning of a word is displayed in its normal use. The latter assumption is, however, contrary to the realist account, which drives a wedge between meaning and use, so that according to it the meanings of our words can be hidden from us.

Consider again the case of the space travellers who forgot the atomic weights of the two metals they had brought with them and thereafter referred to their molybdenum as 'aluminium' and vice versa. Putnam, as we saw, concluded that 'aluminium' has a different meaning in [their] community than in ours'. But this change of meaning would not have been known to the space travellers. Hence they would not have known the meaning of this word, in spite of their regular use of it.

In the time before modern chemistry no one could have known that water consists of oxygen and hydrogen; and on Twin Earth (assuming parallel histories) no one could have known that their water consists of XYZ. Even so, claims Putnam, since the real nature of the two waters was different in those times just as it is now, the meanings of 'water' differed accordingly. Hence two persons on Earth and Twin Earth, even if wholly identical, could not have used this word with the same meaning. They would have

> understood the term 'water' differently in 1750 *although they were in the same psychological state* and although . . . it would have taken their scientific communities about fifty years to discover that they understood the term 'water' differently. (MLR 224)

(The use of 'understood' in this passage is misleading. The difference, according to the realist account, would not be in what they understood but in what they 'really meant': in one case the real meaning would be H_2O, in the other it would be XYZ.) Suppose now that the two speakers met and told each all they knew about water. They might think that 'water' meant the same throughout the conversation, but in this they would be mistaken.

How well is a person living today equipped to know the meaning of such a word? Suppose he knew nothing about H_2O. Then, according to the realist account, he would not know what 'water' means, in spite of the fact that he regularly uses the word in the normal way. Or suppose that, while knowing about H_2O, he disagreed with the realist account, maintaining that what he and others mean by 'water' is a substance having such and such familiar characteristics and not whatever has a particular hidden structure. In this case again, he would fail to know what 'water' really means.

If, on the other hand, we agree with the realist account, then we must accept that our knowledge of meaning, if not downright mistaken, is forever open to doubt. This is because scientific theories are not final; or if some of them are, we cannot know that they are. We cannot be sure that 'H_2O' is the last word on water; and what satisfies the present scientific intension for 'gold' may turn out, in the light of future science, to be merely a more sophisticated version of 'fool's gold' (cf.

NN 119). Even if the present scientific intension of this word coincides with its 'real' meaning, we cannot be sure of it.[9]

A similar denial of knowledge of meaning follows from the requirement of a causal chain, linking the user of a word to an 'introducing event', as described earlier. How can I tell whether you understand the word 'water'? Not, on Putnam's view, by observing how you use it.

> To have linguistic competence in connection with a term it is not sufficient, in general, to have the full battery of usual linguistic knowledge and skills; one must, in addition, be in the right sort of relationship to certain distinguished situations. . . . Linguistic competence is a matter of knowledge plus causal connection to introducing events. (MLR 199, 205)

It follows that neither you nor I could know whether you were 'competent' in the use of a word unless we had suitable knowledge of the causal chain by which it came down to you, all the way from the original introducing event (assuming there was such an event). But this is unlikely in the vast majority of cases. (The same difficulty arises about the causal theory as applied to proper names. On this view, I could not be sure whether you were speaking of Cicero when you used this name, unless I had knowledge of the causal chain linking you to the original naming event.)

In a later work Putnam addressed the difficulty that, on his view, 'we didn't know the meaning of the word "water" until we developed modern chemistry'.[10] This objection, he replied, 'simply involves an equivocation on the phrase "know the meaning"', which may mean either 'the ability to state explicitly what the denotation is' or 'to have tacit knowledge of its meaning, in the sense of being able to use the word in discourse'. In the second sense, he now conceded, we did know the meaning of 'water' before modern chemistry; but not in the first sense. But is the first sense as sense of 'knowing the meaning' at all? By 'the ability to state explicitly what the denotation is' Putnam must

---

9 This was Locke's reason for *opposing* a realist account of meaning, whereby the meaning of a word such as 'gold' must correspond to the 'real essence' of this material. On this view, he argued, 'all . . . properties, which any further trials shall discover in this matter, ought [to belong to] the essence of the species, marked by that name. Which properties, because they are endless, it is plain, that the idea made after this fashion by this archetype, will be always inadequate' (Locke's *Essay*, 3.6.47).

10 Hilary Putnam, *Representation and Reality* (MIT 1991), 32.

mean: being able to state that water is H_2O. But, unless we accept Putnam's verdicts on Twin Earth water and other examples, it still remains to be shown that there is such a sense of 'meaning' and 'knowing the meaning': a sense in which people who are ignorant of the chemistry would fail to know the meaning of 'water'. Suppose someone were unable to state that water is H_2O, though thoroughly able to 'use the word in discourse'. Of such a person we may say that he lacks knowledge: there is something about the nature of water that he fails to know. What we would *not* say is that – even in one sense of 'meaning' – he doesn't know what 'water' means.

Scientific realism and the meaning of 'meaning'

The claim that there may be more to the meaning of a word than what is displayed in its actual use is, as I said, inimical to ordinary language philosophy. In the philosophy of mind, for example, the ordinary language philosopher may draw attention to the ordinary use of such words as 'thought', 'pain', 'belief and 'consciousness'. He will point out, perhaps, that to predicate 'pain' of the mind or brain is nonsensical if this word is understood in its ordinary sense. But to this the scientific philosopher may reply that the ordinary sense is merely that of present intensions, which do not include the hidden structures to which the words really refer. Perhaps, he will say, scientific research will show that 'pain' and 'belief are really the names of conditions of the brain, notwithstanding the facts to which the linguistic philosopher draws attention. Similar separations of meaning from use were noted in Chapter 5, in discussing the claim that there is, or may be, more to the meaning of such words as 'free' than what is displayed in their ordinary use – so that an action may not really be free even if, according to the normal use of this word, it is a paradigm case of free action.

But what should we say about the meaning of 'meaning' itself? This is what the examples of water, gold and the rest were meant to elucidate. (The title of Putnam's main essay was 'The meaning of "meaning" '.) How, then, is the meaning of 'meaning' to be determined? If use is the criterion of meaning, then it is to the *use* of 'meaning' that we must look; and this is what I have done in my criticisms of Putnam and Kripke. Thus, in questioning their claims a bout the roles of 'hidden essences' and 'introducing events' in fixing meanings, I have referred to how 'meaning' and related words would be used in the relevant examples. This also applies to the meaning of 'knowing the meaning', as discussed in the last section, where the conclusion that knowledge of meaning is not attainable was confronted with the fact that this is contrary to the normal use of this phrase.

It might be objected that in relying on the criterion of use I have begged the question. The question is whether the meaning of a word is determined by its use, and to answer it by reference to how the word 'meaning' is itself used, is to assume the point at issue. But how else are claims about the meaning of 'meaning' to be evaluated? Are we to suppose that meaning is itself a natural kind with a scientific essence? It would be hard to make sense of this. However, the assumption that the *use* of 'meaning' is what the argument is about is confirmed by the way in which Putnam and Kripke argue their case. 'After all', writes Putnam at the end of 'The meaning of "meaning"', 'what have been pointed out in this essay are little more than home truths about the way we use words' (MLR 271). To illustrate these 'home truths' the two writers appeal repeatedly to what we would say – how we would 'use words' – in a variety of examples.[11] Whether we would really use words as claimed by them is questionable, as I have shown. But however this may be, the method of pointing out 'home truths about the way we use words' is not a method of scientific philosophy and owes nothing to empirical discoveries; it is as far from that as Wittgenstein's method of 'assembling reminders' (PI 127).

Philosophy and 'intuition'

As I said, appeals to 'what we would say' are prominent in Putnam's and Kripke's discussions of meaning. In Kripke's writings, however, we also find appeals to 'intuition'; and this word has become current in present-day philosophy, where we hear such remarks as 'My intuition about this is . . . '.

What is intuition and how is it related to knowledge of what we say? Let us consider a passage from Kripke. Having introduced the idea that 'a property can be held to be essential or accidental to an object independently of its description', he claimed that this idea is not meaningless because it has 'intuitive content'. 'Some philosophers', he

---

11   The following passage from Kripke is typical: 'If there were a substance . . . which had a completely different atomic structure from that of water, but resembled water in [all other] respects, would we say that some water wasn't H_2O? I think not. We would say . . . ' (NN 323).

went on, 'think that something's having intuitive content is very inconclusive evidence in favour of it'; but he regarded it as 'very heavy evidence'. He 'really did not know what more conclusive evidence one can have about anything, ultimately speaking' (NN 41–2).

But what is intuition? Is it, indeed, a kind of conclusive evidence? What if one philosopher's intuition differed from that of another? Let us consider the role of intuition in Kripke's argument. The question was whether a property can be regarded as essential to a thing independently of the description (intension) under which it is identified. Now an obvious way of approaching such questions is by considering *what we would say* in suitable examples. Such an example is introduced by Kripke. We are to suppose that someone points to Mr Nixon with the words 'That's the guy who might have lost [the presidential election]'. A nearby philosopher comments that whether the man pointed to might have lost the election depends on how he is described. If as 'Mr Nixon', then indeed he might have lost; but if as 'the winner', then this is not so. But Kripke challenges this verdict. He does so by drawing attention to *what one might say* in such a case:

> The first man would say, and with great conviction, 'Well, of course, the winner . . . might have been someone else. The actual winner, had the course of the campaign been different, might have been the loser, and someone else the winner . . . '. (NN 41)

Here is a piece of ordinary language philosophy which contradicts the verdict of the supposed philosopher on the opening statement. This need not be the end of the matter; but however that may be, the question is essentially about *what we would say*, and the talk of 'intuitive content' is confusing and unnecessary. According to Kripke, as we saw, 'the notion of a necessary property' (one that is independent of any identifying description) is meaningful because it has 'intuitive content'. But whether it is true that that notion (or the relevant phrase) is meaningful depends on how the words in question are used and 'intuitive content' contributes nothing.

Another passage in which Kripke appeals to intuition is about the standard metre in Paris. Here he poses the question whether it is 'a necessary truth' that 'stick S is one metre long at t_0', given that 'one metre' has been defined by reference to this stick. He proceeds to consider *what one 'night say'* in such a case. Someone who had just defined 'one metre' in this way, he writes, 'can still say, "if heat had been applied to this stick S at t_0, then at t_0 stick S would not have been one metre long" ' (55). He then poses the question: 'Why can he [say] this?' According to Kripke, the 'simple answer' to *this* question is to be found by appealing to intuition. 'There is an intuitive difference between the phrase "one metre" and the phrase "the length of S at t_0".'

But here again the use of 'intuitive' is obscure and contributes nothing. If there is a relevant difference between the two phrases, this must be shown by reference to how they are used. Similarly, given the original question whether the quoted statement is 'a necessary truth', what is needed are examples of what we would say. One such example purporting to show that it is *not* a necessary truth, is provided by Kripke, as we saw. It is in this way that the question must be addressed, and not by appeals to intuition.[12]

---

12 Parts of this chapter are adapted from my 'Scientific Realism and Ordinary Language', in Philosophical Investigations 1984.

13 'Folk psychology' and the language of science

In Chapter 9 ('Language remade') I examined various attempts to improve on ordinary language by introducing 'more accurate' alternatives for the purpose of philosophical enquiry. And in the last two chapters I have discussed ways in which, according to some writers, meanings may be affected by scientific findings, so that our knowledge of 'what we say' may not be the last word on questions of meaning. The view to be discussed now is that the language in which we speak about human beings may come to be exchanged altogether for a different one, conforming better to modern scientific theories about the human mind or brain and human behaviour. We ordinarily explain human behaviour in terms of such concepts as those of desire, belief and emotion, and this system has been in place, with a few variations, for thousands of years. It is, according to the view in question, a kind of primitive science – a 'folk psychology' – but the time for a more advanced system is now, or may soon be, at hand.

These ideas have developed in the context of the traditional 'mind/body problem'. Are human beings describable wholly in physical terms? Or is the essential person a non-physical entity, a mind or soul, which might be capable of independent existence? On the whole, the latter view has prevailed, in one form or another, in most times and places of human life. But the other view – materialism – also has a long history and became especially prominent with the rise of science in the seventeenth century. In our own time, it has been encouraged by developments in the science of the brain and by popular ideas about the superiority of science over religious beliefs. Advances in computer science have also contributed.

When a materialist tells us that we are our bodies, that the mind is the brain or that consciousness is a brain process, the first question should be, not 'Is this true?', but 'What does this mean?'. The present wave of materialism may be said to have started with two articles in the

1950s, by U.T. Place and J.J.C. Smart,[1] in which it was argued that consciousness and sensation might be brain processes. It was recognized from the start that there was a difficulty about meaning, for obviously our words for sensations do not *mean* the same as expressions denoting brain-processes. Smart, recognizing this, proposed that the identity might be a matter of discovery as opposed to one of meaning, as with the identity of the evening star and the morning star. This proposal was attractive to those who rejected the separation of philosophy from science, for it treated the question of mind–brain identity as a scientific one. On this view it might turn out, as a result of scientific enquiry, that sensations, say, are indeed identical with certain brain processes; and in this way science might provide solutions to a long-standing philosophical problem. There was also, of course, the possibility that the desired identifications might never be made, but this was felt to be unlikely in the long run, given the successes already achieved by the physical sciences in accounting for phenomena of various kinds.

Questions of meaning have, however, continued to pose difficulties for the identity thesis. What, for example, could it mean to say that brain-process B, of which I have probably not the least knowledge, is identical with my belief that it is going to rain, of which I cannot fail to be aware? There are limits to the kinds of things that may be identified with one another without falling into nonsense. A common fallacy in this area is to mistake a necessary condition for an identity. It might be found, for example, that one cannot have sensation S unless one's brain is in state XYZ; but this would not show that sensation S *is* brain-state XYZ. Similarly, a person deprived of oxygen loses consciousness, but this does not show that consciousness is oxygen. That statement would not even make sense; and neither, it has been argued, do the proposed identifications of states of consciousness with states of the brain.

Various attempts have been made to present the identity of mind and brain (sensations and brain-processes, etc.) in a coherent way, without violating the conditions of sense and nonsense as recognized in ordinary language.[2] According to 'eliminativists', however, the way forward is not accommodation but elimination: we are to renounce these conditions and the ordinary ways of speaking in which they are

---

1   U.T. Place, 'Is Consciousness a Brain-Process?', *British Journal of Psychology* 1956; J.J.C. Smart, 'Sensations and Brain-Processes', *Philosophical Review* 1959.
2   See O. Hanfling, 'Consciousness: "The Last Mystery"', in S. Schroeder, ed., *Wittgenstein and Contemporary Philosophy of Mind* (Macmillan 2000).

embedded. The latter are nothing better than 'folk psychology', and if someone rejects materialism because it is not compatible with them, his argument should be turned back against him. Folk psychology may indeed be 'irreducible with respect to neuroscience' – but this would be because the former is 'dead wrong'.[3]

Folk psychology is to be compared, according to these writers, to other systems of 'folk' belief, including 'folk mechanics ..., folk meteorology, folk chemistry and folk biology';[4] and folk medicine might be added to the list. Such systems are often deficient and may be seen to be so in the light of modern science. The same is true, of course, of superseded *scientific* theories, such as that of phlogiston. Now what happens in such cases is not merely the replacement of false beliefs by true ones, but an exchange of concepts. The old concepts, such as that of phlogiston, are abandoned and new ones, reflecting better scientific insights, are introduced. In the same way, it is thought, the present vocabulary in which we describe and explain a person's behaviour may be superseded when the new 'neuroscience', dealing with processes in the brain, is firmly in place. There will be 'a new system of communication ... distinct from natural language, with a new and more powerful *combinatorial grammar* over *novel elements* forming novel combinations with exotic properties'.[5] The change would be justified because 'it would be madness to make it a constraint upon acceptable theory that it explains the "facts" as they [are] currently conceived'.[6] To criticize the new theory for failing to explain folk psychological 'facts' would be like criticizing 'Newtonian physics [for failing] to explain what turns the crystal spheres'.[7] According to another writer, 'literally all of ... the generalizations of commonsense psychology ... will be unstatable' when the new knowledge is in place, but this should be seen as 'an essential step in the growth of a new science'.[8]

We commonly explain a person's behaviour by reference to his beliefs and desires. Knowing that Smith wants a copy of the *Critique of Pure Reason* and believes he can get one at the library, I can explain why he is on his way to the library. I could also have

3   Patricia S. Churchland, *Neurophilosophy* (MIT 1986), 384.
4   Paul M. Churchland, 'Folk Psychology and Scientific Psychology', in John D. Greenwood, ed., *The Future of Folk Psychology* (CUP 1991), 51.
5   Paul M. Churchland, 'Eliminative Materialism', *Journal of Philosophy* 1981, 87.
6   Paul M. Churchland, *Scientific Realism and the Plasticity of the Mind* (CUP 1979), 44.
7   Churchland 1986 op. cit., 385.
8   S. Stich, *From Folk Psychology to Cognitive Science* (MIT 1983), 182.

predicted, from the same knowledge, that he would visit the library. But how reliable are such explanations and predictions? They may serve us well on the whole, but sometimes they let us down. Perhaps we could do better, given suitable advances in the science of mind or brain. In that case one might be able to obtain relevant data from an observation of Smith's brain, put them into a computer, and arrive at a more reliable explanation of Smith's behaviour, which would be couched in the 'new and more powerful' kind of language. Such an overturning of traditional ways of explaining and predicting behaviour would, no doubt, seem unnatural at first and, as with other cases of folk science, there might be much resistance to the change; but this would not affect the superiority of the new system. Eliminativists draw attention to the antiquity of the ordinary ways of explaining behaviour. Can it really be true that a system which 'has been stagnant for at least twenty-five centuries'[9] is the last word in the understanding of human behaviour?

The view just described, with its reference to the brain, is known as 'eliminative materialism'. But eliminativism is not necessarily tied to materialism. Another approach is that of 'cognitive science', in which various 'mental states' and 'mental structures' are posited to explain human behaviour. To posit these it is not necessary to identify the mind with the brain. But, as before, the aim is to produce a scientific theory of mind and behaviour which will be superior to 'folk psychology'.

Advocates of the new theories are aware of the boldness of their predictions and the incredulity they may provoke; but this is put down to a poverty of imagination, such as has sometimes occurred in the face of predictions of scientific progress in the past. Churchland confesses that until recently he himself 'could not clearly imagine a systematic alternative to folk psychology', but he thinks the difficulty has now been surmounted. Since that time, he writes, 'the materials available to imagination have improved dramatically'.

> The microstructure of the brain and the recent successes of connectionist AI [artificial intelligence] suggest that our principal form of representation is the high-dimensional activation vector, and that our principal form of computation is the vector-to-vector transformation, effected by a matrix of differently weighted synapses. In place of propositional attitudes

9   Churchland 1981 op. cit., 76.

and logical inferences from one to another, therefore, we can conceive of persons as the seat of vectorial attitudes . . .. We can already see how such vectorial systems can do many of the things that humans and other animals do swiftly and easily, such as recognize faces and other highly complex stimuli . . .. The possibility of a real alternative now seems beyond dispute: we are already building it.[10]

A need for replacement?

Is folk psychology in need of replacement? What is folk psychology? The term might be applied to old-fashioned sayings such as 'Spare the rod and spoil the child', 'Absence makes the heart grow fonder' and 'Faint heart never won fair lady'. That beliefs of this kind do not take us far in understanding and explaining behaviour will readily be granted; but the resources for improving on them are there in the existing vocabulary. It is the latter, however, that is at stake when eliminativists speak of 'folk psychology'. In support of their view they point out that ordinary ways of explaining behaviour cannot cope with such phenomena as mental illness, creative imagination, the 'intelligence differences between individuals' and 'the nature and psychological functions of sleep'.[11] This is largely true, and in these areas we may indeed hope for enlightenment from scientific research, but it does not follow that the existing vocabulary of belief, desire and the rest is in need of replacement.

What would the new, superior kind of explanation be like? In the passage I quoted it was claimed that it has now become easier to 'imagine a systematic alternative to folk psychology' because of a better understanding of 'representation' and 'computation' in the brain, involving such concepts as 'high-dimensional activation vector', etc.; and presumably the explanations would be in terms such as these. Perhaps they would come in the form of computer printouts with tables of figures, graphs, etc. It seems unlikely that such data could take the place of ordinary explanations, but the eliminativist may reply that this is merely due to lack of familiarity and imagination. Perhaps he would compare it to the difficulty that many people have when starting to work with a computer. At first they are bewildered and frustrated, but

10 Churchland 1991 op. cit., 67.
11 Churchland 1981 op. cit., 73.

in due course they get the hang of it and may even find it more natural than the old ways of working.

There is, however, an important difference between this case and that of explaining human behaviour. In the case of the computer, the deficiencies of the old ways of working can be pointed out to a purchaser, so that he may appreciate the advantage of the computer ways. But in what way, if any, is the vocabulary in which we explain ordinary human behaviour deficient? Does it not enable us to explain such behaviour perfectly well? Suppose, as before, that Smith is on his way to the library. The explanation is that he wants a copy of the *Critique of Pure Reason*. Why does he want a copy of the *Critique*? Because he has to write an essay on Kant's Second Analogy. To explain is 'to make plain or intelligible'; and this is achieved perfectly well in the present example. It is true that such explanations are not always satisfactory. If Smith had been heard to say that he was not writing the essay, then the explanation would be less satisfactory. If his reason for visiting the library were more complicated than merely to get the book (he is attracted by the girl behind the counter, etc.), then the explanation might be deficient in other ways. But these faults could be amended without changing the type of explanation or abandoning the familiar vocabulary of belief, desire and duty. The resources for a better explanation would be there within the familiar vocabulary.

This is not to say that scientific psychology has nothing to contribute in this area. There have, for example, been experimental studies which show that people can be mistaken in the reasons they give for their actions and preferences; and it is sometimes thought that such studies indicate an incipient demise of 'folk psychology'.[12] Now there may indeed be a common assumption that a person always knows, or knows better than anybody else, what he wants and why. That this is a false assumption is apparent, not only from scientific research, but also from a reading of serious novels and, indeed, from a little reflection on one's experience of real life. But what these findings and reflections do is to enrich and augment the understanding of behaviour in terms of belief, desire and the rest; they do not show, or even tend to show, that these concepts should or could be eliminated. To show that what Smith really wanted was X rather than, as he thought, Y, is to use and not to abandon the language of belief and desire.

12   Stich, op. cit., 231–7.

A scientific study may also be fruitful in the prediction, as opposed to the explanation, of human behaviour. This is important in market research, where scientific surveys can enable producers of goods to gain advantage from predictions of behaviour such as could not be made on the basis of common sense, and which might even be contrary to common sense. But these findings, again, are not liable to displace the explanation or prediction of behaviour in ordinary non-scientific ways. Knowing Smith as I do, I may be able to predict with complete certainty how he will act on a given occasion; and in a wide range of ordinary cases, we know what a person will do simply because he has told us what he will do. These ways of predicting behaviour are not in competition with scientific findings.

It is also true that behaviour can sometimes be explained by reference to conditions of the brain. Depression, hyper-sensitivity and other conditions can be caused by substances in the brain and, in some cases, corrected accordingly. But such explanations, again, augment the existing ways of explaining behaviour and do not supersede them, except in abnormal circumstances. If the behaviour is highly unusual, and if an abnormal brain condition is present or suspected, then we may want to say that the *real* explanation for it is to be found in the agent's brain. But this is not so in normal conditions. If a person has good reason to feel depressed, then he can explain, to our satisfaction, why he feels depressed; and while it may be true that a corresponding substance is present in the brain, this fact would not undermine the explanation he gives.

'Folk psychology': a philosophers' myth

It is usual, in criticisms of eliminativism, to argue that the concepts of folk psychology are not dispensable. But to conduct the debate in these terms – endorsing the phrase 'folk psychology' – is already to make an important concession. Eliminativists like to speak of the ordinary concepts of belief, desire and the rest as constituting a *theory* – a proto-science called 'folk psychology' – so as to have a suitable candidate for replacement by a more advanced theory. Now the replacement of an existing theory by a better one is a fact that will be familiar to anyone with some knowledge of the history of science. But is there such a theory as 'folk psychology'? Are the ordinary ways of explaining behaviour in the same business as the sciences to which eliminativists appeal? If not, then they will not be candidates for replacement in the familiar sense of one theory being superseded by another.

What is folk psychology supposed to consist in? Here are examples of 'causal/explanatory laws' which are typical of it according to Paul Churchland.[13]

1   Persons who want that P, and believe that Q would be sufficient to bring about P, and have no conflicting wants or preferred strategies, will try to bring it about that Q.
2   A person who suffers severe bodily damage will feel pain.
3   A person who suffers a sudden sharp pain will wince.
4   Persons in pain tend to want to relieve that pain.
5   A person denied food for any length will feel hunger.
6   Barring a stronger contrary purpose, hunger causes eating.
7   A person who feels overall warmth will tend to relax.
8   A person who tastes a lemon will have a puckering sensation.
9   A person who is angry will tend to be impatient or tend to frown.
10 A person who fears that p desires that not-p.
11 The apprehended loss of a loved one tends to cause grief.

Now one thing we would expect of a theory, psychological or otherwise, is that the propositions comprising it are not such as to be obvious to everyone. But readers who survey these examples may be struck, first of all, by their banality. How, they may ask, can it be a matter of theory that bodily damage causes pain, when this is one of the first things we learn and one that is continually confirmed in everyday life? On the other hand, some of the propositions, such as (7), (8) and (9), are only partly true: their truth will vary with different people and different situations. But this knowledge too is obvious and no theory is needed to confirm it. (In treating such truisms as comprising a causal-explanatory theory, these writers are following in the footsteps of Quine, who also, as we saw in Chapter 11, treated our most ordinary and familiar ideas as comprising a scientific theory – in his case a theory of physics in which we 'posit bodies'.)

A more fundamental difficulty is that many of these 'laws' owe their banality to our knowledge of the *meanings* of the words used in them. Someone who knows the meaning of 'pain', for example, cannot be ignorant of the connection between pain and pain behaviour: this is a necessary condition of knowing the meaning of 'pain'. Similarly, the connection between wanting and trying to get is not a matter of theory; it is part of the meaning of 'want'. The proposition (6) that 'hunger causes eating' may look like a causal law, but here again the

---

13   They are compiled from several of the writings cited above.

connection is one of meaning: hunger is, by definition, a desire to eat. Proposition 9, as I said, is only partly true: one may be angry about, say, the state of the Health Service, without any tendency to be impatient or to frown. Here again, however, the connection between anger and its expression, such as it is, is logical and not empirical.

The distinction between empirical and logical truths is suppressed by eliminativists in their presentation of examples of folk psychology. Empirical generalizations, such as (7) and (8), are mingled with logical truths such as (4); and logical truths are given the appearance of empirical generalizations, as in (6). These assimilations are understandable, given the assumption that the ordinary ways of explaining behaviour constitute a proto-scientific theory, which might be superseded by a more advanced theory.

Is there any reason to think that propositions such as (1), about wanting and trying to get, could be treated as being empirical? It is true that S's desire for X would be an empirical fact, and S's attempt to get X would also be an empirical fact; and knowledge of the first fact might enable us to predict the second. Now according to Paul Churchland, 'any principle that allows us to do this – to predict one empirical state or event on the basis of another, logically distinct, empirical state or event – *has* to be empirical in character'.[14] But the connection between wanting and trying to get is not a matter of empirical discovery: it is not as if we found out from observation that people who want something are inclined to try to get it. The conclusion drawn by Churchland simply does not follow from his premises, and it is idle to insist that it 'has to be' so.

Another argument to undermine the distinction between between logical and empirical truths is designed to show that 'logical' and 'causal' are not incompatible. Thus, if a computer goes through 'a deductive logic program', the successive steps 'are related by logic *and* by cause'.[15] Similarly, it is argued, the existence of a logical relation between, say, desire and action should not prevent us from also describing that relation as causal. Now such relations may be indeed be described as 'causal': there is nothing wrong in saying, for example, that what *caused* someone to act as he did was his desire for X. But this use of 'cause' does not affect the essential difficulty about eliminativism, which is about the contrast between 'logical' and *'empirical'* – or, as we might also say, between 'logical' and 'causal' as used in empirical

14 Churchland 1991 op. cit., 54.
15 Churchland 1986 op. cit., 304.

science. It is the causal-empirical relation that eliminativists want to attribute to the propositions of 'folk psychology', so that it may take its place in the progress towards a more advanced theory.

The difficulty about that programme may indeed be illustrated with the case of the computer. It is true that the steps performed by the computer are related both in a logical and in a causal-empirical way. But could the former be replaced by the latter? Suppose the grammar check on my computer produces a squiggly line under the sentence I have just written. What is the explanation? Two kinds of answers might be given. One is logical: the sentence lacks a subject. The other is causal-empirical: when such and such electric impulses are passed to such and such an arrangement of microchips, etc., the result is the appearance of that line on the screen. But the second explanation would not be suitable as a *successor* to the first, for they are not in the same business. The first tells us what is *wrong* with that sentence, but that is not the function of the second. The second requires a knowledge of empirical laws and theories; but this is not so with the first.

A further argument for regarding ordinary explanations of behaviour as belonging to a proto-scientific theory is derived from the problem of 'other minds'. The problem, as usually presented, is that there is a discrepancy between the ascription of thoughts and feelings to others and the behavioural evidence on which it is based. Might not the other person behave as he does without having the thoughts and feelings that I ascribe to him? Having, like many others, rejected both the behaviourist solution and the 'argument from analogy', Churchland suggests that the attribution of beliefs, desires, feelings, etc., to others is a matter of theory – 'a *theory* of the inner dynamics of human beings'; and this theory is to be judged by 'how well it allows us to explain and predict the continuing behaviour' of other people.[16] On this view, the attribution of beliefs, desires and the rest is like the positing of unobservable entities in a scientific theory. In genetics, for example, it may be fruitful to posit entities called 'genes' even if there is no way of observing them, and similar posits occur in physics. Such entities will, we may hope, become observable, in some sense, in the future, but the usefulness of positing them does not depend on this; and the same would be true of the beliefs and desires that one ascribes to others.[17] In this case, however, the posits belong to the present 'folk'

16 Churchland 1979 op. cit., 91.
17 As we saw in Chapter 11, such views about mind and behaviour are to be found already in the writings of Quine, who questioned whether 'there is a case for mental events and

theory which, according to eliminativists, is due to be superseded. Thus a future 'neuroscience is unlikely to find … anything that answers to the structure of individual beliefs and desires'. Folk psychology is likely to be 'false and … its ontology chimerical. Beliefs and desires are of a piece with phlogiston, caloric and the alchemical essences.'[18]

But is the theoretical attitude one that we have, or could have, towards other people? If I tell you sincerely that I believe that p, then you know that I believe that p. But this knowledge is not mediated by a theory: you do not posit a theoretical entity or process in my mind or brain – or if you do, this is not relevant to your knowing what I believe. Similarly, if my daughter demands an ice cream, then I know she wants an ice cream; but this knowledge is not about a posited entity in her mind or brain. Again, beliefs and desires are often *shared*. Do you share my belief that computers are a mixed blessing? This is not a question about your 'inner dynamics'; it is about whether you are prepared to agree with me about this matter.

Eliminativism and the first person

If belief, desire and the rest were theoretical concepts when ascribed to others, how should we account for the ascription of them to oneself? The reason for regarding them so in the case of others was the alleged discrepancy between ascription and evidence, but this cannot be so in the case of oneself. I do not ascribe to myself the belief that p because I heard myself say that p, or observed myself behaving in a way appropriate for that belief. Should we conclude that the words in question ('belief', 'desire', etc.) have different meanings when applied to oneself? This could not be right. Suppose I told you 'I believe that p'. This would, in the normal case, enable you to say 'He believes that p'. But the use of 'believe' in this case would not be *equivocal*: what you say about me would be the same as what I said about myself. The 'theoretical' approach may be appropriate when we are dealing with processes of the brain or other parts of the body. Here it may be useful to posit unobserved entities or processes to explain what we observe.

mental states'. If there is a case for them, then, he thought, 'it must be just that the positing of them, like the positing of molecules, has some indirect systematic efficacy on the development of theory'. (He warned, however, against multiplying such posits unnecessarily: 'The bodily states exist anyway; why add the others?') W.V. Quine, *Word and Object* (MIT 1960), 264.

18 Churchland 1991 op. cit., 65.

But our beliefs and desires are not like this, and the idea that the ordinary language of belief, desire and the rest embodies a theory of 'inner dynamics' is an illusion.

The case of the first person is also important with regard to explaining behaviour. Why am I going to the doctor? Because I have a pain in my leg. Could this explanation be replaced by one referring, say, to processes in the brain or other parts of the body? Suppose the doctor examines me and can't find anything wrong. Would this mean that the explanation I gave may have been mistaken? No; my reason for visiting the doctor was the pain and not a belief about the physical state of an organ. That might have been the reason, but it was not. Moreover, I may still have my reason for seeking the doctor's help: perhaps he can do something to relieve the pain, even though he can't find the cause of it.

How could this explanation of my behaviour be eliminated in favour of a better one? Suppose that knowledge of the associated brain processes became extremely detailed and reliable: this would not affect my explanation of what I was doing. My reason for seeking the doctor's help would still be the pain and not the brain process. The account of the latter, whatever it might be, would not be in competition with the reason I gave for my behaviour and could not replace it: they are not in the same business. It is also an illusion to suppose that the scientific explanation, or any other, could be an *improvement* on the one I gave. The explanation 'because I am in pain' was as clear as an explanation could possibly be: it was a paradigm case of explanation. (A similar point was made earlier about Smith's reason for visiting the library.)

These statements are contrary to the view taken by Davidson in an influential article. According to him, there is an obscurity in the concept of rational explanation, and the only way to understand such explanations is in terms of cause and effect.[19] He points out that the mere existence of a suitable reason is not sufficient to explain why someone acted as he did. 'A person can have a reason for an action, and perform the action, and yet this not be the reason why he did it' (op. cit. 85). What is further needed is that he 'performed the action *because* he had the reason'. But how are we to 'account for the force of

---

19 Donald Davidson, 'Actions, Reasons and Causes', in A.R. White, ed., *The Philosophy of Action* (OUP 1968). He quotes a remark of Hampshire's on the connection between reasons and action: 'In philosophy one ought surely to find this . . . connection altogether mysterious' (87). For an excellent discussion of Davidson's position, see S. Schroeder, 'Are Reasons Causes?', in S. Schroeder (ed.) *Wittgenstein and Contemporary Philosophy of Mind*, (Palgrave 2001).

that "because" '? The only way, according to Davidson, is by invoking 'the pattern of cause and effect'. This pattern is one 'that we understand as well as any', whereas that of 'reason and action' has still to be 'identified' (86). (In Davidson's argument the cause of an action is typically a 'pro attitude ... or the related belief ... or both' (80). His account would belong to 'folk psychology' and not to the more advanced science.)

Now it is true that reason R may not be one's reason for doing A, even though one is aware of R as a suitable reason; but it does not follow that when R (or S or T) *is* the reason for doing A, we must resort to the language of cause and effect to explain the connection. Nor is it true that the pattern of cause and effect is better understood than that of reason and action. The connection between A and R is established when the agent *gives* R as his reason for having done, or being about to do, A; and this is understood as well as anything could be.

It has also been claimed, by Nagel, that the rational kind of explanation 'doesn't really explain the action at all'.[20] He refers to cases in which there are 'reasons on both sides' – both for doing and not doing A. In such a case, we can explain the doing of A by reference to the reasons in favour of A. Yet, as Nagel points out, 'we could equally have explained his *refusing* [to do it], if he had refused, by referring to the reasons on the other side'. Thus the explanation 'says I did it for certain reasons, but it does not explain why I didn't decide not to do it for other reasons'. This is true; but does it follow that the doing of A would *not* have been explained? This would be a strange complaint to make. What would be left unexplained would not be *why I did it*, but merely why the reasons on one side prevailed over the others. The explanation I gave would be perfectly good, unless there were some reason for challenging it. (In any case, the problem of 'reasons on both sides' arises only for some actions. Even if it were true that an action could not be explained when there are reasons on both sides, it would not follow that this is so when the reasons are all on one side.)

Explanation and justification

The difference between the two kinds of explanation is commonly referred to as being about 'reasons' versus 'causes'. This is a convenient but inaccurate label, since both words are used on both

20   Thomas Nagel, *The View from Nowhere* (OUP 1986), 115.

sides of the intended distinction. The *relevant* sense of 'cause' is that of empirical science, where causal connections, and causal laws, are discovered by observation and experiment, and phenomena are explained by reference to such laws. This kind of explanation, as I have tried to show, cannot be a substitute for explanation of the other kind.

An important role of the latter is that of justification. In explaining why I went to the doctor I was *justifying* my action: presenting it as reasonable in the circumstances; but this is not so in the case of scientific explanation. An explanation of what I did in terms of the mechanisms of my brain and nervous system would not be a justificatory explanation. The relevant distinction also arises in the case of beliefs. Asked why S believes that the thoughts of Chairman Mao can enable us to surmount all obstacles, one might give an empirical explanation: 'He was brought up and indoctrinated in the People's Republic of China.' (It is an empirical fact that such beliefs can be caused in such a way.) But usually this is not what is wanted – especially when the question is addressed to the believer. Asked why he believes that p, he would probably be expected to *justify* the belief, as one that is likely to be *true*. The other kind of reply might be acceptable in some cases. Religious people, asked why they believe as they do, sometimes reply 'Because I was brought up to it'; and this may be reasonable in the circumstances. But such a reply would have no bearing on the truth of the belief, and an explanation of the justificatory, truth-related kind might still be demanded. The relevant distinction is also important in the case of actions to be done in the future. 'Why are you going to do that?' Here it would be absurd to answer in terms of brain-washing or physical states of the brain. What is wanted is a *reason for* doing that; and someone who could not provide such reasons would not count as a rational agent.

It is true that in certain cases scientific evidence may be held to override a justificatory explanation. A scientific survey of shoppers may reveal that the reasons they give for preferring brand B are contrary to what emerges from their behaviour. Asked why I buy brand B rather than brand C, I may justify my choice by saying that the contents of B are more wholesome; but scientific research may show that what really makes the difference is the picture on the package or the plastic toy inside it. This, however, is a special kind of case, which could not be generalized. The normal case remains that in which we are *not* deceived about our reasons. But even in cases where we are so deceived, the 'real reason', as established by the researcher, is still on the justificatory side of the divide; for to say that my 'real reason' was the plastic toy is to invoke a reason that *might* be given to justify one's choice. This reason might be regarded as a poor one, but we are not here concerned with good or bad reasons. What matters is that it is intelligible: it can be recognized *as* a reason – an attempt to justify one's choice. By contrast, the fact that one's brain is in condition C, would not be so recognized; it would not provide an intelligible reply to 'Why do you prefer brand B?'.

A justificatory reason need not, then, be a *good* reason. But it is important that such reasons *can* be assessed as good or bad, mature or ill-considered, childish, etc. As a responsible person, I must be prepared to justify what I say and do, and to change my behaviour if my reasons are shown to be false or inadequate. (I must see that this is what I *ought* to do, even if I fail to do it.) But these normative ideas are not in place when we explain a person's behaviour by reference to his brain or nervous system. In doing this we are not attempting to justify what he is doing, or to put his actions in a reasonable light.

The question 'Why?', in the justificatory sense, governs our lives to a large extent. We are responsible, in the literal sense of 'answerable', for our actions, beliefs and emotional feelings. A child cries out in the night. 'Why are you crying?' – No answer. – 'There must be some reason. Why don't you tell us?' Perhaps, on this occasion or the next, the child will think of something. 'I'm frightened.' – 'What are you frightened of?' – Silence. – 'There must be something you are frightened of. You can't be frightened of *nothing*.' In due course the child will learn this lesson too and produce something suitable. What then? Perhaps the parents will argue 'But that's nothing to be frightened of . . .' In these and similar ways we are inducted into the logical requirements of this and other concepts.

Causal and justificatory discourse are connected in various ways and it would be futile to ask whether one is more fundamental than the other. It is, however, inconceivable that the justificatory kind might disappear with the advance of science. Science is itself a rational activity and the scientist must be prepared to defend his statements in rational terms. His statements, like any others, are put forward as reasonable and likely to be true; and we expect him to have reasons which make them worthy of belief, both by him and by ourselves. These concerns are essential to scientific discourse, as to any other.

In Western philosophy since Hume it has been common to observe a fundamental distinction between 'fact' and 'value', 'is' and 'ought'. According to Kant,

'*Ought*' expresses a kind of necessity and connection with grounds which is found nowhere else in the whole of nature. The understanding can know in nature only what is, what has been or what will be. We cannot say that anything in nature *ought to be* other than what ... it actually is. When we have the course of nature alone in view, '*ought*' has no meaning whatsoever. It is just as absurd to ask what ought to happen in the natural world as to ask what properties a circle ought to have.[21]

Kant, Hume and others have located 'ought' especially in the moral sphere, and have distinguished moral from empirical discourse by reference to evaluative terms such as 'ought'. But evaluative language – 'ought', 'good', etc. – is not confined to the moral sphere; it enters into discourse of nearly every kind. An empirical statement does not itself *say* that something is good or right, and in this respect it differs from moral statements which do; yet in making the empirical statement one is committed to the claim that it is justified – that one is in a suitable position to make it. (One is also responsible for the act of making the statement – the judgement that it was right to speak when one did.) A similar point was made in Chapter 5 about the concept of *validity* – an evaluative concept which is essential to the notion of argument. Arguments are necessarily good or bad, valid or invalid; and in this way evaluative ideas enter into any discourse in which argument occurs. This normative vocabulary is not replaceable by the language of scientific theory; but it is essential to the existence of our language.

Throwing away the ladder

It might be thought that my objections to eliminativism are all irrelevant because they are themselves expressed in the unreformed Oldspeak of folk psychology which is to be superseded as a result of the new scientific insights. It is true that my discussion has been conducted in Oldspeak, but the same is true of the positions I have criticized: the advocates of eliminativism argue, and must argue, their case in the existing language. This is not merely because Newspeak has not yet been perfected; it is because in that language the very concept of argument, with its justificatory components of a good reason, a sound objection and so on, would be lacking. The reader of eliminativist philosophy might well be advised to approach it in the

---

21 I. Kant, *Critique of Pure Reason*, transl. N. Kemp Smith (Macmillan 1964), B575.

spirit recommended by the earlier Wittgenstein: 'Anyone who understands me eventually recognizes [my propositions] as nonsensical, when he has used them – as steps – to climb beyond them. (He must, so to speak, throw away the ladder after he has climbed up it.)'[22] Similarly, the 'folk' language in which the case for eliminativism is argued would have to be thrown away if that case turned out to be sound.

Eliminativists argue that just as there are really no such things as witches or phlogiston, so it may turn out that 'there really are no such states as beliefs'.[23] But when the eliminativist says this, must he not *believe* what he says? And how could he do that if there were really no beliefs? This objection is anticipated but underestimated by Patricia Churchland. She replies that in the new vocabulary the eliminativist's point 'could be stated with greater sophistication' and without self-refutation. Instead of saying that he does not *believe* in beliefs, the eliminativist 'might declare "I gronkify beliefs ...", where gronkification is a neuropsychological state defined within the mature new theory' (397). But how is the word *'declare'* in this sentence to be understood? If the Newspeak 'I gronkify ...' is a declaration, then it must be expressing a *belief*. This is what makes the difference between declaring (asserting, etc.) and other speech acts or utterances. The Newspeak eliminativist would have to be held, no less than the old, *responsible* for what he declares: to have good reasons for it, etc. If the word 'declare' is not to be understood in this sense, then we do not know what it means; and neither can we understand the statement, quoted above, in which it occurs.

Such arguments have been compared to an argument that might have been offered in defence of the theory, prevalent in medieval times, that life depends on 'an immaterial vital spirit'. A defender of the theory might, it is suggested, have argued that to deny it would be incoherent. If the denial were true, he would argue, then the person making the denial would 'not have vital spirit, and must therefore be *dead*. But if he is dead, then his statement is just a string of noises, devoid of meaning or truth.'[24]

Such a defence would, of course, be question-begging; it would assume the truth of what was being questioned: that life depends on an immaterial spirit. But the connection between asserting and believing

---

22 L. Wittgenstein, *Tractatus Logico-Philosophicus* (Routledge & Kegan Paul 1961), 6.54.
23 Churchland 1986 op. cit., 397.
24 P.M. Churchland, *Matter and Consciousness* (MIT 1984), 48.

is not like that between being alive and having a vital spirit, as posited by the medieval theory. The former is analytic. Someone who asserts that p – where p might be the eliminativist thesis – is taken to express a belief that p: this is part of the meaning of 'assert'. But there is no such analytic connection between being alive and the possession of an immaterial spirit, any more than between being alive and the possession of adrenalin (though the latter may be essential to life as a matter of fact). Someone who used the word 'alive' in medieval times, or who uses it now, need have no knowledge of vital spirits or adrenalin. But he could not be competent in the use of 'assert' if he did not acknowledge the connection between assertion and belief.

The concepts of assertion, belief, reason and justification are such that one could not survive without the others; and the concept of truth also belongs in this company. Hence it is not surprising to find, in another eliminativist writing, the speculation that true and false might vanish and that, instead of 'spoken language [with] sentences and arguments', communication would be by neural connections between brains, 'in roughly the same fashion that your right hemisphere [of the brain] "understands" ... your left hemisphere'.[25] The scare quotes around 'understands' are appropriate, for this interaction between parts of the brain does not satisfy the logical conditions of understanding any more than other physical interactions in the bodies of human beings, animals and plants.

Is it conceivable that our language, with its standards of validity and justification might vanish from the earth? Yes, such a catastrophe is conceivable. It would also be compatible with the continued existence of systems of input and output of great complexity, such as exist, for example, in the world of plants. Such an elimination might be the result of some natural or man-made catastrophe. But it could not follow from a better understanding of the workings of the brain or other bodily organs.

---

25 Churchland 1981 op. cit., 87–8.

Index